The Ruin of
Sir Walter Scott

THE RUIN OF
SIR WALTER SCOTT

Eric Quayle

Clarkson N. Potter, Inc./Publisher NEW YORK

DISTRIBUTED BY CROWN PUBLISHERS, INC.

TO
Davina and Christine

O what a tangled web we weave,
When first we practise to deceive!

Marmion Canto VI. v.xvii.

Illustrations

Frontispiece
Sir Walter Scott (by Andrew Geddes)

Between pages 162–163
James Ballantyne (by his nephew, John Ballantyne)
John Ballantyne (artist unknown)
Ballantyne's first printing commission from Scott
Paul's Works (by John Ballantyne)
Wooden press used in printing the *Waverley* Novels
John Gibson Lockhart (by Sir Francis Grant)
Archibald Constable (by Andrew Geddes)
One of the many accommodation notes signed by Scott
Abbotsford from the south
Entrance Hall, Abbotsford
Sir Walter Scott and his friends at Abbotsford

Acknowledgments
The drawings of James Ballantyne and Paul's Works are reproduced
by permission of the Board of Trustees of the National Galleries of
Scotland; the portraits of Scott, John Ballantyne, Lockhart, Constable,
and Scott and his Friends are reproduced by permission of the Scottish
National Portrait Gallery; the views of Abbotsford from the south,
and the Entrance Hall, Abbotsford are reproduced by permission of
Messrs Valentine & Sons Ltd.

Introduction

FEW FIGURES IN literature present a more baffling enigma to a would-be biographer than that of Sir Walter Scott. Both as a man and as an author he commands alternately respect and condemnation; a genius in many aspects of his work as a novelist, and a weakling beset with traits of character that allowed a consuming self-interest to dictate modes of conduct that finally brought ruin on himself and many lesser men.

In his day he was accorded a reverence that very few writers have ever had bestowed upon them during their lifetime, and after his death his son-in-law, Lockhart, made certain that a shroud of immaculate whiteness protected his memory from the inquisitive generations that were denied the delight of knowing him as a man. I have written this fresh biography of the Wizard of the North, not with any iconoclastic idea of toppling the best loved and most popular author of his day from the seat of literary honour he occupies while serenely contemplating the passing crowds in Princes Street; but in the belief that much still remains to be told about the underlying personality of the man. He last limped his way through his magnificent mansion at Abbotsford nearly one hundred and forty years ago, a monument he had painstakingly erected to his name on the banks of the Tweed he loved so well. It is startling to discover, after the passage of nearly a century and a half, that Scott still has admirers who are prepared to reject out of hand any biography of the Laird of Abbotsford that is not also by way of being a hagiography, apparently preferring that any defects in his character should be allowed to remain hidden in the glory surrounding his genius.

Scott knew his native land, the prose and poetry of it, its history and legends, and above all, the idiomatic qualities of its people, as no other writer except the immortal Robert Burns has ever known them before or since. But the iconic portrayal of his image as one of spotless integrity and untarnished respectability, which Lockhart presented to the world in 1837, conceals the fact that the great Sir Walter was just as human as the rest of us, and just as open to the temptations that beset us all. Two years ago I was lucky enough to discover (in true fictional style) the whereabouts of the battered tin trunk containing many of the letters and papers of the Ballantyne family, some of whom were close friends and business acquaintances of Scott from his schooldays in Kelso until his death at Abbotsford in 1832. Evidence came into my hands at that time that painted an entirely different picture from that presented by John Gibson Lockhart to explain the downfall of the man whose daughter he married. It soon became obvious that not only had Scott's first biographer slanted the facts of the case he presented in a way no fair-minded judge would ever permit, but he had also manufactured situations and incidents that had never occurred during his father-in-law's lifetime. With the publication of his *Memoirs of the Life of Sir Walter Scott, Bart.* a myth was born that still gains acceptance to the present day: one family in particular, he tells us with solemn assurance, was responsible for Scott's downfall, and theirs were the guilty fingers that rifled the treasure chest his genius had worked so hard to fill.

I have traced from the beginning the path that eventually led to that fatal January morning in 1826, when Scott's dream of being able to maintain a vast estate on the banks of the Tweed, commensurate with the position he had attained in society, dissolved like the mirage of prosperity with which he had for so long surrounded himself. With his fall there tumbled many of the minor figures in the Edinburgh of his day. To discover who was really responsible for the catastrophe which overwhelmed them all is what this book is about.

Eric Quayle
Zennor
West Cornwall
1968

1

THE YEAR 1805 was a momentous one in European history, witnessing the battles of Trafalgar and Austerlitz and finding Britain in the midst of a wartime boom in which commercial speculation was rife. Shrewdly patriotic gentlemen, whose business interests enabled them to offer the supplies necessary for the continuation of the glorious struggle against the French, quickly made their fortunes. Credit was everywhere plentiful; partners and time-expired apprentices branched out on their own, and young and newly established businesses mushroomed into growth in a way that jostled the High Streets of the towns and cities with a plethora of shops and offices on a scale unprecedented in the past. With money plentiful, there was a revival of interest in literature and the arts, and the reading public, growing rapidly in numbers every year, were soon spending increasing sums on newspapers, magazines and books of all sorts. Booksellers, whose title in those days was synonymous with publisher, flourished to an even greater degree than rival trades whose interest it was to cater for the arts; printers set up extra presses to cope with the seemingly insatiable demand for the printed word, and the boarded and labelled quartos and octavos filled shelves in libraries and drawing-rooms that were as new as the volumes they housed.

The modish taste for literature in all its forms was a stimulating trend that was noted with a sharp-eyed interest by a partly self-educated, heavily built young man, who, seventeen years before, had arrived in the city of Edinburgh from Fife. At the age of fourteen, Archibald Constable had been bound an apprentice to serve in Peter Hill's bookshop in the High Street, a dusty emporium of inter-connected rooms in which the shelves of massive folios towered above the constantly picked-over Dutch walls of books with which the floors and tables were littered. For his keep and a pittance to clothe him, plus the occasional gratefully accepted tip, the rapidly growing lad had passed the years

15

of his apprenticeship in the dim recesses of the back room where the parcelling and despatching were contrived with saved string and discarded paper, later to whistle his way through the crooked streets of the Old Town as errand boy for his master. But he kept his eyes open, read avidly whenever he could find the time, and, well before the end of his term, was trusted to conduct business with all but the most important clients. At the age of twenty he had the wit to marry the daughter of a wealthy printer in the city, and made immediate use of her tocher to set up in business on his own account.

Edinburgh had by this time become justly celebrated for the quality of its printing. Orders for books produced there poured in from all parts of Britain, and, within the space of a few years, Constable had made himself head of a prosperous and ever expanding publishing house. He had a keen commercial sense, coupled with a nose for a bargain in any form: he took calculated risks that sometimes appalled his competitors, but which usually, on the rising tide of public speculation, paid handsome dividends. By hard work and sometimes ruthless enterprise, within a few years he commanded a business that was rapidly overhauling in size those of his largest rivals. His ambitions were boundless and he was gifted with the drive to carry even the most grandiose schemes through to a successful conclusion, only providing the capital could be raised to cover the period until the returns came flooding in.

Once established as one of Edinburgh's leading publishers, Constable looked around for a means of widening his business interests in the same field. He had the sense to perceive which way the wind was blowing the inclinations of the newly emerging middle-class, and made sure that his firm acquired a reputation for a liberal approach to the political affairs of the day. With this in mind, he needed little persuading to agree to become the publisher of the newly founded *Edinburgh Review*, then edited by Sydney Smith, a man whose Whiggish sympathies were already well known to the public at large, and who was steering the paper firmly on an anti-Tory path. When Smith was succeeded in the chair by Francis Jeffrey, one of the most brilliant literary critics of his time, the magazine soon came to the forefront as a popular journal, gaining a circulation that enabled it to commission as contributors some of the best known names of the period. The now portly and confidence-inspiring figure of

Archibald Constable, gifted with what seemed the golden touch, before long stood at the head of the Scottish publishing world, his name commanding increasing attention and even a measure of respect in some of the largest of London's financial houses.

Amongst the stable of authors and poets who were regular contributors to Constable's *Edinburgh Review* were many of the most fashionable and successful writers of the day, and the un-heard of prices the publisher paid for their articles attracted what was then considered the cream of the literary world, irrespective of their political sympathies. The risen star in Scottish literary circles and a name now on everyone's lips was the young Sheriff-deputy of Selkirkshire, Walter Scott, whose poetical romance *The Lay of the Last Minstrel*, published early that year, was enjoying an unprecedented success with the reading public. This metrical romance in six cantos was welcomed in almost rap-turous terms by the vast majority of reviewers, copies of the heavy quarto being snapped up by an enthusiastic public who made it an instant and enduring success. The opening lines became a favourite piece of recitation for declaiming between sentimental songs at supper parties, with their dramatic and finely drawn picture of an ageing minstrel who narrates the sixteenth-century legend of the feud between the Buccleuchs and the Cranstouns:

> *The way was long, the wind was cold,*
> *The Minstrel was infirm and old;*
> *His wither'd cheek and tresses grey,*
> *Seem'd to have known a better day.*
> *The harp, his sole remaining joy,*
> *Was carried by an orphan boy.*
> *The last of all the Bards was he,*
> *Who sung of Border chivalry;*
> *For, welladay! their date was fled,*
> *His tuneful brethren all were dead;*
> *And he, neglected and oppress'd,*
> *Wish'd to be with them, and at rest.*

The ballad contained many oft quoted lines glorifying a Scot-land the author feared would soon be dead and gone. It revealed Scott's innate reverence for the feudalism of a privileged aristo-cracy, to the more influential members of which he dedicated so many of his books. The thirty-four-year-old poet's stiff conservatism was already hardening into an attitude of mind that was to colour the character of his ballads and romances for the remainder of his literary career, but despite this, Constable was able to overcome whatever scruples the author might have in contributing to a Whig magazine by offering the highest rate per page ever paid to any writer in his *Review*.

Scott had been born of middle-class parents in a dingy set of rooms set high up in the College Wynd off the Cowgate in Edinburgh, on the 15th August, 1771. A turnpike stair in the corner of the perpetually dirty little court led to where the boy's father, Walter Scott, Writer to the Signet, and a somewhat eccentric but painstaking member of the Edinburgh legal profession, lived in an atmosphere of austere simplicity with his wife Anne, and the remnants of what should have been a large family of growing children. The entry below, more often than not, was wet with the slops of basins and chamber-pots tipped from the windows above, and the flight of broken stairs leading to their apartments was the playground and refuge on rainy days of a horde of unkempt, unwashed and raucous children who thrived and wilted in the warren of overcrowded rooms that composed the tenement.

No less than six of the children born to the Scotts succumbed to the effects of being reared in such insanitary conditions; but the parents, bemused by the superstitions of a religion that taught them that bereavements must be accepted as a manifestation of God's Will, embraced their adversity with a stoical piety that calls more for pity than applause. But soon after their lusty young son Walter arrived, they moved to a newly built house in the modern George Square, a site surrounded with trees and trim gardens and where there were days when the air still retained a tang of the Pentlands and the Firth.

Despite being coughed over by a consumptive maid, whose condition was realized in time to prevent him contracting the disease, the infant Scott attained the age of eighteen months in seemingly robust health. At first he thrived in his new surroundings, but shortly after the family had taken up residence in their spic and span new home, he was suddenly laid low with a fever. This illness was at first thought by his parents to be nothing worse than one caused by his cutting several teeth, but there is no doubt that it was an attack of poliomyelitis, not then recognized as a specific disease. When she came to bathe him some days later, his mother was shocked to find that her little son's right leg was hanging limp and useless. Nothing she and her husband tried restored its use; physicians and surgeons were consulted, numerous remedies were prescribed and diets and exercises faithfully carried out; but all to no avail. From that day forth the small boy crawling round the house used only one knee to propel himself, his other seemingly healthy leg dragging behind him like a broken-stringed puppet's. The use of his right leg never returned and his limp remained to clump stolidly beside him for the rest of his days.

Although the position given him by birth was, as G. R. Gleig put it,[1] 'neither among the very high nor the very low, but in the middle class which constitutes the backbone of society,' young Scott could nevertheless boast in later years that he had in his veins the blood of the most historic of the Border lairds of Murray, Rutherford, Swinton, and Scott. From the clans of MacDougal and Campbell there was a strain direct from the ancient Celts, while amongst his forebears were the grizzled saints and sinners of a bloody and tumultuous past. Retreat in time for a few generations and you were surrounded by knights and cattle-lifters, Whigs and Jacobites, Cavaliers and Quakers, and the glowering portraits of dour and rough-hewn men who would have oathed their way to their claymores if one had so much as questioned their right to claim a gentle birth. It was even possible to trace his line through the Buccleuchs back to the great noblesse of Scotland (a somewhat laborious genealogical exercise but one in which it gave him pleasure to indulge). When a grown man, this child who entered life in what was little better than an eighteenth-century Edinburgh slum, was able to encrust his ceilings in his magnificent mansion at Abbotsford with a galaxy of painted shields depicting a pedigree as resplendent as many a peer could claim, and one which no member of the College of Heralds was able to gainsay.

By the time he reached his twelfth birthday, the lad in the round black hat, gaudy waistcoat, and the brown corduroy breeches of the Edinburgh High School uniform, had grown into a tall and thick-set young man, crowned with an unruly mop of long, sand-coloured hair, and with the distinctive facial features of a high domed forehead and deep upper lip that were to mark him out in any company to the end of his days. His

[1] *The Life of Sir Walter Scott*, G. R. Gleig, Edinburgh, 1871.

health had been far from good during the previous year, and his parents, believing that he had outgrown his strength, sent him to stay with his Aunt Janet at a little house standing near the banks of the Tweed at Kelso in Roxburghshire, at that time owned by the boy's father. It was here, during the summer of 1783, that Scott arrived to spend six months' holiday. This pleasant sojourn in Kelso was destined to have far-reaching effects on his future career; for it was here that the boy who was later to become the darling of the *literati* of every country into whose language his books were translated, first met the sons of John Ballantyne, draper and general merchant, and laid the foundations of a friendship with those whose fortunes were ultimately to founder with his own.

The Ballantyne shop in Kelso had been growing in size since the 1760s, when John Ballantyne's father had first painted the sign 'Grocer' over the front parlour window. At his death, John had managed to purchase the house next door, knocking the two front rooms into one, and modernizing the exterior by the provision of large bull's-eyes of greenish glass behind which the goods for sale were displayed. 'Draper and General Merchant' was now blazoned in letters of gold beneath the bedroom windows; and, by the time Scott came to Kelso, the store had become the largest in the town, standing on a corner of the main square in a spot now occupied by the British Linen Bank. According to the advertisements that appeared in the local paper, its windows must have been full of everything from 'Taplin's Genuine Horse Medicine' to 'The Very Latest London Fashions in Millinery'; these last mentioned feminine garments being dispensed by his bustling little wife Jean, whose hands must have already been fully occupied with the task of rearing their three young sons.

These brown haired, good-looking boys, James, John, and Alexander, proved from their earliest days to be both artistic and musical by nature, looking, as their grandmother Agnes Ballantyne put it, 'like the wee gentlemen in Angelica's Ladies Library rather than a grocer's bairns.' Each in his turn attended Kelso Grammar School, and it was here that young Scott found himself sharing a desk with James, the eldest of the trio. The two boys rapidly became firm friends, a friendship that was to last almost to the end of the author's life. Both boys later attended Edinburgh University, James Ballantyne returning to Kelso in 1795 to start his own solicitor's practice, and then a newspaper devoted to the Tory interest, the *Kelso Mail*; while Scott, at the age of seventeen, discovered that his father had decided that he should enter the highest branch of the legal profession. The lad's two elder brothers had chosen careers in the Army and Navy, and, although Walter was only too eager to do the same, his lameness made this impossible. He therefore accepted the third of the callings open to the sons of gentlemen, that of the law, and, on the 11th July, 1792, after three years' work of varying degrees of intensity and a great many late nights carousing with his fellow students, Scott passed his finals and proudly assumed the gown of an advocate.

As a lawyer he proved himself sound but by no means brilliant. His love of reading had enabled him to cover a wide expanse of subjects, and it is doubtful if there was another young man his age who had a more comprehensive knowledge of history of the British people, especially of events in the past that had occurred north of the Border. He had been gifted since early childhood with a prodigious memory, a memory that enabled him to store away details of the annals of his native land that he could recall with an almost photographic clarity years after the books of reference he had used had been closed and forgotten. He could now read German, speak a little French, and knew some Spanish and Italian, while his knowledge of Latin rivalled that of the professors at the University.

His boyhood was now behind him and, by the time he celebrated his twenty-first birthday, he was not only a leading member of several of the most noisy and boisterous clubs in a city at that time noted for the exuberance of its social life, but had gained a considerable reputation amongst his drinking companions for the amount of whisky he could imbibe without disappearing under the table. In later life he was apt to complain that these dusk-to-dawn bouts of over-indulgence were partly responsible for his frequent stomach troubles, and the son who later bore his name was more than once warned of the perils of drinking to excess. Young Scott's often extremely tardy appearances at the family breakfast table led his irate father on one occasion to accuse him of being 'born nae better than a gangrel scrape-gut!' But he certainly did not fritter away the hours he spent in the libraries of Edinburgh, and he passed into manhood with a head full of a most remarkable accumulation of knowledge covering practically every field of human endeavour.

After falling head over heels in love with a pert and extremely attractive young lady, Miss Williamina Belsches, daughter of Sir John Stuart-Belsches, he found himself summarily rejected in favour of a wealthy young banker. A hurt and wounded Scott soon afterwards became engaged to a Miss Charlotte Margaret Carpenter, a dark-haired, well-rounded young woman of French extraction. She was a ward of Lord Downshire, a nobleman whose relationship with the girl's mother has remained a mystery. They were married on Christmas Eve, 1797, in St Mary's Church, Carlisle. Despite an imagined broken heart, Scott outwardly appeared quite happy during his engagement, and there is little doubt that the marriage began with much tenderness on both sides. In October, 1798, the young parents were brought closer by sharing their grief over the death of their first baby, a boy who survived only a short period after his birth. Even so, it seems certain that Scott's heart had not been affected to anything like the extent it had been with his earlier love. In a letter to Lady Abercorn, written some twelve years later, he admits:

> Mrs. Scott's match and mine was of our own making, and proceeded from the most sincere affection on both sides, which was rather increased than diminished during twelve years marriage. But it is something short of love in all its forms, which I suspect people only feel once in all their lives; folk who have been nearly drowned in bathing rarely venturing a second time out of their depth.

They settled in Edinburgh, finally in 39 North Castle Street, a house which was to remain their city home until the dark days of 1826. Scott's meagre earning at the Bar now averaged about £150 a year; but, added to an allowance made him by his ailing father, plus an annuity of several hundreds of pounds which his wife received from her brother in India, they had more than enough to live on. At a tiny country cottage he purchased at Lasswade on the Esk, some six miles from the city, he translated two ballads from the German of Burger, entitled *The Chase* and *William and Helen* which later appeared in Edinburgh in the form of a slim quarto volume. This first literary effort attracted little attention, but it was the start of a career that brought him immeasurable fame throughout the world. The friend of his schooldays, James Ballantyne, now successful as the proprietor of the *Kelso Mail*, helped with the production of his next ephemeral pamphlet, published at Kelso in 1799, entitled *An Apology for Tales of Terror*, a satirical reference to the long delayed appearance of M. G. Lewis's book[1] to which Scott had been asked to contribute. The pamphlet marked an important milestone in the careers of both men, for with its appearance came the birth of the Border Press (later renamed the Ballantyne Press) a printing house which was soon to become famous throughout the British Isles.

Scott was so pleased with the excellence of style and typographical beauty of the finished booklet, with its meadows of margin, wide leading, good spacing and colour, and attractive appearance, that he had no hesitation in advising Ballantyne to keep his presses in play during the part of the week when they were normally idle, by obtaining booksellers' work. He promised James, provided a publisher could be found, to collect together as many of the Border ballads 'as might make a neat little volume, to sell for four or five shillings.' This was a subject that had interested him ever since his schooldays in Kelso, when he had sat hour after hour under the huge platanus tree in his aunt's garden, engrossed in a battered three-volume copy of Bishop Percy's *Reliques of Ancient English Poetry*. Much of his leisure time had been spent collecting the fast disappearing and half-remembered ballads stored only in the memories of some of the oldest inhabitants of the Border lands. But, aided by his friends John Leyden, William Laidlaw, and the redoubtable James Hogg, by the autumn of 1801 he had amassed sufficient to fill two large octavo volumes.

Early in 1802, after months of painstaking effort in the press-room and careful and meticulous proof reading by James Ballantyne, whom Scott came to rely on more and more in this respect in later years, the first edition of *Minstrelsy of the Scottish Border* was at last sent to the booksellers. It proved a steady if unspectacular success and within twelve months the whole 850 copies of the first printing had been sold. The imprint 'Kelso' on the title-pages was read with astonishment by many of its readers, some of whom wrote to Cadell and Davies, the publishers, saying they were amazed at the quality of typography which so obscure a town could produce. Ballantyne was naturally extremely pleased with the reception the work received, for he

[1] Under the title *Tales of Wonder*, M. G. (Monk) Lewis's collection of ballads and poems appeared in London in 1801. Scott had been asked to contribute verses to it as early as 1798; hence his exasperation at its non-appearance. Few copies (according to Lockhart not more than a dozen) were printed of *An Apology for Tales of Terror*, and of these only five are known to have survived.

had awaited the outcome of the sale of the first edition before finally making up his mind whether to try even more ambitious projects in the city of Edinburgh. This was a course Scott had been urging on him since the spring of 1800, when he had written to James:

> It appears to me that such a plan, judiciously adopted and diligently pursued, opens a fair road to an ample fortune. In the mean while, the *Kelso Mail* might be so arranged as to be still a source of some advantage to you; and, I dare say, if wanted, pecuniary assistance might be procured to assist you at the outset, either upon terms of share or otherwise.

He had painted a rosy picture of the fortune awaiting Ballantyne in Edinburgh, but was unable to immediately lure James to the city, although the printer took the first steps to make such a move possible in the future. His youngest brother, Alexander, (always known as 'Sandy') was given a place as second-in-command at the *Kelso Mail*, James going to great pains to teach him all he knew about the editorship of the newspaper. But, for the moment, Ballantyne stayed where he was, and Scott's first tentative attempt to buy a share in the printing enterprise came to nothing.

At that time Scott was financially far better off than he can ever have imagined possible so early in life. Due to the influence of the Duke of Buccleuch and Lord Melville, both of whom he could count among his friends, he had been appointed Sheriff-deputy of Selkirkshire. So, at the age of only twenty-eight, he found himself in receipt of a thousand pounds a year, made up of his wife's allowance, his earning at the Bar, and the residue of his late father's estate; his annuity from the sheriffship bringing in £250 a year. He was now comfortably settled in life, happily married, with a healthy young family, and surrounded by a large circle of friends. Yet he was already consumed with financial ambitions that stemmed from an inate greed, perhaps prompted by a sense of insecurity brought about by his physical disability which had made him the butt of coarsely shouted facetious remarks for much of his early childhood. An unexpected windfall in the summer of 1804 increased his bank balance by £5,600,[1]

---

[1] Walter Scott's uncle, Captain Robert Scott of Kelso, died, leaving his nephew Rosebank Cottage, together with thirty acres of fine pastoral land. This he immediately sold for £5,000, the residue of his uncle's estate making up the balance.

and soon afterwards he moved to Ashiestiel, a rented property of far more imposing proportions than the humble cottage at Lasswade. He now had a growing family, a son aged three, named after himself, a five year old daughter, Sophia; and a baby girl of just over twelve months whom they had called Anne. They settled in Ashiestiel in the late summer, furnishing it in a manner suitable for a Sheriff of the county to reside in, and before long he was deeply immersed in a major literary work he had on hand.

It was from this peaceful setting that he despatched to Ballantyne the completed manuscript of the metrical romance that was to bring him nation-wide fame. James had finally been persuaded by his friend to take the plunge and move to Edinburgh, Scott advancing him £500 as a loan to increase the liquid capital of the business. The printer had set up his presses in two crowded rooms in Holyrood House, but the close association with Edinburgh publishers and the increasing amount of Session work which Scott was able to channel in his direction soon rendered these too small. He was obliged to move again; first to Foulis Close in the Canongate, and later to much larger premises in Paul's Works nearby. Here, according to a letter of Scott's, written in July 1806, James finally found the space his rapidly expanding business required, having 'established a hall, equal to that which the genie of the lamp built for Aladdin in point of size, but rather less superbly furnished, being occupied by about a dozen presses'.

Archibald Constable had taken note of the young advocate's literary success soon after the three-volume second edition of *Minstrelsy of the Scottish Border* had issued from Ballantyne's press in Holyrood House in 1803. He was astute enough to persuade Longman, Hurst, Rees, and Orme, the London publishers, to let him take a share of the risk in publishing *The Lay of the Last Minstrel*, and when the volume appeared in January 1805, his firm's name was on the title-page in small print. He had noted with his usual perception that the Border Sheriff appeared to be pioneering new poetical paths that were largely in accord with modern taste, and he marked him as a man whose acquaintance it would be wise to cultivate, epecially as the poet had not yet bound himself to any rival publisher.

Meanwhile, the little printer was finding that things had gone almost embarrassingly well since the Ballantyne Press had moved to Edinburgh. The phenomenal success of the *Lay* had put a heavy strain on the firm's financial resources and orders from other publishers waiting to be executed were now held up by lack of capital to purchase the materials for their completion. Money was slow in coming in; booksellers and other customers often demanded long credit before placing their orders, and it soon became obvious to its proprietor that his firm was grossly under-capitalized. Paper, inks, type-faces, extra presses, machinery of all sorts, needed to be bought and paid for to keep the printed sheets flowing and they were struggling to cope with the demands of a large turnover on liquid resources of only a few hundred pounds. James Ballantyne, with order books full to overflowing, was sometimes hard pressed to find sufficient funds to meet the weekly salaries of his employees, and he was finally compelled to write to Scott to acquaint him with his difficulties.

JAMES'S REQUEST CAME at a fortuitous time. Scott was still in possession of the majority of the £5,600 he had received under the terms of his late uncle's will, having previously earmarked most of it to purchase the moderately sized estate of Broadmeadows, situated near the ruins of Newark Abbey on the northern bank of the Yarrow. But his hopes of investing the money in a larger country house eventually came to nothing, and when Ballantyne's letter arrived he immediately seized the chance to procure a share in what he knew to be a business whose future profits seemed assured. To finance a rapidly growing enterprise, whose reputation for the typographical beauty of its products was already bringing in more work than its owner could handle, was an opportunity not to be missed, and he envisaged a large and increasing return on his capital.

Any ambitions he might have had of carving a niche in the legal profession as a successful young advocate had receded during the last few years. His biographer, Lockhart, states that Scott attributed his lack of clients to the prejudice of Scottish solicitors to employing a barrister who devoted so much of his time to literary pursuits. A more likely reason was his lack of enthusiasm for the day-to-day duties of an advocate who had yet to make a name for himself at the Bar; another, the fact that he made a comparatively poor showing in the cut and thrust of court debate. His well-grounded knowledge of the jurisprudence of his country was not coupled with any flair for cross-examination and legal oratory; he had a lukewarm approach to a side of the profession in which he had never evinced much interest, and the distractions of a literary career further dimmed his chances of finding wealthy clients with causes to argue and grievances to redress.

The reasonably prosperous solicitor's business which his father had left in George Square had gradually dwindled away due to the incompetence of his brother Thomas, so that the regular work which had come his way from this source was reduced to a mere trickle. As his literary reputation advanced, so did his professional work at the Bar diminish. But he had no intention of retiring as a barrister and devoting his time solely to writing; although at this period, with a fixed income from various sources of about £1,000 a year, he might very well have done so. 'I determined,' he said, 'that literature should be my staff but not my crutch, and that the profits of my literary labour, however convenient otherwise, should not, if I could help it, become necessary to my ordinary expenses. Upon such a post an author might hope to retreat, without any perceptible alteration of circumstances, whenever the time should arrive that the public grew weary of his endeavours to please, or he himself should tire of the pen. I possessed so many friends capable of assisting me in this object of ambition, that I could hardly over-rate my own prospects of obtaining the preferment to which I limited my wishes; and, in fact, I obtained, in no long period, the reversion of a situation which completely met them.'[1]

He had set his heart on obtaining the post of Clerk of Session, a position at that time carrying a salary of £800 per annum, the duties of which consisted of 'a few hours' labour in the forenoons when the Court sits, leaving the evenings and the whole vacation open for literary pursuits.' The present holder of the office was a rather deaf and decidedly doddery old gentleman, Mr George Home by name, and Scott diplomatically suggested to him that he should take over his duties gratuitously during his lifetime, leaving Home to draw the salary which the author would succeed to at his death. This was mulled over for some time but finally agreed; the Treasury also sanctioning the arrangement, thus giving Scott an assured income, over and above what he already held, as soon as Mr Home should pass to a better world.

In the meantime the author had thought over the contents of Ballantyne's letter requesting a further loan, and had replied 'that he was not quite sure that it would be prudent for him to comply, but in order to evince his entire confidence in me,' so James later told Lockhart, 'he was willing to make a suitable advance to be admitted as a third-sharer of my business.'[2] If the firm was to meet its obligations and eventually expand, Ballan-

---

[1] Introduction to the 1830 edition of the *Lay of the Last Minstrel*.
[2] *Memoirs of the Life of Sir Walter Scott, Bart.*, Vol. II. Fuller publication details of works consulted are provided in the select Bibliography.

tyne, who had lived well off the profits, had to find fresh capital as quickly as possible, so to this suggestion he had perforce to agree. A valuation of the machinery, type-founts, and other assets, taken to reassure Scott as to the soundness of the enterprise, revealed property totalling £2,090, and negotiations were completed on Whit Sunday, 26th May, 1805. On that day a partnership agreement was signed whereby the author advanced a further £1,500, making his total investment £2,000 as his previous loan of £500 was now converted into share capital. The contract admitted him into partnership as owner of one third of the stock of James Ballantyne and Company, drawing profits in the same proportion, and, with the help of this welcome influx of money, the printing house prospered for the next few years. Scott advanced the firm's interests in every way he could, but kept the agreement a close secret from even his most intimate friends, only William Erskine sharing the knowledge of his entry into the world of commerce.

Here we can perceive Scott's consuming desire asserting itself; his impatient need to acquire the wealth that would enable him to maintain a position in society to which he imagined he was fully entitled by reason of his illustrious forebears that had honoured the family name. It was not to help a friend in need or from any altruistic and noble-minded wish to further the cause of literature and the arts that he advanced Ballantyne the money. His action in this case, as in many others later in life, was no more than a straight-forward commercial speculation; a gamble that he hoped might double or treble his investment in a matter of a few years and give him the capital he needed to advance his status in a world where money commanded respect and a gentleman must provide for his guests on a scale that did not permit invidious comparisons to be made with the entertainment provided by those of his wealthier friends.

Even before the agreement was actually signed, he had plunged into an enthusiastic appraisal of their future prospects, proposing to his partner-to-be a number of grandiose schemes to keep his presses well supplied.

He succeeded at first in arousing even the interest of the shrewd Archibald Constable in a gigantic plan for a hundred or more volumes edition of the British poets, only to discover that Cadell and Davis of London had a similar, though much smaller, plan afoot, and had approached Thomas Campbell to write the biographical prefaces. Undismayed by this news, Scott immediately proposed that the Edinburgh and London publishing houses should join forces for the venture, and that the task of editing the work should be shared between himself and his brother poet; an idea which initially had the tentative approval of the publishers and to which Campbell warmly assented.

It is difficult to imagine that such an ambitious undertaking could ever have been a commercial success; there were too many imponderables in a scheme of this size, and once having advertised the scale of the venture and supplied the first volumes, it would have been most difficult to withdraw before completion of the series. But the whole grandiose design eventually came to nothing in the face of the publishers' refusal to sanction unappealing titles such as Chaucer, which both Scott and Campbell insisted must be included. It was perhaps a happy escape for all concerned; but it serves to show how Scott's desire to feed a lucrative printing order through the presses of James Ballantyne & Company, in whose profits he now shared, clouded his judgement as to the merits of an enterprise that could well have turned out to be a white elephant of monstrous proportions.[1] Campbell ultimately contented himself with preparing for the press a seven-volume edition of *Specimens of the British Poets*, which appeared in 1819, while Scott turned his attention to new fields of literary endeavour.

A projected edition of the works of Dryden had also come near to foundering, but a Mr Miller of Albemarle Street, London, was persuaded to commission Scott to edit an eighteen-volume series at a price of forty guineas a volume. The author accepted, but on one rigid condition; namely, that Mr Ballantyne of James Ballantyne & Company be given the order for printing the work. To this stipulation William Miller had no option but to agree, while the two partners in the printing concern winked knowingly and mentally counted the profits on a very sizable order. On open tender it may never have come their way.

For the next few years Scott became an extremely active miscellaneous writer, devoting most of his free time to furthering a diversity of literary enterprises. He undertook many tasks that could be described as little better than hackwork, but most of

[1] Scott wrote to Ellis: 'As for the British Poets, my plan was greatly too liberal to stand the least chance of being adopted by the trade at large, as I wished them to begin with Chaucer. The fact is, I never expected they would agree to it.'

which helped to swell the turnover at Paul's Works in a way he hoped might one day make his fortune. A host of comparatively minor publications flowed from his pen; tasks in which he was aided by the many impoverished amanuenses and down-and-out authors whom he employed to do the routine tasks of copying for the press, or checking the countless bibliographical details he needed for the texts. 'It was enough to tear me to pieces,' he once told Lockhart, 'but there was a wonderful exhilaration about it all; my blood was kept at fever-pitch—I felt as though I could have grappled with anything and everything; then there was hardly one of my schemes that did not afford me the means of serving some poor devil of a brother author. There was always huge piles of material to be arranged, sifted, or indexed—volumes of extracts to be transcribed—journeys to be made hither and thither, for ascertaining the little facts and dates—in short, I could commonly keep half-a-dozen of the ragged regiment of Parnassus in tolerable ease.' Like coal-waggons linked to an engine, Lockhart suggested. 'Yes,' retorted Scott, 'but there was a cursed lot of dung-carts too.'[1]

Concurrently with the 'Dryden' he somehow found sufficient time to edit *Original Memoirs written during the Great Civil War* by Slingsby; *Memoirs of Capt. George Carleton*; *Memoirs of Robert Carey* by Sir R. Naughton; *The State Papers of Sir Ralph Sadler* (edited by Clifford but with historical notes by Scott); *The Life of Lord Herbert of Cherbury*; *Queenhoo Hall, a Romance* by Joseph Strutt; and a mass of tracts, magazine articles, and various antiquarian curiosa. All these works of specialist interest delighted him as a historian and provided much well-paid work for the Ballantyne Press, but they made little if any profit for the publishing houses he persuaded to sponsor them. There was even some talk of a vast edition of the British novelists, an idea first mooted by the young and comparatively inexperienced publisher John Murray; but this, fortunately for all concerned, came to nothing. 'I like well,' Constable once exasperatedly exclaimed, 'Scott's ain bairns, but Heaven preserve me from those of his following!' Of all these works probably only *Queenhoo Hall* had any considerable bearing on the course of his future career, for through working on this romance of ancient times he must have learned much of the art needed for composing historical novels. This knowledge was to stand him in good stead when he came

[1] *Life of Scott*, Vol. II.

to write *Waverley* and the rest of the long series of immensely popular Scottish tales.

John Ballantyne, the middle brother of the trio, thin and undersized but possessing the type of sensuous good looks that many women found irresistible, had earned himself the reputation of being the black sheep of the family; a title he cheerfully accepted and did nothing to disown. He was gifted with such a devil-may-care, happy-go-lucky personality that his host of friends had a genuine affection for the little man, finding him an inexhaustible fund of amusement. Scott thoroughly enjoyed his sometimes outrageous misbehaviour, his antics and eccentricities being a continual source of delight after the humdrum affairs of the Court of Session, and to the end he never tired of 'Jocund Johnny's' mercurial company. The author, who took pleasure in pegging nicknames to all his friends, dubbed him 'Rigdumfunnidos' and loved to regale his more serious minded companions with tales of John's latest escapades, some of which read like a scene from a Restoration comedy.

Since leaving school he had spent some time in the office of a London banking house, an apprenticeship he had loathed, finding the dry-as-dust environment boring in the extreme. On his return to Kelso his father, against his better judgement, had been forced to give him a place in the management of the family store, and at the age of twenty-one, due to his mother's influence, he had been grudgingly taken into partnership. But in 1797, there had been a violent quarrel between him and his strictly conformist father, the old man having strongly disapproved of his son's proposed marriage with a Miss Hermione Parker, a local lass who had gained a reputation for being scandalously modernistic in her conduct and most unladylike in her general deportment. She was a highly intelligent and artistic young miss, very good looking as a teenager, and gifted with a flow of worldly-wise repartee that exactly suited the high-spirited, hard-drinking young grocer's idea of a partner in matrimony. Their engagement precipitated an immediate row, and their marriage resulted in the dissolution of the business arrangement between the two men, the outraged father refusing any longer to recognize John as his son.

Perhaps to spite him, the newly-weds opened their own shop

within a few yards of that of John Ballantyne senior,[1] taking with them half of the stock-in-trade from the family store and using Hermione's marriage portion to supply counters and fittings for the new premises. Above their freshly painted little haberdashery the two set up home, dealing in millinery, soft furnishings and fancy goods of all descriptions. For a time they prospered, but John was never satisfied for long with a quietly respectable life and was soon leaving the management of the business more and more in the hands of his precocious young wife who was temperamentally unsuited for the task. As often as three times a week her husband donned his gilt-buttoned green coat and doe-skin leggings and rode off to follow the hounds. He was unfailing in his attendance at local race meetings, incensing his father and causing numerous violent rows with Hermione by light-heartedly running up gambling debts, which, though eventually paid, did much to destroy the credit of both their shops. Coupled with a too free indulgence in the delights of the brandy bottle and expensive amorous weekends with the daughter of a local farmer, these vicious amusements gradually began to take their toll, and, despite his wife's single-handed efforts to continue the business, by 1806 they were very near ruin. The greatest drain on John's resources was fulfilling the expensive demands of the spoilt and petulant girl he had made his mistress, the attractive daughter of a Kelso farmer, who eventually deserted him for a richer friend.

With his business in ruins, his wife now estranged, and the girl he loved in the arms of another man, for once John's gay spirited optimism deserted him and he dejectedly resolved to attempt a new life in Jamaica; only the intervention of his brother James, to whom he revealed his plan, preventing him from emigrating. He accepted the offer of a job in his brother's printing office at a salary of two hundred pounds a year; but it was conditional on his mending his ways and returning to live with his wife. His mother successfully effected a reconciliation between the two, knowing full well that this was bound to make her son adopt a more sober mode of existence. The quarrel between John and his father was patched up at the same time, Hermione being grudgingly accepted as a member of the family from that time onwards. The old man had fared no better than his son in business; ill health, competition from John's shop, and bad

[1] John's shop was at 48 Market Place, The Square, Kelso.

debts, had all combined to increase the worries which a dwindling turnover brought in its trail and he had turned increasingly to the bottle as a means of forgetting his difficulties. His intemperate habits and surly bad temper on the days when he was fit to serve, had estranged many of his best customers from the long established Kelso store, and he was driven to trading and purchasing stock by accommodation notes and promises-to-pay. These means of obtaining credit meant that he was forced to pay high rates of interest for the loans he was able to raise, and inevitably he fell deeply into debt, finally having to sell up in order to clear himself. He too, was now employed by his son James, earning a hundred pounds a year as proof reader and ledger clerk, while his wife acted as her son's housekeeper and lived rent free with her husband in St John Street.

Hermione, whose total inability to resist the more fattening forms of both food and drink had by this time rendered her decidedly on the plump side, promised to forgive her philandering husband his sins, and to outward appearances the breach between them was sealed. They rented a villa at Trinity Grove on the Firth of Forth,[1] about three miles from Paul's Works in Edinburgh, and, no doubt with his tongue in his cheek, John promptly renamed it 'Harmony Hall'. But the atmosphere inside must have been anything but harmonious for he gleefully devised a scheme which enabled him to share the same roof with his wife, but was instrumental in keeping her at a safe distance. Although typical of the comicality of his nature, it must often have brought tears of rage to her eyes and it certainly cannot have benefited their marital relationship. Taking advantage of her absence for a few days in Kelso, wee Johnny Ballantyne had the door leading to one wing of the house made so narrow that he could himself only pass through it sideways, while poor stout Hermione was barred as effectively as a camel at the needle's eye. Into this refuge he scuttled whenever she uncovered one of his amorous intrigues, leaving her ranting outside while he was safe within.

After the spring recess of 1806 Scott had for the first time assumed his duties as one of the Principal Clerks of the Court of

[1] John later purchased the villa from the trustees of a Mr William Creech, (bookseller and ex-Lord Provost of Edinburgh).

34

Session, a post he subsequently filled to the entire satisfaction of the members of the Bar for the following twenty-five years. Henceforth he was to sit for about five hours a day at the table below the judges' bench, recording in dry legal language their lordships' decisions, and taking written note of the progress of the various cases that came before them. There was a team of six Principal Clerks amongst whom the work of the various courts was divided, and their tasks, although monotonous, were certainly not of an exacting nature. The Court of Session did not sit on a Monday, that day being reserved for criminal trials in the High Court; and Scott also had free every other Wednesday, 'Teind Wednesday' as it was called, when the judges assembled to hear legal pleas regarding tithes. The Court was in recess for a full six months of every year, so he found plenty of free time for both literary and political pursuits. And at this period he took an extremely active interest in the political affairs of the day.

A new Whig government had just been elected, and one of its first measures was to impeach Scott's close friend and benefactor, Lord Melville, on the grounds of fraudulent conversion. It was alleged that large sums of public money intended for the Navy had found their way into his Lordship's pockets during his term of office as Treasurer, and the case aroused wide interest, especially in Scotland. But on the 12th June, 1806, after a trial before his fellow peers lasting fifteen days, they acquitted him by majority verdicts of all the charges laid against him. As may be imagined, this news was received with particular satisfaction amongst his Tory friends in Edinburgh; Scott taking it upon himself to write a triumphant ballad in his honour. He persuaded James Ballantyne, who was noted for his rich brown baritone voice, to sing it at a public dinner arranged to celebrate Melville's acquittal, and, no sooner was the last course served, than the stout little clean-shaven printer hoisted himself on a chair and banged with the butt end of a bottle on the table-cloth to call for some sort of order in the crowded room. Before long, to the rollicking tune of 'Carrickfergus', the choruses were roared out by the well-wined, well-dined well-wishers there assembled, with Scott's voice joining in as loud as the rest.

Since here we are set in array round the table,
Five hundred good fellows well met in a hall,
Come listen, brave boys, and I'll sing as I'm able,

How innocence triumphed and pride got a fall.
 But push round the claret,
 Come, stewards, don't spare it,
With rapture you'll drink to the toast that I give:
 Here, boys, join with me instantly,
 Off with it merrily—
MELVILLE *for ever, and long may he live!*

Their shouts and cheers nearly raised the roof at the end of the seven verses. But some of the expressions used in the song gave particular offence to many sincere friends of the composer of the lyric when they read them a few days later. A number of his closest acquaintances were strong supporters of the Whig administration, and the last verse especially aroused their anger in no uncertain measure, causing the author many regrets when he realized how deeply he had wounded their feelings.

 In Grenville and Spencer,
 And some few good men, sir,
High talents we honour, slight difference forgive;
 But the Brewer we'll hoax,
 Tallyho to the Fox,
And drink MELVILLE *for ever, as long as we live!*

At the time these words were being drunkenly bawled through the streets of Edinburgh, the Whig statesman Charles James Fox was known to be in very precarious health, and in fact was dying of a disease of which dropsy was one of the more distressing symptoms. It is not therefore surprising, that the penultimate line of the last verse was deemed to be in the worst of taste, and the expression 'Tallyho', with its implication of an imminent 'kill', lost Scott several friends and caused a coldness in the attitude of others that the passage of time never really overcame. The local Tories were delighted, however, and made sure that the whole composition appeared in as many newspapers as would print it; their darling George Canning writing Scott to the effect that all of his party 'are thankful for your exertions in a cause which they have much at heart, [and] owe it to themselves, as well as to you, that the expressions of their gratitude and pleasure should reach you in as direct a manner as possible.'

During the short reign of the Whig administration Scott took an extremely active interest in the politics of his county; canvassing electors, addressing meetings, and being especially to the fore whenever he considered the interests of his great and noble and almightily influential patrons the Buccleuchs were in any way threatened. Not all his energies were expended in defence of the Duke and Duchess; he worked hard in other directions, and in February, 1808, his epic poem *Marmion* was published and immediately proceeded to race through edition after edition. It was a stirring ballad of Scottish chivalry, culminating in the bitter defeat on Flodden field; some of the stanzas depicting the battle having been hastily noted down after a wild gallop he took with his Volunteer regiment across the sands at Portobello. Although the critics were divided as to its merits, the public swamped Ballantyne's presses with their demands for copies and for some weeks there was a backlog of orders which the booksellers were clamouring to see filled. Constable had characteristically taken a chance, believed that it might well prove a best seller, and had offered the author the round sum of one thousand pounds for the poem without having actually seen one word of the manuscript. He was well satisfied with his bargain.

The following year was in many ways a momentous one for Scott and those with whom his literary activities brought him into contact. John Ballantyne, a little worn at the elbows but doing his best to live a gay life on two hundred a year, had been chafing as a clerk in his brother's printing office for two years. Any opportunity which might present him with the chance of proving his true worth by the use of his own initiative would be more than welcome, as he let all and sundry know. He was now determined to break out of the stifling drudgery of office routine and had formulated a dozen glittering business schemes which needed only the capital to light the train to financial success. Meanwhile, his brother Sandy Ballantyne back in Kelso had married in 1806 a Miss Anne Randall Scott Grant, 'a lass wi' a lang pedigree', whose dowry enabled him to purchase from his brother James his entire interest in the *Kelso Mail*. James in his turn found himself in pocket from the sale of the newspaper at a time when additional funds were extremely welcome. His hopes, and those of brother John, were centred on Walter Scott's reaction to the proposals they had put to him some months before, that he should consider acting as his own publisher and partake of the very large profits that at present were finding their way into the pockets of Archibald Constable and his partner.

For some time the author had been less than happy that he was in any way associated with Constable's *Edinburgh Review*. Its politics he detested, and although he knew the editor, Francis Jeffrey, and treated him as a personal friend, his criticisms of some of his poetry had undoubtably rankled in the past. The influence of the *Review* was now so great that it could damn a new work almost completely in the eyes of the reading public, and the pronouncements of contributors such as Sydney Smith, Henry Brougham, or Jeffrey himself, were always awaited with considerable anxiety by those struggling to make a living by the pen. Scott was now too well established as a poet for the remarks in the *Review* to have much effect on sales of his latest work, however cogently they might be expressed, and the editor did not hesitate to despatch a copy of his article on *Marmion* to him before it appeared in print. With it went a note saying—'If I did not give you credit for more magnanimity than any other of your irritable tribe, I should scarcely venture to put this into your hands. As it is, I do it with no little solicitude, and earnestly hope that it will make no difference in the friendship which has hitherto subsisted between us.'

What Scott thought of the review, with its description of his poem as 'a broken narrative—a redundancy of minute description—bursts of unequal and energetic poetry—and a general tone of spirit and animation, unchecked by timidity or affectation, and unchastened by any great delicacy of taste or elegance of fancy' it is not now possible to tell with certainty. The article highlighting the shortcomings of *Marmion* was published on the very day when Jeffrey was expected to dine with the Scotts at their house in Castle Street, the invitation having been sent and accepted some time before. Mrs Scott was strangely silent throughout the meal, but at the end of the evening, when their guest rose to take his leave, she turned to him suddenly, saying in her attractive continental accent—'Well, goodnight, Mr Jeffrey—dey tell me you have abused Scott in de *Review*, and I hope Mr Constable has paid you very well for writing it.' In the embarrassing silence that followed her words the editor made an apologetic departure. It is more than likely that her attitude, together with the annoyance expressed by many of his well-wishers, had a lasting effect on Scott's future conduct towards Constable, despite his previous boast that he considered himself impervious to criticism.

Matters were finally brought to a head between the owner of the *Review* and himself over remarks made by the publisher's partner, Mr Alexander Gibson Hunter. Scott had been seeking an excuse to sever the relationship between himself and Archibald Constable and Company for some time; ever since, in fact, he realized that he could get his fingers on a share of the profits derived from the publication of his own and other literary works. The dispute began shortly after Constable had offered him the sum of £1,500 for an edition of Swift's works, which was to include a biography. 'It will occupy me occasionally for two years,' Scott noted in February, 1808, 'but labour is to me really pleasure, and the profit is not to be despised.' Hunter was appalled at the price his partner had offered for the work, and made it quite plain that he considered that Scott should concentrate all his energies on completing it within a reasonable time; if necessary shelving all other projects until it was finished. This was the opening the author had been looking for in order to put in hand his plans for setting up a rival concern, and he wrote a preliminary letter on the 2nd January, 1809, to set the ball rolling.

In this he requested, that if, on reflection, the publishers thought they had made a bad bargain and had committed themselves too hastily, they would forthwith cancel the contract he had made with them. Constable wrote back on the 11th of the same month with a conciliatory reply.

Sir,

We are anxious to assure you that we feel no dissatisfaction at any part of our bargain about Swift. Viewing it as a safe and respectable speculation, we should be very sorry to agree to your relinquishing the undertaking, and indeed rely with confidence on its proceeding as originally arranged.

We regret that you have not been more willing to overlook the unguarded expression of our Mr Hunter about which you complain. We are very much concerned that any circumstances should have occurred that should thus interrupt our friendly intercourse; but as we are not willing to believe that we have done anything which should prevent our being again friends, we may at least be permitted to express a hope that matters may hereafter be restored to their old footing between us, when the misrepresentations of interested persons may cease to be remembered.

At any rate, you will always find us, what we trust we have ever been, Sir, your faithful servants,

A. Constable & Co.

By return Scott wrote a curt reply, stating that he was 'only happy that the breach has taken place before there was any real loss to complain of,' and asking for a settlement of his outstanding account. Constable was bitter about the way he had been treated, believing that Scott had only used his firm until he was strong enough to dispense with their services. 'We have merely reared the oak until it could support itself,' he told his friends; but he was far-sighted enough to say nothing that would make an eventual reconciliation impossible.

THE WHIG WRITERS who contributed to the *Edinburgh Review* almost without exception supported a policy of non-intervention in Spain, where the Peninsular War had recently started. Some of the articles that had appeared were frankly defeatist in tone, putting the intensely patriotic Walter Scott nearly beside himself with rage. He followed the campaign with the eager enthusiasm of an armchair general, passing sleepless nights when things seemed to be going badly, and cursing the incompetent War Office martinets who had initially recalled Arthur Wellesley (later the Duke of Wellington) from his command. Then came Jeffrey's celebrated condemnation of the war, which appeared in the *Review* under the heading of 'Don Cevallos, on the usurpation of Spain'. This to Scott was the last straw, and he wrote immediately to Constable, telling him to strike his name from the list of subscribers, and adding that his magazine was such that 'I can no longer continue to receive or read it.'

To George Ellis, his close friend, he now confided a secret; first setting out some of his reasons for his course of action.

Ashiestiel, Nov. 2d, 1808

Dear Ellis,

We had, equally to our joy and surprise, a flying visit from Heber, about three weeks ago. He staid but three days—but, between old stories and new, we made them very merry in their passage.

During his stay, John Murray, the bookseller in Fleet Street, who has more real knowledge of what concerns his business than any of his brethren—at least than any of them that I know—came to canvass a most important plan, of which I am now, in 'dern privacie,' to give you the outline. I had most strongly recommended to our Lord Advocate to think of some counter measures against the *Edinburgh Review*, which, politically speaking, is doing incalculable damage...

The *Edinburgh Review* tells you coolly, 'We foresee a speedy revolution in this country as well as Mr Cobbett;' and, to say the truth, by degrading the person of the Sovereign—exalting the power of the French armies, and the wisdom of their counsels— holding forth that peace (which they allow can only be purchased by the humiliating prostration of our honour) is indispensible to the very existence of this country—I think, that for these two years past, they have done their utmost to hasten the accomplishment of their own prophecy. Of this work 9000 copies are printed quarterly, and no genteel family can pretend to be without it, because, in- dependent of its politics, it gives the only valuable literary criticism which can be met with. Consider, of the numbers who read this work, how many are there likely to separate the literature from the politics—how many youths are there upon whose minds the flashy and bold character of the work is likely to make an indelible impression; and think what the consequence is likely to be.

Now, I think there is balm in Gilead for all this; and that the cure lies in instituting such a Review in London as should be conducted totally independent of the bookselling influence, on a plan as liberal as that of the Edinburgh, its literature as well supported, and its principles English and constitutional. Accordingly, I have been given to understand that Mr William Gifford is willing to become the conductor of such a work, and I have written to him, at the Lord Advocate's desire, a very voluminous letter of the subject...

Ever yours,
Walter Scott

The following year saw the birth of the *Quarterly Review*, a paper Tory to its backbone, with behind it many of the old staff of the ultra right-wing 'Anti-Jacobin' which had ceased publica- tion in 1798. George Canning, who became Prime Minister in 1827, was associated with it from the start, as was Hookham Frere, Robert Southey, Samuel Rogers and a host of other well known names. Under the editorship of the vitriolic William Gifford, whose rigorous adherence, as a critic, to the old school of literature and whose implacable hatred of all radical ideas lent added force to his often bitter denunciations of the rising generation of poets and authors, the *Quarterly* advanced from strength to strength, eating into the circulation of the *Edinburgh Review* in a way that must have caused Constable and Jeffrey increasing concern. Scott, Heber, Ellis, and others who had no love for the *Edinburgh*'s political views, all contributed articles, their names lending prestige to the magazine in its early days and doing much to establish its name in the minds of the reading public. Several of Scott's friends were dismayed that he should so pointedly support this new pillar of the Tory party, believing this was bound to antagonize many of those who admired his literary talents and would certainly do nothing to assist his career as a writer. Lord Dalkeith wrote to him, asking that he 'talk not, think not of Politics. Go to the hills and converse with the Spirit of the Fell, or any spirit but the Spirit of Party, which is the fellest fiend that ever disturbed harmony and social pleasure.'[1] But Scott paid no need to his aristocratic friend and subsequently found himself involved in the souring rancours of political strife at a time of life when what he needed before all else were the peaceful quietudes of worry-free days.

By the end of January, 1809, he had broken with Constable completely and was busy with his plans for setting up the rival publishing house. The ubiquitous John Ballantyne was delighted to be offered the post of co-partner and manager of the new business venture, and he jumped at the chance of once again becoming his own master. He celebrated his long awaited good fortune by arriving home that evening with a concourse of extremely genial and very noisy friends, who finished a raucous night of wining and dining by a series of arm-linking choruses, grouped round a dish of broiled bones and a vast bowl of steaming punch, in which his wife, Hermione, shiny and red-faced, dipped the ladle with the rest. But he was determined to make a success of his new career and for the first few months diligently applied himself to the task of establishing the firm in its Hanover Street premises.

Scott took a half share in the new enterprise which he had decided should trade under the name of John Ballantyne and Company; James and John being allotted a quarter share each, the last named receiving a salary of three hundred pounds per annum for his duties as manager. Any profits made were to be divided in the same proportion as the shareholding of the partners, and all matters of policy were supposed to be decided jointly. But in practice, Scott, having subscribed £1,000 as his share of the floatation capital, plus a loan of £1,500 to increase its liquid assets, had the last word in all matters of importance, including the vital one of which titles the company should market. James, by reason of the money received from his brother Sandy in respect of his purchase of the *Kelso Mail*, was

[1] *Familiar Letters*, 1.

able to invest the sum of £500 in payment for his quarter share in the business, and he loaned John a similar amount to pay for his share.[1] Having secretly become James Ballantyne's partner in the printing enterprise, Scott was now about to steer the commercial affairs of the new publishing house from behind the figurehead of the diminutive John, but with results that were disastrous for all concerned.

First, however, he wished to make his position quite secure in the prosperous printing establishment, a firm whose turnover was increasing every year and which was only held back by its chronic lack of liquid capital. Its future prospects looked very bright indeed, provided funds could be found for expansion; James was an honest and efficient manager of a business turning out a high quality product, and Scott had heard praise of the typographical beauty of the finished sheets from many sources, none of which had any idea he was connected with the enterprise. He now proposed a new partnership agreement between them, this time giving him a fifty per cent share of the assets of the company, although the ratio of profit sharing was to remain as before. A balance sheet proved their holdings in the firm to be equal, previous withdrawals and advances by both partners having left a balance in favour of each amounting to the same value. They were both quite satisfied that this was so, each having signed the yearly sets of accounts; but whereas Scott had other sources of income, James Ballantyne relied entirely on his share of the profits of the printing house. For several years these had averaged about £1,500 for each twelve months trading, James being entitled to two thirds of this and his partner the remainder. If at any time Ballantyne had overdrawn his credit he had always made this up by the advance of fresh funds, borrowing from a Mr Creech, a Miss Bruce, and later from his brother Sandy, in order to keep his balance straight in the firm's books. The 'accurate cash book and ledger' which Scott had asked to be kept was always open to his inspection, and he knew enough of accountancy to be able to interpret a balance sheet when it was put before him.

James agreed to sign a new contract on the terms put forward by his friend: in fact he could not very well refuse. With the new

[1] In a letter to Scott, dated 20th March, 1813, John stated: 'I entered the business with nothing, and of course, must expect nothing, unless it is realised on a final balance.' (*Ballantyne Humbug Handled*, pp. 28–9).

publishing house just commencing to trade, with his brother John comfortably in the saddle, and the fact that the printing business was once again sorely in need of fresh funds (for both partners had drawn heavily on its resources and had ploughed little or nothing back during the past few years), he was quite resigned to having to lose effective control of the firm. For with this new agreement Scott became owner of James Ballantyne and Company in all but name; if at any time he had threatened to withdraw his capital the company could not have continued to trade, as both he and James were well aware. The boot could not be on the other foot, for Ballantyne relied solely on the business for his own support; for him to try and withdraw either his capital or his services would be tantamount to putting himself out of work. However, at the time the agreement was signed there was no thought but that the enterprise would go from strength to strength, with increasing yearly profits enabling them both to reap a rich reward.

At a meeting of the parties, held 13th December, 1809, these accounts having been examined, and the balance thereon accruing to each partner found equal; it was determined that the accounts should be closed, and their amounts, forming together the sum of £7684, considered as the permanent capital stock of the company, invested in buildings and materials, whereof each partner possesses one-half. It was further determined that the divisible profit on the trade should be, and remain until altered in another written minute in this book signed by both parties, £1350 annually; whereof £900, being two-thirds, should be paid to James Ballantyne, and £450, being one third, to Walter Scott, Esquire; and that the further balance of profit arising on the trade should remain within the current year in the first place, and thereafter to accumulate towards the permanent capital stock.

    (Signed) Walter Scott
              James Ballantyne[1]

Beneath this was a minute, signed by both partners, in which they agreed that the stock of the firm should be reconstituted at £6,000, of which £3,000 was to be held as the stock of each: and it was further stipulated that:

…in the event of either partner's placing, or allowing to be in the funds of the company, any sum exceeding their share of the capital, such partner is to receive on such advance a trade profit of fifteen per cent.

[1] *Reply to Mr Lockhart's Pamphlet*, p. 20.

The effect of this latter proviso was that either could place extra funds at the disposal of the company, or allow his credit balance to rise above £3,000, and, at the end of each twelve-month period, receive a swingeing return of fifteen per cent on the loan. At this time there would have been no difficulty in borrowing money from the banks, on the usual security, at from six to seven per cent. Any firm that was forced to pay over twice this amount in interest charges was bound to feel an adverse effect on its finances, unless its profits were so great as to make the matter of small significance. Scott must have known quite well when he asked for the minute to be appended to the agreement that it was most unlikely that Ballantyne would be able to make any use of this liberal concession in the foreseeable future; he was aware of the difficulty James had experienced in the past in keeping his capital holding on a par with his own. Nothing had occurred since then to make Ballantyne any richer and his partner must have considered it highly improbable that James would be able to make use of the clause. But Scott had drawn up the minute in the knowledge that, on his own part, it offered a ready source of additional income at a rate more than twice what a finance house would expect to receive in charges. Within a short period he had invested a total of £1,800 of his own and borrowed a further £1,200 from his brother, Major Scott, pledging to him, as security for the loan, the stock-in-trade and machinery of the printing house. For this £3,000 advance he netted £450 per annum. There is little doubt that the Ballantyne Press made full use of these extra liquid resources in order to clear its debts and increase its turnover by the purchase of new machinery; but one can feel sympathy for James for later evincing angry annoyance at what he considered the usurious conduct of his partner.[1] From Whit Sunday 1808 to the end of 1811, Scott received a total of £1,446 in interest, and for only part of that period did his loan stand as high as £3,000.[2] He extracted the maximum he could procure, and in business matters was as hard-headed and exacting as a gentleman in his position could afford to be.

During this period he was working at Ashiestiel and elsewhere to finish his six canto poem *The Lady of the Lake*; a work which

[1] *Reply to Mr Lockhart's Pamphlet*, p. 11 et seq.
[2] *Ibid.*, p. 31.

46

not only gave new lustre to his name, but did much to establish the Western Highlands of Perthshire and Loch Katrine in particular as a tourist centre from that time on. He electrified his readers with his descriptions of the scenery to be found in the more remote regions of Scotland, Robert Cadell writing that 'crowds set off to view the scenery of Loch Katrine, till then comparatively unknown; and as the book came out just before the season of excursions, every house and inn in that neighbourhood was crammed with a constant succession of visitors. It is a well-ascertained fact, that from the date of the publication of *The Lady of the Lake* the post-horse duty in Scotland rose in an extraordinary degree, and indeed it continued to do so regularly for a number of years, the author's succeeding works keeping up the enthusiasm for our scenery which he had thus originally created.'

Of all his long poems, this was the most popular, his love for the land of his birth lending a force to his words which led him to pen some of his most admired descriptive lines of rural scenery.

> *The western waves of ebbing day*
> *Rolled o'er the glen their level way;*
> *Each purple peak, each flinty spire,*
> *Was bathed in floods of living fire.*
> *But not a setting beam could glow*
> *Within the dark ravines below,*
> *Where twined the path, in shadow hid,*
> *Round many a rocky pyramid...*
>
> *The broom's tough roots his ladder made,*
> *The hazel saplings lent their aid;*
> *And thus an airy point he won,*
> *Where, gleaming in the setting sun,*
> *One burnished sheet of living gold,*
> *Loch Katrine lay beneath him rolled;*
> *In all her length far winding lay,*
> *With promontory, creek, and bay,*
> *And islands that, empurpled bright,*
> *Floated amid a livelier light;*
> *And mountains, that like giants stand,*
> *To sentinel enchanted land.*

The story tells of a knight of old, James Fitz-James, who falls in love with Ellen, daughter of the outlawed Lord James of Douglas, a maiden whose hand is also sought by the fierce Highland chief Roderick Dhu, to say nothing of young Malcolm Graeme to whom the fair Ellen has already lost her heart. The stirring descriptions of stag hunts, fierce duels in remote and lovely glens, mysterious signet-rings with the power of granting favours from the king himself, and the dramatic deaths of Highland chiefs, followed by a happy ending, all added up to a work which suited the public mood exactly. Strangely enough, Scott is believed not to have read this or any other of his own poetry to his children, preferring to recite them lines of George Crabbe who was an especial favourite of his. 'Well, Miss Sophia, how do you like *The Lady of the Lake*?' James Ballantyne once asked his friend's eldest daughter. 'Oh, I have not read it!' the young lady replied. 'Papa says there's nothing so bad for young people as reading bad poetry.' And when his son Walter, then aged nine, was asked to explain his father's immense popularity amongst his fellow men, the lad thought for a while and then replied, 'Well, it's commonly *him* that sees the hare sitting.'

In many ways it is to be regretted that *The Lady of the Lake* proved such a money-spinner for the newly founded publishing house. It appeared early in May 1810, as a finely printed quarto at two guineas a copy, carrying as a frontispiece Saxon's portrait of the author. This first edition of over two thousand copies was sold out almost immediately and was quickly followed by no less than four octavo editions the same year, so that in the space of a few months some twenty thousand volumes had been disposed of. The enthusiastic John Ballantyne positively crowed the news of what he made out to be his firm's stupendous financial breakthrough into the publishing world, thus helping to establish not only the company's credit in the eyes of those to whom they owed money, but also that of his own. Unfortunately, his wildly optimistic assessment of the company's rosy future as a commercial undertaking earning fat profits was not to be born out by its subsequent progress, but both he and his partners were more than satisfied with the way things were going. As *The Lay* continued to be demanded by booksellers from one end of the British Isles to the other, they could perhaps be forgiven for feeling pleased with themselves, but this never-to-be-repeated windfall of profits lulled them into a totally false estimate of their future prospects. For the copyright of the work the poet received two thousand guineas, but as John Ballantyne and Company, (of which he owned a half share), retained three-quarters of the property for themselves (Longmans, and William Miller of London purchasing the other quarter between them), Scott must have received considerably more than this on the division of the publishing house's profits. As a secret partner in the firm of James Ballantyne and Company, who of course printed the work, he benefited once again; therefore receiving substantial sums from all three sources from the publication of a single work.

Archibald Constable must have viewed with dismay this rich harvest that might so easily have been his; but he kept his feelings to himself, and even advised the cheeky John Ballantyne (who had unblushingly asked his advice on such technical matters as to the method of advertising the work, and many other professional details) how he could market the volume to the best advantage. As the wily publisher no doubt knew he would, Scott heard from John how helpful Constable had been, and upon receiving a letter which once again conveyed Hunter's apologies for any offence he may have given, Walter wrote a conciliatory reply which put an end to the misunderstanding between them.

Castle Street, 13th March, 1810

Dear Sir,

I am sure if Mr Hunter is really sorry for the occasion of my long absence from your shop, I shall be happy to forget all disagreeable circumstances, and visit it often as a customer and amateur.

I think it necessary to add (before departing from this subject, and I hope for ever), that it is not in my power to restore our relative situation as author and publishers, because, upon the breach between us, a large capital was diverted by the Ballantynes from another object, and invested in their present bookselling concern, under an express assurance from me of such support as my future publications could give them; which is a pledge not to be withdrawn without grounds which I cannot anticipate.

But this is not a consideration which need prevent our being friends and wellwishers.

Yours truly,
W. Scott

But if Archibald Constable was out of the running as a professional partner, John Ballantyne was very much in. With the sudden flush of ready money which the division of the first half-year's profits brought him, he made immediate use, translating

49

himself into the gay whirl of Edinburgh high life with a *bonhomie* which quickly surrounded him with a bevy of new-found friends. From the first he was recklessly extravagant with any personal funds which happened to come his way, dressing himself in styles he considered the fashion of the moment and appearing in outfits which were not only comical in their eccentricity but often frankly weird. It was not long before his antics became the topic of conversation at many a social gathering, as were the midnight parties he organized at his house on the Firth of Forth. Sumptious alterations were carried out at Harmony Hall, for many of which he must have promised to pay out of the future profits of the publishing company, his connection with Scott being sufficient to ensure him credit for a considerable time.

In spite of Hermione's half-hearted protests and her prophesies of their ultimate ruin, her over-generous husband acted as host at a series of expensive Parisian-style dinners, offering his guests everything from roast boar's head to baked swan. These four hour gargantuan meals were often followed next morning by one of his roistering hunts, at which the irrepressible little man delighted to gallop the countryside with a hunting horn swinging from one side of his ornate saddle and a leather brandy bottle swinging from the other. Before long these activities had completely scandalized his dourly Calvinistic neighbours, giving rise to whispered talk of orgies and tales of muffled screams coming from the darkened bedrooms of the now infamous Hall. Yet, notwithstanding the solemn head-shaking of his more sober-minded friends, there is no doubt that Scott cherished towards this handsome pint-sized gallant a most sincere attachment, seeking his company as light relief from the cares of an often sombre world. He readily forgave him his worst excesses and took a grim pleasure in shocking some of his acquaintances with recitals of wee John's latest escapades, chuckling over such details as his hurried departure through bedroom windows and down drainpipes, clad only in a nightshirt, on the unexpected appearance of the husband of his latest lady friend. 'A more reckless, thoughtless, improvident adventurer never rushed into the serious responsibilities of business,' wrote the heavily biased J. G. Lockhart about the mercurial manager of John Ballantyne and Company, 'but his cleverness, his vivacity, his unaffected zeal, his gay fancy always seeing the light side of everything, his imperturbable good-humour, and buoyant elasticity of spirits, made and kept him such a favourite, that I believe Scott would have as soon ordered his dog to be hanged, as harbour, in his darkest hour of perplexity, the least thought of discarding "jocund Johnny." [1]

Although the trials and exigencies of running the administrative side of a publishing business efficiently meant little to John, whose attitude to life in general and work in particular was one of easy indulgence and sybaritic indifference, he was gifted with a verbal dexterity and quickness of brain which made him more than a match for even the shrewdest of the London booksellers when it came to striking a bargain. In this respect, Walter Scott held him in the highest esteem and he never failed to employ his services to negotiate the best possible terms for the marketing of his works.

In the early summer of 1810, with the plaudits of the critics and the reading public still ringing in his ears, the poet departed to the Hebrides with members of his family and a few friends. Here he braved sea-sickness on trips to Mull, Staffa and Iona and other islands, taking the opportunity to obtain details of a factual background for a new poem to be set in the Highlands which he entitled *The Lord of the Isles*. He worked on it on his return to Edinburgh, where he was now a frequent visitor at the Hanover Street premises of John Ballantyne and Company. Had he only left the selection of titles to be published to his two partners the subsequent history of the firm might have been quite different; but Scott seems to have had a blind spot for the imperfections and indifferent quality exhibited in the literary work of many of his contemporaries. He told James Ballantyne, 'If you wish to speak of a real poet, Joanna Baillie is now the highest genius of our country,' [2] an assessment which appears little short of ludicrous today; and his judgement was equally clouded when he came to consider the merits of Anna Seward, the so-called Swan of Lichfield, whose works he persuaded his reluctant partners to publish in three octavo volumes in 1810.

This publication, on which the firm made a considerable loss, was only the first of a long series of unfortunate speculations sponsored by the majority shareholder of John Ballantyne and Company. The *Edinburgh Annual Register*, which had been a brain-child of Scott's even before the publishing business had

[1] *Life of Scott*, Vol. II.
[2] *Ibid.*, Vol. II.

been formed, was to prove a constant drain on their resources, showing a yearly loss on average of well over a thousand pounds. A new periodical of this type, appearing in two large volumes annually, was doomed to failure unless it had the incisive editing of a man of the calibre of Jeffrey of the *Edinburgh Review* or Gifford of the *Quarterly*, or of Scott himself. But, although he devoted some of his time to the preparation of the first few volumes and contributed several long poems and articles, he lacked the leisure to keep an ever watchful eye on its preparation for the press. Before long its sales started to sag in an alarming way, but against all advice to the contrary, Scott insisted on its continuance long after it was apparent to all concerned that the enterprise had failed to gain a worthwhile readership.

From that time onwards the history of the firm proved to be one of almost unmitigated disaster, notwithstanding the excellent profits it derived from the sale of Scott's own works. Within a year or two of its inception, its warehouse was filled with a growing mountain of unbound and unsold sheets which the Ballantyne Press had printed for the publishing house. Included were such horrors as Weber's[1] fourteen-volume edition of the plays of Beaumont and Fletcher, about which both James and John expressed particular alarm. 'How Scott should ever have countenanced the project of an edition of an English book of this class, by a mere drudging German,' Lockhart wrote despairingly, 'appears to me quite inexplicable...Weber's text is thoroughly disgraceful, and so are all the notes, except those which he owed to his patron's own pen.'

They managed to sell only a few sets of this monument to turgidity; the rest stayed on the shelves, with amongst others, a hulking quarto entitled *Tixal Poetry*, which Scott had personally sponsored and which both his partners agreed must be got rid of at any price. 'We could not now even ask a London bookseller to take a share, and a net outlay of near £2,500, upon a worse than doubtful speculation is surely most tolerable and not to be endured.' Yet another ill-starred venture was the publication of *The History of the Culdees*, an abstruse work dealing with the clergy of the primitive Scoto-Celtic church, a subject calculated

[1] Henry William Weber (1783–1818), son of a German father and an English mother, whom Scott had befriended in 1804 when Weber was a half-starved bookseller's hack. He indulged in bouts of heavy drinking, once threatening his patron with a pistol, finally going insane in 1814 when he was confined in York lunatic asylum until his death.

to interest only a handful of scholars and with no commercial prospects whatsoever. It had been written by Scott's worthy old friend, Dr John Jamieson, the author of the celebrated dictionary, and, despite James Ballantyne's protests, had been printed in a considerable edition in consequence of the interest Scott felt, not for the writer's hypothesis, but for the author personally. A number of other works shared the same melancholy fate; most of these should never have been allowed to see the light of day.

In November, 1810, depressed by the ill-success of so many of his cherished book-publishing schemes, and annoyed at the coming changes in the administration of the Scottish courts of law, he wrote to his brother Thomas saying that, if Robert Dundas, soon to succeed his father as the second Viscount Melville, were to be appointed Governor-General of India as he had reason to hope he would, 'and were he willing to take me with him in a good situation, I would not hesitate (although I by no means repine at my present situation) to pitch the Court of Session and the booksellers to the Devil and try my fortune in another climate'. He was not yet forty, still young enough to make a fresh start, and he may well have conjured up visions of the kind of active life abroad which had often filled his youthful dreams. Coupled with the certainty of a High Court judgeship in Calcutta which his close friend Dundas would make sure would be his for the asking, was the possibility of returning to his native land after a few years' service in India with his pockets lined and an ample fortune made, more than enough to give him the chance to live exactly as he desired for the rest of his days. But the moment of pique passed quickly; all thoughts of emigration left his mind, and he was roused sufficiently by the sufferings of the Portuguese during Massena's campaign in the Peninsular, to promise a London Relief committee the profits from a poem in Spenserian stanzas he was writing on their behalf. This 'patriotic puppet-show' as he termed it, he entitled *The Vision of Don Roderick* and it raised the sum of one hundred pounds for the unfortunate Portuguese by the sale of the first edition; the author later having it reprinted in its entirety in the *Edinburgh Annual Register*, in an effort to stimulate interest in that rapidly wilting journal.

A superannuation scheme had at last been introduced into the Scottish judicature, so that from the first day of 1812 he expected to be able to draw the full salary from his Clerkship of Session, amounting to £1,300 a year. The nominal holder of the office, the aged Mr George Home, whose duties Walter had performed gratuitously for far longer than he had hoped, would undoubtedly avail himself of the chance to resign and live on a handsome pension. If Scott added his new salary to his sheriff's stipend and his wife's income, he could now count on a clear £2,000 every twelvemonth—in those days a substantial income for a country gentleman. And he had high hopes of doubling this by his literary earnings, his loan interest, and the profits he thought might be his from the printing concern.

The lease of Ashiestiel was up, and although he would probably have had little difficulty in renewing it had he so desired, he made use of its expiration to forward what had long been his most cherished ambition—that of being acknowledged as a Tweedside laird. He had recently heard that a farm a few miles from Ashestiel would soon be up for sale; one that stood on the road between Melrose and Selkirk and which overlooked the Tweed a little above where it met the Gala. It stood nearly on the site of a famous clan battle that had changed the course of Scottish history; one that had involved the Earls of Angus and Home, helped by the two chiefs of the race of Kerr, in bitter strife against the young Buccleuch and his clan. Now he had it in his power to acquire for a Scott of the clan of Buccleuch a part of this ancient heritage and he seized the chance with an eagerness that almost conjured the purchase money from the skies.

He wrote to James Ballantyne on the 12th May, 1811, apologizing for the delay in returning proof sheets he had been sent, and telling his partner that his attention had been distracted as he had 'resolved to purchase a piece of ground sufficient for a cottage & a few fields....There are two pieces,' he went on, 'either of which would suit me, but both would make a very desirable property indeed. They stretch along the Tweed near half-way between Melrose and Selkirk, on the opposite side from Lord Somerville, & could be had for between £7000 and £8000—or either of them separate for about half the sum. I have serious thoughts of purchasing one or both, and I must have recourse to my pen to make the matter easy. The worst is the difficulty which John might find in advancing so large a sum as the copyright of a new poem, supposing it to be made payable in the course of a year at farthest from the work going to press,—[which] would be essential to my purpose. Yet The Lady of the Lake came soon home. I have a letter this morning from Mr Dundas, giving me good hope of my Treasury business being carried through: if this appointment takes place, I will buy both the little farms, which will give me a mile of the beautiful turn of Tweed above Gala-foot—if not, I will confine my purchase to one. As my income, in the event supposed, will be very considerable, it will afford a sinking fund to clear off what debt I may incur in making the purchase. It is proper John & you should be as soon as possible apprised of these my intentions, which I believe you will think reasonable in my situation—& at my age, while I may yet hope to sit under the shade of a tree of my own planting. I shall not, I think, want any pecuniary assistance beyond what I have noticed, but of course my powers of rendering it will be considerably limited for a time.'

The decaying farm, complete with barn, kailyard and duck-pond, which he finally settled to purchase, consisted of a stretch of meadow along the bank of the river, backed by about a hundred acres of undulating land composed of marshy haugh, rough hill pastures, and a solitary line of newly planted firs. The property was known as Clarty Hole by reason of the muddy duckpond which was such an obvious feature, and was owned by a Dr Douglas, the minister of Galashiels. Having prudently decided that for the time being, he would content himself with this single purchase, Scott paid the astonishingly high price of £4,200 for the privilege of taking possession and becoming laird of Abbots-ford, as he renamed his new estate. Half this sum he borrowed from his eldest brother, the retired Major; the rest John Ballantyne skipped around and managed to raise on the security of the still unwritten *Rokeby*, a poem on which Scott lavished special care in the hope that it might clear his publishing business of the mounting debts with which it was encumbered.

THE SCOTT FAMILY left Ashiestiel for the last time at the end of May 1812, not without regrets for they had passed some very pleasant years there. They were well loved and respected in the surrounding villages, the rustic inhabitants of which turned out in strength to wish them health and happiness in their new home. A long waggon-train of twenty-four horse-drawn vehicles of the most varied types conveyed their heaped belongings the five miles to the Tweedside farm, paced by a horde of eager ragamuffins who kept up a constant hullabaloo of shouts and whistles to urge on the slow-moving farm animals and prevent them falling too far behind. Nearing the end of their journey they splashed through the shallows of the river at the spot after which Walter had named Abbotsford, for the whole of the land in the area had once been owned by the Abbot of Melrose Abbey, and both he and the monks must have used this ford on many occasions. 'The neighbours have been much delighted with the procession of my furniture,' he wrote a few days later to Lady Alvanley, 'in which old swords, bows, targets, and lances, made a conspicuous show. A family of turkeys, was accommodated within the helmet of some preux chevalier of ancient Border fame; and the very cows, for aught I know, were bearing banners and muskets. I assure your ladyship that this caravan, attended by a dozen of ragged rosy peasant children, carrying fishing-rods and spears, and leading ponies, greyhounds, and spaniels, would, as it crossed the Tweed, have furnished no bad object for the pencil, and really reminded me of one of the gypsy groups of Callot[1] upon the march.'

Laid across one of the waggons was one of the master's proudest possessions, Rob Roy's long-barrelled gun; while another treasured relic, which the crafty John Ballantyne had managed to secure for him by refusing to conclude the purchase

---

[1] Jacques Callot (1594–1635), engraver. His most celebrated works are 'Miseries of War' and 'Gypsies'.

of a library unless the owner threw it in as a makeweight, was the sword which Charles I had presented to the Marquis of Montrose for his great services to the royalist cause. Antiques of every description had been accumulating at Ashiestiel pending their removal to what their owner hoped would one day be a worthy setting in which to house them. Many of these had been purchased in London by the actor Daniel Terry, whom Scott had befriended in Edinburgh and was to help on many future occasions.

When this motley cavalcade finally arrived at its destination, the utmost confusion reigned, for the builders whom the architect[1] had set to work to convert the dilapidated farm into a country house were nowhere near finished, and most of the rooms were uninhabitable. The horses took fright at their strange surroundings; the pump was found to be blocked with workmen's debris and would give no water; the cows and sheep found a gap in the hedge and meandered over half a square mile of unfenced marsh land; while poor Charlotte was reduced to tears at the hopeless mess she found the house in. Her husband at first locked himself away to unpack his books in the room that for the present had to do duty as his study, refusing to act as general in what had become a melee until the most valuable of his treasures had been safely stowed. But at last he could stand the shouting and noise no longer. He dashed out, cursed the workmen, his servants, and the wandering livestock; hobbled, waving his stick, after horses, chased hens, rounded up cows; and in the end restored peace to a weary household who were more than thankful to find bed-space for the night.

Before the end of the year, despite the din of carpenters' hammers and the chisels of a dozen masons hard at work on the very extensive rebuilding he had now commissioned, Scott had nevertheless managed to finish two new poems, *Rokeby* and *The Bridal of Triermain*. The last of these pieces was published anonymously a few weeks after the first, with the deliberate intention of laying a trap for Jeffrey of the *Edinburgh Review*. The writer hoped to hold the critic up to ridicule by persuading him to make comparisons between this 'unknown poet's work' and that of the author of *Rokeby*, thus revenging himself for the reviewers' wounding remarks about *Marmion*, and his defeatist

[1] Mr Stark of Edinburgh, who died shortly after building operations commenced.

views regarding British intervention in the Peninsular War. But the trick failed to work; Francis Jeffrey was away in America when the two volumes appeared, and on his return proved far too astute to be caught, only a few minor critics ascribing *The Bridal* to the wrong author.

The poet's main hopes were centred on his major work of *Rokeby*, a long romance of Cavalier versus Roundhead set in an English scene which he believed would give it a wider appeal than his Scots pieces. He had titled it after the magnificent country seat at Greta-Bridge in Yorkshire owned by his wealthy friend John Morritt, a mansion at which the writer was frequently a guest. On its first appearance in January 1813, Scott waited with considerable anxiety for the reviews, for he was well aware how important it was that this new poem should have an enthusiastic reception from a wide and applauding public. It was necessary for it to enjoy a success at least as great as that accorded to *The Lady of the Lake* if it was to show a financial return sufficient to reverse the tide of their fortunes and rescue the publishing house from disaster. Money had been borrowed from several sources in order to market the work, including a substantial sum from Morritt to whom a grateful Scott had dedicated the poem. At first all seemed to be going as he and his partners had hoped, and the author wrote to his friend in high spirits.

Edinburgh, 12th January, 1813

Dear Morritt,

Yours I have just received in mine office at the Register-House, which will excuse this queer sheet of paper.

The publication of *Rokeby* was delayed till Monday, to give the London publishers a fair start. My copies—that is my friends'—were all to be got off about Friday or Saturday; but yours may have been a little later, as it was to be what they call a picked one. I will call at Ballantyne's as I return from this place, and close the letter with such news as I can get about it there.

The book has gone off here very bobbishly; for the impression of 3000 and upwards is within two or three score of being exhausted, and the demand for these continuing faster than they can be boarded. I am heartily glad of this, for now I have nothing to fear but a bankruptcy in the Gazette of Parnassus; but the loss of five or six thousand pounds to my good friends and school-companions[1] would have afflicted me very much. I wish I could whistle you here

---

[1] John Morritt was a school-fellow of Scott's when they attended Edinburgh High School.

today. Ballantyne always gives a christening dinner, at which the Duke of Buccleuch, and a great many of my friends, are formally feasted. He has always the best singing that can be heard in Edinburgh, and we have usually a very pleasant party, at which your health as patron and proprietor of Rokeby will be faithfully and honourably remembered...

On calling at Ballantyne's, I find, as I had anticipated, that your copy, being of royal size,[1] requires some particular nicety in hot-pressing. It will be sent by the Carlisle mail *quam primum*.

Ever yours,
Walter Scott

P.S. Love to Mrs Morritt. John Ballantyne says he has just about eighty copies left, out [of] 2250, this being the second day of publication, and the book a two guinea cut.

Within four months of his writing this letter *Rokeby* had passed through five editions and had sold over ten thousand copies in various sizes and prices; a figure high enough to turn the head of any other poet in the land. But its immediate success was not on a scale commensurate with that of *The Lady of the Lake*, which Scott was using as a measuring-stick of the book's popularity; and, after the first flush of anticipation had died away, there was little clamour for extra copies as there had been for the earlier work. He had lavished more time and effort on this 'pseudo-romance of pseudo-chivalry' as he came to call it, than on any other poem, destroying the completed draft of the first canto in the belief that he had corrected all the spirit out of it, then sitting down and starting afresh with the daunting whiteness of the first blank sheet before him once again. His efforts to be original had led him to contrive so complicated a plot as to make the action of the story difficult to follow for the majority of his readers; his elaborate descriptions of the English countryside lacked the harsh realism of his Border and Highland scenes; and the leaden octosyllables he employed seemed to have deadened whatever poetical merit the verses may have had. It was not a work of which he was proud in later years, and in the introduction to the 1830 reprint he ascribes its comparative failure to the radically unpoetical character of the Roundheads which peopled the tale; an excuse so shallow as not to be worth refuting. To give Scott his due, he never entertained a particularly high estimation of his own poetical genius. Five years after *Rokeby* first appeared

[1] Only twenty-five large-paper copies were printed, all for presentation purposes.

he wrote Maria Edgeworth, saying—'I have not read one of my poems since they were printed, excepting last year *The Lady of the Lake*, which I liked better than I expected, but not well enough to induce me to go through the rest, so I may truly say with Macbeth:

> *I am afraid to think of what I 've done—*
> *Look on't again I dare not.'*

One or two of his friends tried to persuade him that *Rokeby* was the best thing he had written, but the reading public certainly did not endorse this view, and he was too wise a man not to perceive that his star as a poet was slowly setting. Parodies of the piece quickly appeared, one of which, *Jokeby*, written by John Roby of Rochdale, in its first year passed through as many editions as the original it lampooned. Tom Moore, in his *Two-penny Post-Bag*, made the sarcastic suggestion that Scott was preparing a topographical guide by working his way south through the seats of the landed gentry. This was put in verse and, at least in London, must have had an effect on the sales of the original.

> *Should you feel any touch of poetical glow,*
> *We've a scheme to suggest—Mr Scott you must know,*
> *(Who, we're sorry to say it, now works for the Row),*
> *Having quitted the Borders to seek new renown,*
> *Is coming by long Quarto stages to town,*
> *And beginning with Rokeby (the job's sure to pay),*
> *Means to do all the gentlemen's seats on the way.*
> *Now the scheme is, though none of our hackneys can beat him,*
> *To start a new Poet through Highgate to meet him;*
> *Who by means of quick proofs—no revises—long coaches—*
> *May do a few Villas before Scott approaches;*
> *Indeed if our Pegasus be not cursed shabby,*
> *He'll reach, without foundering, at least Woburn Abbey.*

To be laughed at and held up to ridicule in this way was a new and sobering experience; it was a disquietening trend and one he had no doubt the publishing houses would be quick to notice. But, for the moment, he had more pressing things to attend to, for a spate of letters arrived whose contents showed him that the affairs of John Ballantyne and Company were going from bad to worse. Their warehouse was full to overflowing with dead and unsaleable stock, most of it fathered by the poet himself against the advice of his partners. And although the initial sales of *Rokeby* indicated a reasonable return on the capital invested in it, it was essential, if he was to keep faith with his personal friends, that the loans they had made to help its publication should be paid back with interest on the dates promised. Unfortunately, the large profits made from their one completely successful publication, *The Lady of the Lake*, instead of being ploughed back into the business to allow for future contingencies, had almost immediately been divided between the trio of partners, without, as now seems clear, fully reimbursing the Ballantyne Press for printing and casing up the work. This otherwise prosperous printing business, with a turnover that was the envy of many of its competitors, was now being hamstrung by renewing loans made in its earlier days at outrageously high rates of interest; loans its chronic lack of liquid capital made it unable to pay back. This weight of interest effectively milked its profits to an extent that left little or nothing for expansion, with the result that any major publication dislocated other orders and quickly had their finances in difficulties when it came to paying for the materials used.

There is no reason to suspect that James gave other than a factual picture of his firm's position to his senior partner; but his brother John was an incurable optimist when it came to assessing the future prospects of the publishing concern. His psychological aversion to conveying any but the most joyful tidings made him invariably present the rosiest possible picture of John Ballantyne and Company's finances to his brother and Walter Scott. Nothing damped his exuberance and his optimism quickly infected his more sober-minded partners who were pleased to be able to believe what he so gaily told them. James later gave his version of the situation as it then existed in a letter he sent to Lockhart.

My brother, though active and pushing, was not a cautious bookseller, and the large sums received never formed an addition to stock. In fact, they were all expended by the partners, who, being then young and sanguine men, not unwillingly adopted my brother's hasty results.

By May, 1813, in a word, the absolute throwing away of our own most valuable publications,[1] and the rash adoption of some injudi-

---

[1] Certain of the copyrights of Scott's works had been disposed of in order to raise capital to continue publishing.

cious speculations of Mr Scott, had induced such losses and embarrassments, that after a very careful consideration, Mr Scott determined to dissolve the concern.[1]

How exactly this was to be done without incurring a public scandal and perhaps endangering his own position in society by revealing himself as a partner in the debt-ridden enterprise, was difficult to perceive. Loans raised from various sources some twelve months before had now to be repaid; other creditors were pressing their claims and demanding immediate payment and there was little or nothing in the kitty with which to fob them off. The financial standing of the firm was now so low that it was proving quite impossible to raise fresh loans at the banks or elsewhere. Scott was finally forced, much against his will, to approach Archibald Constable in the hope that he might be persuaded to take over what was left of the assets of the Company. As early as Christmas 1812, James Ballantyne had proposed that they open negotiations with the rival publishing house by asking them to purchase a share both in *Rokeby* and in the ill-fated *Edinburgh Annual Register*. Hunter, whom Scott disliked intensely, had died earlier in the year, but even so the writer hesitated to make an approach to a man he believed to be slick and crafty when it came to a business deal and whose whole personality exuded the type of commercialism the Laird of Abbotsford found distasteful in the extreme. He wrote to James: 'You must be aware, that in stating the objections which occur to me in taking in Constable, I think they ought to give way either to absolute necessity or to very strong grounds of advantage. But I *am* persuaded nothing ultimately good can be expected from any connexion with that house, unless for those who have a mind to be hewers of wood and drawers of water. We will talk the matter coolly over, and in the mean while, perhaps you could see W. Erskine, and learn what impression this odd union is like to make among your friends.'

Constable had now taken in a new partner, a cautious but extremely ambitious young man named Robert Cadell, who, in a memorandum written later, summed up the situation as it was in the days when bankruptcy seemed imminent.

Prior to this time the reputation of John Ballantyne and Co. had been decidedly on the decline. It was notorious in the trade that

[1] *Life of Scott*, Vol. III.

their general speculations had been unsuccessful; they were known to be grievously in want of money. These rumours were realized to the full by an application which Messrs B. made to Mr Constable in May, 1813, for pecuniary aid, accompanied by an offer of some of the books they had published since 1809, as a purchase, along with various shares in Mr Scott's own poems. Their difficulties were admitted, and the negotiation was pressed urgently; so much so, that a pledge was given, that if the terms asked were acceded to, John Ballantyne and Co. would endeavour to wind up their concerns, and cease, as soon as possible, to be publishers.

I need hardly remind you that this was a period of very great general difficulty in the money market. It was the crisis of the war. The public expenditure had reached an enormous height; and even the most prosperous mercantile houses were often pinched to sustain their credit. It may easily, therefore, be supposed that the Messrs Ballantyne had during many months besieged every banker's door in Edinburgh, and that their agents had done the like in London.

Constable was well aware of their pressing difficulties, but he would not be rushed into any precipitate action; he took his time, hinted that he would prefer to deal only with Mr Scott, and no doubt savoured the pleasure of having his prophecies of their ultimate ruin proved correct. After protracted negotiations a hard fought bargain was concluded. He had intimated that he was willing to step in and help—but on his own terms. They must give their word that John Ballantyne and Company would be wound up as soon as practicable, for he obviously could not do business that would be the means of helping a rival publishing house regain its feet. He would certainly have nothing to do with the *Annual Register*, which he pointed out had been losing, according to their records, a steady thousand a year since its inception. However he offered to advance £1,300 for part of their stock of books and printed sheets at present lying unsold in their Hanover Street storerooms, providing Mr Scott would allow him to purchase a quarter share of the copyright of *Rokeby* for an extra £700. Beyond this price he would not budge, although he promised to cast a critical eye over the accounts of the firm and let them have the benefit of his expert opinion as to its liabilities. Neither Scott nor the Ballantynes were in any position to argue with him, and to these terms the senior partner had perforce to agree. At the time Scott believed that Constable had gained a great advantage, writing to John: 'It is a sacrifice, but being pennyless and without credit what could we do?... James has behaved very well during this whole transaction & has been most steadily attentive to business. I am convinced that the more he works the better his health will be. One or other of you will need to be constantly in the Printing office hence forward. It is the sheet anchor.'

The quire stock from which Constable had selected his bargains at knock-down prices was composed of a miscellaneous lot of slow-selling titles. When the publisher's waggons arrived to collect, John supervised the loading of dozens of sets of Weber's unhappy edition of the works of Beaumont and Fletcher; fifty of the massive twelve-volume sets of Defoe's novels; one hundred volumes of *Tales of the East* printed in small type in double columns; a vast quantity of a similar work entitled *Popular Tales*; nearly eight hundred copies in various sizes of *The Vision of Don Roderick*, of which they had printed far too many sheets; about three hundred six-volume sets of the *Edinburgh Annual Register* reduced to thirty shillings a set; plus a mixed lot of old titles to make up the total. But even when they had thankfully said goodbye to this large quantity of bales of printed paper and boarded books, their storerooms were still three-quarters full of similar trash. They were by no means yet out of the woods financially.

For a short interval they had earned a breathing space, and Scott was able to write that 'for the first time this many weeks I shall lay my head on a quiet pillow.' He had been depressed and anxious while the negotiations were in progress, and had written more than one letter to John Ballantyne berating him for not keeping him better informed as to the true state of the publishing house's finances. After the deal was concluded, Scott wrote his partner again in more conciliatory tones, finishing up with a gentle homily as to his future conduct.

> Adieu my dear John. I have the most sincere regard for you & you may depend on my considering your interest with as much attention as my own. If I have expressed myself with irritation in speaking of this business, you must impute it to the sudden extensive & unexpected embarrassments in which I found myself involved all at once. If to your real goodness of heart and integrity, and, above all, to the quickness & acuteness of your talents, you added habits of more universal circumspection, and, above all, the courage necessary to tell disagreeable truths to those whom you

hold in regard—I pronounce that the world never held such a man of business.

These it must be your study to add to your other good qualities. Meantime, as someone says to Swift, I love you with all your failings. Pray make an effort & love me with all mine.

Yours truly,

W.S.

Printing Office 19 May (1813)
We have just £1500 to go on with, & £1770 to pay & more before 31st. But there be debts recovered & James is to do your bidding about the discount. Damn the very name—I shall hate it while I live.[1]

The two thousand pounds received from Constable was quickly dissipated in satisfying the more demanding of their creditors, but other bills were falling due, and within a month or two they were once again in deep water. Throughout this period they were unable to call on the resources of the Ballantyne Press for financial help as it was as impoverished as the publisher's company. In fact it stood in the books as one of the publisher's largest creditors, although it was desperately short of money itself. The vast quantity of volumes it had printed for its sister company had mostly remained unpaid for; James Ballantyne and Company had to wait at the tail-end of the queue as far as John Ballantyne and Company were concerned. As a creditor it would never turn savage and bite—but the opposite held true for the many outside interests to whom they owed such considerable sums.

Amazingly, in the midst of his manifest and increasing financial troubles, we find Scott blithely entering into negotiations for the purchase of a large and expensive tract of land bordering his Abbotsford estate. Most of it was composed of desolate and treeless marshland, useless for agricultural purposes, but containing at its far extremity the lonely and romantic waters of Cauldshields Loch. The chance to obtain this lake at one end of his estate in contrast to the lovely stretch of Tweed at the other, was too great a temptation to resist, and he became determined that the money to acquire the extra acres should be found even if he had to mortgage his future literary work to procure it. On the 20th June he wrote to Constable, who had already been told verbally of what he had in mind, stating that he was most anxious to close the deal for the purchase of the land from a Mr

[1] *Letters of Sir Walter Scott*, edited by H. J. C. Grierson, Vol. I. Appendix.

Grieve, who was 'a very capricious person' and might change his mind about selling. He then went on to offer Constable the copyright of a (as yet unwritten) new poem for the sum of £5,000, with Longman's of London being given the chance to acquire fifty per cent of the holding for half this sum. He stated that he considered this a fair price, as 'it is considerably less than I have made on the share of *Rokeby* sold to yourself & surely that is no unfair measurement.' But when Constable had, a few days earlier, informed his partner Robert Cadell of the proposal, the young man was at first incredulous and then furious that the poet should have had the nerve to ask such a ridiculously high price for a work of which he had not yet written a single word.

I am perfectly astonished at Mr S asking, nay, even hinting at such an idea as our paying six or twelve months in advance for a Poem not written – perhaps scarcely thought of [he wrote his partner]. In what sort of a situation would Longmans and ourselves stand in if engaged to him for say £3500, as in July, and to be renewed till the Poem is published, if Mr S was to be summoned to the other world, and not a sheet at Press – how would we look? What would the world say to it? You will say I am a very gloomy fellow, but Mr Scott is not like his poems – immortal. The B[allantyne]s, it was said, advanced for *The Lady of the Lake* and *Rokeby*. But they could not refuse and must either do that or go to pot. Mr S has cheated us in Swift, humbugged us in *Rokeby*, &c., and will continue to do so the greater the halo he gets to creep in at... I think that £5000 is too much for his proposed poem. He wishes to squeeze us as he has done the Bs. They thought *Rokeby* was to perform wonders in their finances, but the cream has gone to Mr S and what is left to them is very thin. I am of opinion we should, in the most genteel manner, say that we could not make an offer for the Poem till further progress is made in it. We will be most happy to treat on the most liberal terms, but our other great engagements are so heavy that we cannot increase them at the moment. As to his *Register* – we have already got bit with it, and I think to receive it in at present would only put us in a disagreeable situation.

Cadell's opinions coincided with those of his partner, who had himself been more than a little taken aback at the poet's audacious proposal. Constable thereupon wrote Scott a letter of polite refusal. The publisher's bargain for the purchase of part of John Ballantyne and Company's stock of books had not turned out nearly so well as the buyer had expected. After hawking them round the trade for some months, Cadell had been forced to dispose of them for less than half the figure his firm had paid, so neither of them were disposed to be outstandingly benevolent to a man whom they came to suspect was not nearly such a fool in financial matters as he was sometimes at pains to appear. And so, for the time being, Walter Scott had to be content to let the land purchase deal hang fire; but he was quite determined to enlarge the boundaries of his riverside estate once he had the means to satisfy the land hunger which gripped him with increasing force as the years passed by.

In July he left Edinburgh to take up residence once again at his beloved Abbotsford; there to await the arrival of a large quantity of ancient armour and old books which he had commissioned Daniel Terry to buy for him in London. He settled down contentedly to enjoy his holiday with his family, hoping to start work on his new poem and perhaps finish it in time to prevent Mr Grieve offering his desirable acres elsewhere. He indulged in a little hunting and fishing, and drew up elaborate plans for further extensive plantations of trees to clothe his ground. He limped round his estate, inspecting the young saplings they had planted the previous autumn, and suffered the annoyance of discovering that the crop of acorns they had sown in one corner of a patch of meadow had all fallen victim to field-mice some months before. For the moment all his urgent financial problems had been relegated to the background. Nevertheless, he had despatched John Ballantyne to London in the hope of his being able to play one publisher off against another, thus raising a substantial advance on the projected poem. This was a type of manœuvre at which the ubiquitous John soon became an expert, and which stood him in excellent stead when he came to bargain with various booksellers for the publication rights of the *Waverley* novels. He was back in Scotland before the end of the month without being able to report any definite progress other than a keen interest on the part of several publishers to be allowed to acquire at least part of the copyright as soon as the poem was in manuscript. Despite this somewhat disappointing news, which killed any immediate hope Scott may have had for buying more land, he was, nevertheless, happier than he had been for some considerable time; his horizon seemed clearer now that the publishing business was in the process of being wound up, and the complicated legal difficulties which had prevented the final settlement of his late father's estate were well on the way to solution. Once his father's will was proved he hoped to find himself in pocket by perhaps a thousand pounds. The Duke of Buccleuch had just been gracious enough to invite both him and Mrs Scott to Drumlanrig Castle for a few days, and, all in all he was finding life very pleasant after the troubles of the last few weeks. Then suddenly, without prior warning of any kind, a hurried note arrived from John Ballantyne, stating that a batch of long-dated bills were due for payment in Edinburgh next day and that as Sir William Forbes, their banker, had refused to grant them further credit, he had been unable to raise the money to meet them.

The abuses to which the payment of one's debts by means of post-dated bills of exchange lent itself were the cause of innumerable bankruptcies in the first half of the nineteenth century, before the rules governing the granting of credit were tightened by the government. The methods then used allowed what were sometimes unsound commercial enterprises and impoverished private individuals to present a totally false picture of their real financial worth to the world at large; often living and trading by means of an increasing snowball of credit which grew with every passing month, then suddenly melted to reveal a hopelessly inadequate core of assets. The struggling proprietor of the village grocer's shop indulged in the practice as frequently as the seemingly wealthy owner of an inflated business in the city: the Ballantynes, Constable, Walter Scott, and hundreds of others had become enmeshed to greater or lesser degree in a process that depended for its continuance on the unquestionable assumption that all participants in the cycle were men of financial worth – or would be when their bills became due for payment. Scott's latest bargain with Archibald Constable & Company will serve to show how the system operated. The publisher had agreed to pay the author £2,000 for the stock of books he had selected, this amount including a quarter share in the remaining copyright of *Rokeby*. But there was never any question of Constable paying cash on the nail for the goods and privileges he had purchased. He gave instead to Scott, bills drawn on his firm's bank account amounting to a total of £2,000, but post-dated for payment at intervals of six, twelve and eighteen months ahead. This means of obtaining extended credit was not in itself open to criticism providing the bills themselves were supported by sufficient securities to cover the amount the issuing party had stipulated to pay, or

68

credit was available at his banker's to meet them in full when they fell due. But very often this was not the case. Many of the smaller Scottish banks were themselves unsound, being able, at that time, to grant credit and issue banknotes without retaining sufficient gold and securities in their vaults to back the value of the loans they made. Grossly inflated rates of interest were charged if the bills they guaranteed had been issued by a firm whose financial standing was in any way suspect; but certain of the banks which buttressed the rickety edifice of houses trading upon credit would themselves have been revealed as insolvent in any impartial audit.

When a post-dated bill was issued it was quite possible to cash it immediately provided the payee was willing that the broker deducted a discount, sometimes of considerable amount, to compensate him for the risk he ran. The further forward the bill was dated, the larger the discount deducted for immediate payment; and once let a firm's credit become even slightly suspect and the difficulty in cashing their bills increased enormously—and so did the rate of discount charged. Scott experienced this with Constable's bills at a later date to the extent of having to ask John Ballantyne to hawk them to several banks before finding one that would accept responsibility; with the result that he began to insist on being paid with bills drawn on London houses whose credit he knew was sound. One of the evils of this system of doing business was the facility offered by certain banks of renewing bills when they became due for payment—'keeping 'em floating' as the commercial houses dubbed it—and by this method, providing a swingeing rate of interest was paid, it was possible to avoid retiring a bill for several years after the due date for repayment. A flimsy mass of paper promises-to-pay and I.O.U.'s was constantly flowing backwards and forwards between various business houses and private individuals, supported in many instances by banks that were themselves built only of straw. Provided nobody pricked the bubble, all was outwardly well, but once let a bill remain unpaid by default, then the façade collapsed with a crash that caused repercussions often extending far beyond the original creditor and debtor.

John Ballantyne's urgent message saying that their banker's action in refusing to honour further drafts had made him short by a considerable amount to meet the firm's debts due next day threw its recipient at Abbotsford into a flurry of anxious activity, while he wrote cheques on his personal account to be rushed into the city to cover them. It was late in the afternoon when John's frantic appeal arrived, and too late to send the money into town the same day. At the latest, it had to be paid into the bank when it opened its doors next morning (which was a Saturday) and Scott worried himself into a sleepless night by wondering if any mishap would prevent it getting there in time. At three in the morning he could stand the strain of inaction no longer, and he dressed and hurried to the stables to wake one of the grooms, telling him to ride post haste the thirty miles with the precious packet of signed cheques. The following day was spent in waiting the lad's return with the news that he had delivered them safely into John Ballantyne's hands, and only when he was told all was well could he once again relax and take an interest in the farm's affairs. Scott well knew the penalty they would all have to pay if the cash had not arrived on time. The unsettled bills would be 'noted', as it was termed, by the bank concerned, and the information published for all to read. Nothing could then save them from ruin. All confidence in their credit would be destroyed, both in Edinburgh and London; short dated accommodation bills previously granted to them would not be renewed as they fell due, and they would be instantly besieged with demands for payment by their other creditors. The screen of I.O.U.'s and promises to pay, behind which their publishing and printing houses sheltered, would be revealed for all to see, and the whole uncertain edifice would collapse around their ears. Little wonder, therefore, that he sat down fuming with anger to write an exasperated letter to Ballantyne, warning him of the consequences of leaving the collection of funds to meet their obligations to the very last minute. 'All I desire,' he told him, 'is unlimited confidence and frequent correspondence, and that you will give me, weekly at least, the fullest anticipation of your resources...Omit no exertions to procure money, even for a month or six weeks, for time is most precious...The greatest risk we run is from such ill-considered despatches as those of Friday. Suppose that I had gone to Drumlanrig? Suppose the pony had upset? Suppose a thousand things—and we were ruined for want of your telling your apprehensions in due time.'

In August, Constable sent the Ballantynes his report of the financial state of the printing and publishing companies, and

James duly delivered a copy of his verdict to Walter Scott. It made most unhappy reading. In his statement reviewing their position, the publisher made it very clear that it was not the slightest use their raising money in driblets. Notwithstanding his previous purchase, there was still, at face value, over twelve thousand pounds' worth of printed sheets and finished books in the Hanover Street warehouse, most of which were practically unsaleable unless they were prepared to take a quarter of that sum in the open market. But to realize even this amount would be extremely difficult at short notice, and bills were shortly to be presented for payment amounting to many thousands of pounds. These were the sums they had borrowed to enable them to buy and produce the books which now lay unsold in the stockrooms. In a nutshell, either they must raise the amount of four thousand pounds almost immediately, or declare themselves bankrupt. As a publisher he would help them all he could with advice as to the best means of disposing of their stock, but to raise such a large sum of money at short notice was quite beyond his resources.

This, to all three of them, was shocking news, but especially so to Walter Scott. He had visions of seeing himself dragged into the open as a partner in unsound commercial enterprises; his secret manipulations whereby he drew profits from three directions for every book he wrote would be held up for an incredulous world to see; and finally his forced resignation from the well-paid post of Clerk to the Court of Session made a matter of certainty. He must try and avoid such an exposure at all costs, but, if the worst came to the worst, he would stand his ground like a man and brave the consequences. He refused to entertain any thought of running away from what he considered to be his responsibilities. 'I should hope no one can possibly be a loser by me,' he wrote to James Ballantyne. 'I am sure I would strip myself to my shirt rather than it should be the case.'

Just as things seemed at their blackest, a letter arrived by order of the Prince Regent, offering him the post of poet laureate left vacant by the recent death of Henry Pye. Of late years this office had fallen into disrepute by the lamentable efforts of the unfortunate Mr Pye to compose annual patriotic odes in honour of his Sovereign's birthday, full of the most humble and irreproachably correct sentiments, but without any poetical merit whatsoever. Their allusions to vocal groves and feathered choirs fluttering round the monarch were the source of unrestrained laughter and ridicule in literary circles and George Steevens mimicked one of the earliest in the words of the nursery song:

> *And when the Pye was open'd*
> *The birds began to sing,*
> *And was not this a dainty dish*
> *To set before the King!*

Although Scott was sensible of the honour the Prince Regent had accorded him by offering him the post, the only consideration that made him pause before turning it down was his erroneous belief that the laureateship carried with it a salary of between three and four hundred pounds per annum. In the midst of all his troubles, with the possible bankruptcy of the firm of which he was senior partner staring him in the face, to have to consider accepting such a ridiculous office rather than lose the few hundreds he believed it would bring him, must have been humiliating in the extreme. But beggars could not be choosers. Unless he was prepared to sell the remaining copyrights of his works, probably at bargain prices, he had to find security for the sum of four thousand pounds within the next few days. This fact was inescapable and, if he failed to secure backing for this amount, then the salary of poet laureate might be very acceptable in days to come. This was the position as he debated the matter in his study at Abbotsford; and it was then that a letter from John Ballantyne arrived, containing a suggestion from Constable that there was one man who, at the stroke of a pen, could dissolve the author's difficulties and would doubtless be more than pleased to be given the opportunity to do so.

At this lowest point in his fortunes, Scott was cornered; he had no alternative but to comply with Constable's suggestion, and he wrote immediately to Drumlanrig Castle, to the chief of his clan, the Duke of Buccleuch, acquainting him with his plight. As usual when begging financial favours from his friends, he was careful not to reveal that he was in any way connected with the commercial concerns of the city; he knew the simple fact that had he informed them that he stood in need of the money would be sufficient explanation to any gentleman of his own class to remit the required amount if he could possibly afford it. In the Duke's case, Scott had rendered him a similar service in the past, and he was confident that his plea would not be made in vain. 'I am not asking or desiring any loan from your Grace,' he wrote, 'but merely the honour of your sanction to my credit as a good man for £4000....I trust your Grace will not suppose me capable of making such a request as the enclosed, upon any idle or unnecessary speculation; but, as I stand situated, it is a matter of deep interest to me to prevent these copyrights from being disposed of either hastily or at under prices. I would have half the booksellers in London for my sureties, on a hint of a new poem; but bankers do not like people in trade, and my brains are not ready to spin another web. So your Grace must take me under your princely care, as in the days of lang syne; and I think I can say, upon my sincerity as an honest man, there is not the most distant chance of your having any trouble or expense through my means.'

For a few days there was no reply and Scott's fears and anxieties rapidly mounted. But the fifth day brought the prayed for relief, for with the coach came Buccleuch's reply, stating in generous terms that he was only too willing to be of assistance in the matter of guaranteeing Scott's overdraft. At the same time he took the opportunity to strongly advise his friend to have nothing whatsoever to do with the laureateship. The knowledge that he held this official post, he told him, 'would stick to you and your productions like a piece of court plaster. Your muse has hitherto been independent,' he went on, waxing to his subject, '—don't put her into harness. You know how lightly she trots along when left to her natural paces, but do not try driving.' Even without his noble friend's advice the poet's mind had been made up. With his immediate financial anxieties removed, he needed no second bidding to refuse the proffered laurels. He excused himself to the Court Chamberlain, pointing out that he already held two offices of profit under the Crown, and saying that he considered himself 'inadequate to the fitting discharge of the regularly recurring duty of periodical composition'. In other words, the thought of having to write an annual ode to mark the birthday of His Royal Highness, or to be called upon to furnish verses to commemorate other State occasions, was too invidious a task to contemplate. Through Croker and others he pushed the claims of his impoverished friend Robert Southey, to whom any additional regular income would be more than welcome. 'I am not such an ass as not to know that you are my better in poetry,' Scott wrote him, 'though I have had, probably but for a time, the tide of popularity in my favour.' In due course Southey was appointed to the office, but instead of the four hundred a year his friend expected him to receive, he discovered that the emoluments amounted to little more than a quarter of that amount.

The war with Napoleon was going well at the end of 1813, and now offered hopes of a speedy victory. The city of Edinburgh sent a deputation to give their thanks to the Prince Regent on the improved military situation and Scott was asked to write an address to mark the occasion. The city magistrates declared themselves delighted with its elegant style and well turned phrases, and before long the writer found himself being presented with the freedom of Edinburgh coupled with the right to select a handsome piece of plate as a memento. He promptly ordered from the silversmith's a massive silver tankard with a capacity of half a gallon. Charlotte thought his choice of a tankard inexpressibly vulgar, but, as might be expected with one of her husband's physique, it matched in size the massive meals he consumed during his sojourns at Abbotsford. He took less exercise in the city and was more careful with his diet, but once in the country and he ate like a farmer. He indulged in heavy breakfasts, and it was not a matter for comment to find his early morning table loaded with plates containing thick slices of beef, pig's trotters, perhaps a cold sheep's head, and a thick wedge of cheese flanked by a coarse brown loaf and a flaggon of ale to wash them down. Not that the laird consumed all before him, but most mornings he certainly made considerable inroads into the victuals before rising to continue a hard day's work. At lunch he ate very little, but more than made up for this abstinence when it came to the evening meal, at which, especially in later years, there were often guests to share his table. His well-stocked wine cellar could cater for the most fastidious tastes, but he himself usually stuck to his favourite whisky-and-water after he had finished his share of the claret. But he was never adverse to a glass or two of champagne, and the evening seldom closed without his smoking at least one large cigar.

5

THE CRISIS IN the financial affairs of John Ballantyne and Company was not subdued until the late autumn. On Archibald Constable's fresh advice, Scott persuaded his 'princely Chief', as he now termed the Duke of Buccleuch, to stand guarantor behind a redeemable annuity for the sum of £4,000. This involved the payment of heavy yearly premiums, in addition to which the author was forced to insure his life for a similar amount in order to guard Buccleuch from liability in the event of his death. By this device confidence was at last restored in the ability of the publishing house to meet its obligations, and Scott was able to save the copyrights of his works from being disposed of to meet his debts. The annuity bond was not signed until the middle of November, by which time all sorts of wild rumours had spread regarding Scott's deep involvement in the Ballantyne's affairs. It was confidently predicted that he would be called upon to find over £20,000, and his bankruptcy was said to be only a matter of time. He began to receive letters from his friends, sympathizing with his troubles and offering help; and John Morritt wrote anxiously, telling him that he had heard in London 'that your poor friend Ballantyne had failed & with great grief that you were likely to be a sufferer to a very great extent by his failure, indeed to an amount which, if true, must be very distressing. For God's sake then, my dear friend, let not the consideration of the money advanced by Hoare upon Ballantyne's bill & my security increase your embarrassment for a moment. I will settle with Hoare when the time of payment comes & I trust you will allow me to a sufficient claim on your friendship to gratify my feelings in this instance by sharing yours; & that you will not on any account endeavour to repay me till it is perfectly convenient to you'.

Some weeks elapsed before Scott was able to reply, but when all was signed and sealed he sat down to write a letter of thanks to his friend,

I did not answer your very kind letter, my dear Morritt, untill I could put your friendly heart to rest upon the report you have had — which I could not do entirely untill this term of Martinmas was passed.

I have the pleasure to say that there is no truth whatsoever in the Ballantynes reported bankruptcy. They have had severe difficulties for the last four months to make their resources balance the demands upon them, and I, having the price of *Rokeby* and other monies in their hands, have had considerable reason for apprehension and no slight degree of plague and trouble. Their balances, however, have been so favourable at this term and they have been so well supported, that I have got out of hot water upon their account and have not the least doubt of extricating my cash without any eventual loss as the funds greatly over balance the claims upon them and will make an ample reversion. They are winding up their bookselling concern with great regularity & are to abide hereafter by the printing office, which, with its stock &c, will revert to them freely...

This matter has set me thinking about money more seriously than ever I did in my life & I have begun by insuring my life for £4000 to secure some ready cash to my family should I slip girths suddenly. I think my other property, library, &c., may be worth about £12000 & I have not much debt...

The Ballantynes have behaved very fairly & honestly & I trust will do very well.

> Ever yours truly,
> Walter Scott[1]

In this letter Scott was forced to deceive Morritt, as he did nearly everyone else, as to his true position in the business affairs of the Ballantynes, concealing from him the fact that he was himself the senior partner in both enterprises, while James and John were no more than managers who could be dismissed at will. John had already been sent packing; James was on tenterhooks that the same thing might happen to him. The weight of capital shown against the author's name in the ledger of the Ballantyne Press, and the fact that it was his influence that secured them some of their most profitable orders, as well as easier credit, gave Scott a most powerful lever when it came to shaping the policy of James Ballantyne and Company. As in the case of the publishing firm, where his superior shareholding

---

[1] *Letters of Sir Walter Scott*, Vol. III.

gave him the right to insist on having his own way in the selection of titles for publication (often against the most strenuous advice of his two partners), so it proved to be with the printing establishment. In matters of financial policy, James could remonstrate gently and politely if he disagreed, but he was in no position to act against the wishes of his illustrious partner. Ballantyne was his own master in technical matters and in the day-to-day administration of the business, but the hidden hand of his master steered the firm's financial course. It was Scott who decided which of their numerous creditors should be paid the first; from whom they should raise loans; the interest the partners should be permitted to draw on any money left in the firm; and the way in which the profits of the company should be divided or employed. These decisions were Scott's own prerogative, for in all but name he was the owner of the Ballantyne Press. The protection he afforded the firm can be witnessed in the letter quoted above. Here he was able to allay suspicion in the mind of one to whom they were obliged for backing a loan, by giving him reassuring information about companies with which his correspondent had no knowledge he was directly connected. His friend would have stood by him whatever happened, but it was essential to restore confidence in the firm's ability to pay its debts, for a run on its funds would have meant disaster. From the tone of Scott's letter Morritt must have gained the impression that the most the writer could lose was the £3,000 the Ballantynes had agreed to pay him for *Rokeby*, which sum was still 'in their hands', plus 'other monies' of unspecified but seemingly minor amounts. Actually, the author had received the equivalent of this £3,000 from the firm before *Rokeby* was even published, and the 'other monies' involved were his proper share of the company's debts which he had authorized John Ballantyne to incur on behalf of all the partners. Such soothing phrases as 'Their balances, however, have been so favourable at this term and they have been so well supported' and also, 'the funds greatly over balance the claims upon them and will make ample reversion' were only true if one threw into the scales the immense weight of assistance received from the Duke of Buccleuch, Charles Erskine, Matthew Hartsonge, Morritt himself, and a number of equally close friends of the writer, none of whom were aware that aid had been given from other quarters.

His statement to Ballantyne that he would not go 'mendicating from the booksellers a contract for a new poem' appears to have been soon forgotten, for in October the same year he wrote to James telling him he had reduced the price of the still unwritten work to four thousand guineas. 'I have no objection that £1050 shall be made dependent on the success of the work,' he went on, 'as I have no wish to have any undue advantage....But as my coming under an engagement of this sort at present is owing to my wish to realize a sum of money for a particular purpose, it would be necessary that Messrs. C & D should accept for the whole sum in four bills at 12, 15, 18 & 24 months for £1050 each. The last bill I shall relieve them from if the work proves unsuccessful.' Here he was asking Ballantyne to approach Cadell & Davies, the London publishers, to see if they were willing to advance this amount in post-dated bills of exchange. 'You may shew Messrs. C & D that I have been always paid in advance & am making no new rule for them,' he concluded, apparently hoping, by proving that John Ballantyne and Company had paid him in full before receiving the completed manuscripts of his earlier works, to induce the London house to do the same. When one calculates what such a sum would be worth in modern values, it seems unbelievable that any writer should dare to ask such a price for a work of which only the rough outline existed in the poet's mind. The fact that publishers were at least willing to consider the acceptance of such outrageously expensive terms, goes far to prove how uniquely popular Scott's poems had earlier become. It is known that by 1813 no less than 27,300 copies of *The Lay of the Last Minstrel* had been sold, and about 17,000 of *The Lady of the Lake*. Even after his star as a poet had begun to wane, *Rokeby* still managed to sell over 11,000 copies by 1815, and, with the knowledge of such unequalled sales to spur him on, it is no wonder that he felt himself justified in demanding fantastic sums for further compositions. In this instance none of the publishers the Ballantynes approached rose to the bait, and Scott was forced to reduce the price of the poem-to-be still further, this time to three thousand guineas. At this price John Ballantyne was ultimately successful in striking a bargain with Constable, who agreed to buy half the copyright (sharing this portion with his London agents, Longman and Company) while Scott retained the other half. He had already agreed to pay in advance for the nineteen-volume edition of the works of Swift on which Scott and his literary hacks had laboured for several years, this massive compilation being at last sent to the press in 1814.

The poet's statement that he wished 'to realize a sum of money for a particular purpose', refers to the fact that, amid all his manifest worries about finance, he was seriously contemplating at this time purchasing several hundred additional acres near Abbotsford. These Darnick lands were called Kaeside, which he was finally successful in acquiring from John Moss in May 1816. One may well ask how any man in his right mind could be so ill-advised as even to toy with the idea of making a purchase costing several thousands of pounds at a time when he was up to his ears in debt. But Scott, where land to increase his estate was concerned, could never resist the temptations which the various small landowners nearby were quick to dangle before him as soon as they realized his weakness. In this he displayed a totally amoral attitude towards the well-being of his family and those others with whom his fortunes were linked. If the land offered was adjacent to his estate, he could not resist for long no matter how difficult it was to raise the purchase money. Once the Scottish Cock-lairds who were his neighbours discovered this he was seduced into expensive follies at regular intervals, and he seemed quite powerless to resist the desire to say 'Yes' to the grossly inflated prices they demanded.

The difficulty he had experienced in finding a backer for the new work he had promised to produce, at a price he thought it should merit, only confirmed Scott in his belief that his place as the most popular poet of his day was in process of being usurped by others. The first two cantos of Lord Byron's *Childe Harold's Pilgrimage* had appeared in 1812, and he was quick to realize that here was a poet of incomparably greater eloquence than himself. Three years before Scott had read 'English Bards and Scotch Reviewers', a brilliant satirical attack by Byron on Jeffrey and others who, in the *Edinburgh Review*, had criticized in contemptuous terms his poem 'Hours of Idleness' when it first appeared. Not only was Jeffrey verbally castigated, but also Southey, Wordsworth, Coleridge and Scott himself. After taking a tilt at *The Lay of the Last Minstrel* by describing the narrator as playing his 'whining half-strung harp', Byron turned his attention to the poet himself and his *Marmion* in particular.

And think'st thou, Scott! by vain conceit perchance,
On public taste to foist thy stale romance,
though MURRAY and his MILLER[1] may combine
To yield thy muse just half-a-crown per line?
No! when the sons of song descend to trade,
Their bays are sear, their former laurels fade.
Let such forego the poet's sacred name,
Who rack their brains for lucre, not for fame:
Low may they sink to merited contempt,
And scorn remunerate the mean attempt!
Such be their meed, such still the just reward
Of prostituted Muse and hireling bard!
For this we spurn Apollo's venal son,
And bid a long, 'good night to Marmion'.[2]

Emanating from the pen of a brother poet, these harsh phrases hurt and rankled far more than they would have done had they been uttered by a professional critic, and Scott was none too pleased that his pressing need for ready cash at the time *Marmion* was published should have been so bluntly revealed to the public. Most of the money had gone to help his brother Thomas, who without it may very well have landed in jail. 'It is funny enough,' Scott wrote to Southey, 'to see a whelp of a young Lord Byron abusing me, of whose circumstances he knows nothing, for endeavouring to scratch a living with my pen. God help the bear if, having little else to eat, he must not even suck his paws. I can assure the noble imp of fame it is not my fault that I was not born to a park and £5000 a year.' Nevertheless, *Childe Harold*'s Spenserian stanzas profoundly impressed him, and he was warm-hearted and generous enough not to allow a private grievance to warp his judgement of literary worth. When the publisher John Murray later reported to him a conversation he had with Byron in London, in which the poet had told him how much he endorsed the Prince Regent's recent praise of Walter Scott's poems, he immediately seized the opportunity of making friends with his former critic by writing to Byron to congratulate him on his newly published autobiographical poem. Byron replied by giving him an account of his talk with the Prince, and concluded by saying: 'To be thus praised by your Sovereign must be

[1] John Murray and William Miller, the London publishers.
[2] 'Good night to Marmion', was Henry Blount's farewell to his friend and leader on finding him dying on Flodden Field.

gratifying to you, & if that gratification is not alloyed by the communication being made through me, the bearer of it will consider himself very fortunately and sincerely, etc.' From this time onwards the two men became firm friends and met on several later occasions in London. It made a strange sight to see them, both with a deformity of gait, limping arm in arm downstairs from the rooms of the publisher John Murray. Here were the middle-aged Scottish lawyer and the handsome young nobleman, engrossed in animated conversation and happy in each other's company. Their friendship was maintained by a correspondence lasting many years, and was cemented by Scott refusing to abandon his friend after Byron had been forced by his estranged wife's scandalous tongue to leave the country as a social outcast.

Meanwhile, with about forty workmen of one sort and another chipping at the oaken beams and shaping the stonework of an ever expanding Abbotsford, Scott was forced to buckle down in an endeavour to earn more money with his pen. He made a determined start on *The Lord of the Isles*, as he had entitled his much discussed new work, although he confessed in a disheartened way to Ballantyne: 'James, Byron hits the mark where I don't even pretend to fledge my arrow.' Up to this point in his literary career, poesy had served him generously and well; he had devised a new type of poetical narrative by ingeniously adapting the form used in the old ballads—but he had employed this tramping measure so often that there was now a staleness about his lines that had begun to bore his readers. All novelty had long since departed; his style had grown tediously familiar to a public whose enthusiasm had been quenched by the interminable ramblings of the latter half of *Rokeby*, whose complicated plot would have been far more suitable for a novel's prose. Only a radical alteration in his mode of composition and lilt of expression could recapture the imagination of a readership who demanded to be amused and entertained. Unless he had within himself the capacity to evolve something entirely different to what he had produced in the past, he foresaw that the future held the threat of rapidly diminishing financial returns. He was now aware that his verses could never attain the lofty heights of poetical excellence so evident in the stanzas of Byron, and any comparison between the two of them was bound to result in the laird of Abbotsford being relegated to second place. Some years later he confessed to his readers '...his Lordship is a cut above me—I won't run my horse against his, if I can help myself.'[1]

It was at this juncture in his literary affairs, when his will to write in verse had been blunted by the knowledge of his cramping limitations, that he made a discovery that completely altered the course of his career as a writer. While rummaging through the drawers of an old cabinet in an upstairs room at Abbotsford, he came across the partly completed manuscript of an historical novel which he had thrown on one side some years before. Those to whom he had previously shown the opening chapters had either damned it by faint praise, or, like his friend Erskine, condemned it outright as being prosy and dull. Any reader who has been forced to wade through the sludge of verbosity that characterizes the greater part of the first volume of this tale of the Rising of 'forty-five, will have no doubts about the justice of Erskine's criticism; but when Scott sat down and re-read what he had written some eight years before, he decided that the manuscript was of sufficient merit for him to attempt to finish it with some hopes of success. He had provisionally titled it *Waverley: 'Tis Fifty Years Since* and the story had been set in the Highlands in a period of history just outside his own recollection, but within that of many people to whom he had talked as a young man. Those of his readers with the tenacity of purpose to reach chapter seven were at last rewarded for their perseverance, for from that point onwards the action seldom flags, and there is an authenticity in the broken dialogue of the Lowland peasants and the rough outbursts of Highland rank-and-file which brings the tale to life in startling fashion. James Ballantyne was sent portions of the first volume to read and strongly encouraged the author to continue, and, by the time Scott returned to Edinburgh in January, 1814, after the Christmas vacation, the whole of the first section was complete. As the author had emphatically instructed him that his name was not to appear on the title-page, James despatched the manuscript to his brother Sandy at Kelso with a request that he should make a fair copy for the press. Scott had a rooted objection to acknowledging the authorship of any of his fictional prose works (although, as we have seen, he displayed no such reluctance in regard to his poetry) being convinced that to be revealed as a novelist conflicted with his status

[1] From the Introductory Epistle prefixed to *The Fortunes of Nigel*, 1822.

as laird of Abbotsford and Sheriff of Selkirkshire, and that the position he occupied as Clerk to the Court of Session was not to be identified as being in the hands of a writer of romantic fiction. He was resolute in his decision to remain anonymous and when asked outright by friends if he was in fact the author of *Waverley*, he lied to them and strenuously denied all knowledge of the authorship. Each work by him of this type, bore only the words 'By the Author of Waverley' on its title-page, the secret of the writer's identity being known for certain only by the Ballantynes and a small circle of intimate friends.

As soon as the work had been transcribed, John Ballantyne took it to show Constable and, after the usual bargaining, the publisher offered £700 for the copyright. This was reported back to North Castle Street, and Scott, in his hard-headed way, came to the decision that this sum was too much if the novel was a failure but not nearly enough if it should prove to be a success. Ultimately it was agreed that Constable should publish it on the basis of an equal division of profits between himself and the unknown author. At first he was puzzled as to who this could be, for Sandy Ballantyne's hand was strange to him and there was no worming the secret out of John or James. But it was not long before he knew that certain phrases the author had employed had a familiar ring and he realized that the work could only have been written by Walter Scott. Later he was officially admitted into the secret, being pledged to secrecy as were the few others in the know. He advertised that the book would appear in three volumes in March, but its completion was delayed by articles which Scott had promised to write for the supplement to the *Encyclopaedia Britannica*, a publication which Archibald Constable and his partner had recently acquired and which had severely strained their financial resources to do so. It was June before the author was able to resume writing the last two volumes of the novel, the title of which had been slightly altered to bring it up to date, being now *Waverley; or 'Tis Sixty Years Since*. Within three weeks he had completed the task, and this in spite of his having to spend up to six hours a day in Court during each working day of the week.

Lockhart has given us a picture of how diligently the writer toiled during those midsummer evenings. He had been dining with some young advocates in a house which commanded a back view of the window of Scott's study in North Castle Street.

When my companion's worthy father and uncle, after seeing two or three bottles go round, left the juveniles to themselves, the weather being hot, we adjourned to a library which had one large window looking northward. After conversing here for an hour or more, I observed a shade had come over the aspect of my friend, who happened to be placed immediately opposite to myself, and said something that intimated a fear of his being unwell. 'No,' said he, 'I shall be well enough presently, if you will only let me sit where you are, and take my chair; for there is a confounded hand in sight of me here, which has often bothered me before, and now it won't let me fill my glass with a good will.' I rose to change places with him accordingly, and he pointed out to me this hand which, like the writing on Belshazzar's wall, distracted his hour of hilarity. 'Since we sat down,' he said, 'I have been watching it—it fascinates my eye—it never stops—page after page is finished and thrown on that heap of MS., and still it goes on unwearied—and so it will be till candles are brought in, and God knows how long after that. It is the same every night—I can't stand the sight of it when I am not at my books.'—'Some stupid, dogged, engrossing clerk, probably,' exclaimed myself or some other giddy youth in our society. 'No, boys,' said our host, 'I well know what hand it is—'tis Walter Scott's.'[1]

Waverley, the forerunner of what proved to be a long shelf of similar works of romantic fiction, appeared on 7th July, 1814, in three small 12mo volumes priced at one guinea a set. It was only the first of the forty or so 'Waverley Novels' that were to follow and has since been acknowledged as the archetype of the host of imitators cast in the same mould. Without being aware of the fact, Scott had established a new literary form: he had brought forth the first historical novel. By setting the characters of the tale against a factual background of well-recognized historical events he lent an authenticity to the plot that his readers found a refreshing change from the improbabilities they were expected to swallow in the pages of the Gothic novels of the period. It was not long before he found a host of imitators, but he outpaced all his contemporaries by his unrivalled portrayals of the minor characters in his tales, all of them based on the social oddities he had encountered in his travels in the Highlands and Lowlands of the country he loved so well. He more than compensated for his inability to breathe life into a flesh and blood hero or heroine (a glaring deficiency in every story he wrote) by

---

[1] *Life of Scott*, Vol. III.

his characterization of the subordinate roles. Edward Waverley, the asexual hero of the tale, passionless and devoid of colour, is overshadowed by the unforgettable array of rough-shod, lovable humble folk that jostle their way through the pages of the book.

Within less than a week the entire printing of a thousand copies of the first edition had been sold and further orders were pouring in every day. Archibald Constable and Company were in dire need of the money the sales of this best-seller brought them from all over the country, for a number of recent speculations had proved extremely expensive in terms of cash. The senior partner had long since developed a taste for luxury and his private spending was on a scale that made considerable inroads into the company's liquid resources. By offering well-known writers large sums to secure their works, the firm had fallen heavily into debt. As early as May, 1813, Cadell had been horrified to learn the true state of the finances of the house in which he was now a partner. 'At this moment,' he wrote to Constable, 'our engagements in Bills, entirely exclusive of Bonds &c., are above the Sum of £75,000. I know you will be as astonished at this as I was when Mr Fife made it up, and no less so when, during this year, £42,000 and upwards are payable....' There could be no question of paying off all these debts; the vast majority had to be kept floating by renewals, and to do this they were forced to find large amounts of interest which further added to their embarrassments.

Walter Scott had done very well out of Constable, and the publisher had gone to great lengths to be accommodating, advancing sums for his work that were certainly greater than he was able to obtain elsewhere. He was at times more than a little aggrieved that this help did not always seem to be appreciated by the author: on several occasions in the past he considered that Scott had let them down badly. The nineteen-volume edition of the works of Swift was a hopelessly ponderous set to expect a private purchaser to wish to possess, and the firm had only agreed to market it in the expectation of reaping the benefit of the editor's popularity which the success of *The Lady of the Lake* had brought in its train. Scott's quarrel with Hunter, which he had used as an excuse to break with Constable at the time when the firm of John Ballantyne and Company was in the process of being floated, had delayed its appearance. Since then the completion date had been further advanced at Scott's request on several occasions. Shortly before the publication of *Waverley*, Constable had written to Cadell from London, where he had gone to try and interest Longman's in the slow-moving *Swift*. 'Had the work been completed three years ago when the Trade were mad about everything where Mr Scott's name appeared,' he complained feelingly to his partner, 'how very differently should we have stood in this business. But *Don Roderick* helped to damn him & the failure of *Rokeby* completed it. In the meantime Lord Byron carries the laurel & we are left in a considerable scrape...' And, a few days later: 'The first volume of Swift disfigures the whole, if anything can add to the disfigurement of this most vexatious of all Books. It has been a job to somebody and a damnable one to us.'[1]

It is little wonder, therefore, that when, earlier in the year, Scott had sent John Ballantyne round to see them with an audacious plan by which he hoped to clear the £10,000 worth of dead stock still lying in the Hanover Street premises, they should have listened in increasing amazement to the scheme, and then sent a polite but very definite message of refusal. What the two partners said about Scott's plan after his emissary had left can well be imagined. Its essence was contained in a letter he sent to Ballantyne on the 26th February.

Dear John,
    I have been thinking over the plan which I lately formed and talked over this morning, of making our good Stock carry off our heavy by attaching so much of it to future editions... But it has occurred to me that there is a better and more summary mode of winding up which would effectively end these matters.
    Suppose Constable & Longman would take the whole Stock (say £10,000 being £5000 each) at the following terms—

		Bills for 12 mos. to immediately granted for	£2000
Do.	fifteen months		£2000
Do.	eighteen mos		£2000
Do.	twenty one months		£2000
Do.	twenty four months		£2000
			£10,000

Should they be disposed to do this, J. B. & Coy shut shop instantly

---

[1] Constable had paid Scott £1,500 for editing the work. The first edition consisted of 1,250 sets of nineteen volumes each, and the publishers had the utmost difficulty of disposing of them.

86

and leave the field clear, turning over to the purchasers the works of every description which they have now the advantage of publishing—on the same terms of printing in the Canongate and giving the authors half profits...

In future publications, unless in very particular circumstances, or with reasonable grounds of displeasure which there is no chance of occurring, I will certainly consider these houses as my publishers, expecting only in courtesy some share of their countenance in the P[rinting] O[ffice]. As I shall always publish in future for half profits, there is no fear of my having the least temptation to change publishers supposing me to have (as I have not) any wish to do so...

Yours etc
W.S.

In other words, providing Constable and Company, with Longman's to help them, agreed to purchase ten thousand pounds' worth of dead and nearly unsaleable stock from John Ballantyne and Company, the author would agree that in future they were to be considered as his sole publishers, always supposing they contracted that his works should be printed only by the presses of James Ballantyne and Company. It was a ludicrous scheme at which no business man could be expected to look twice; and yet, although they turned it down flat when first presented to them, Scott was later to prove himself astute enough to persuade hard-headed publishers first to nibble and eventually to swallow the whole of the indigestible bait.

All connected with its production were delighted with the success which *Waverley* so quickly achieved, and John Ballantyne, with his shrewd eyes on what might give them the greatest advantage, tried to convince the author that the lustre attaching to his name meant that they would sell even more copies if he allowed it to appear on the title-pages. Scott replied with some doggerel lines of refusal.

> *No, John, I will not own the book—*
> *I won't, you picaroon.*
> *When next I try St Grubby's brook,*
> *The 'A. of Wa—' shall bait the hook—*
> *And flat-fish bite as soon*
> *As if before them they had got*
> *The worn-out wriggler Walter Scott.*

Henry Cockburn, later Lord Cockburn, recalled the sensation

which the first appearance of the novel caused in Edinburgh, in his autobiographical account of Scottish life which he entitled *Memorials of His Time*, published in 1856.

If the concealment of the authorship of the novels was intended to make mystery heighten their effect, it completely succeeded. The speculations and conjectures, and nods and winks, and predictions and assertions were endless, and occupied every company, and almost every two men who met and spoke in the street. It was proved by a thousand indications, each refuting the other, and all equally true in fact, that they were written by old Henry Mackenzie, and by George Cranstoun, and William Erskine, and Jeffrey, and above all by Thomas Scott, Walter's brother, a regimental pay-master, then in Canada. But 'the great unknown', as the true author was then called, always took good care, with all his concealment, to supply evidence amply sufficient for the protection of his property and his fame; in so much that the suppression of the name was laughed at as a good joke not merely by his select friends in his presence, but by himself. The change of line, at his age, was a striking proof of intellectual power and richness. But the truth is, that these novels were rather the outpourings of old thoughts than new inventions.

Someone else who was enjoying life as seldom before was John Ballantyne. Far from allowing himself to be cast down by the abrupt cessation of the activities of the publishing business, within a few weeks of its officially closing its doors he had bounced back into view as a successful auctioneer, complete with a resplendent rostrum of carved mahogany which he set up in his old premises in Hanover Street.[1] Most of the stock of the now defunct publishing company was still stored there awaiting disposal, and the words 'John Ballantyne & Company — Book-sellers' were allowed to remain in letters of gold above the front entrance. But although antiquarian and modern books at first composed the bulk of the lots which came under John's ivory hammer, his catalogues were soon filled with extravagant descriptions of items of furniture, jewellery, pictures and prints, and *objets d'art* of every sort. In his temptingly worded advertisements the goods to be offered for sale were always alluded to as having been sent to his rooms by private clients, but John made a very

[1] Later Ballantyne moved his premises to Princes Street as being a more fashionable address from which to conduct his sales.

good thing out of including articles he had bought for resale on his own account. The sections in his catalogues devoted to books gave him the opportunity to insert lots from the stock in the publishing house storeroom, and by this means he was able to clear several hundred volumes of otherwise unsaleable titles. Scott was elated at his success, the more so as he benefited himself by the sale of the books. 'The Ballantynes are going on prosperously,' he wrote to Morritt on the 17th January, 1814, 'the younger, who is very active, has opened a saleroom for books on commission like Leigh and Sotheby in London & has sold a great part of his own stock by putting it into the catalogues of others...The sales of the younger for fifty days past have run between £50 & £100 a day, on which his own commission must have been a good thing, besides getting rid of lots of his own stock.' John found it hard to credit his own good fortune, for the role of auctioneer exactly suited his ebullient personality and he acted as though he loved every minute of his working day. He went to considerable trouble to gain publicity for his newly decorated rooms. There were occasions when he mounted his rostrum dressed in the full regalia of the hunting field, discarding his hammer in favour of a riding crop which he swished down with a crack to mark the fall of every lot. He managed, without apparent effort, to keep his audience in stitches of laughter by a continual flow of repartee, and could drag extra bids from reluctant purchasers by a combination of salesmanship and impudence. His sales quickly became almost daily affairs, and his 'salon' as he preferred to call it, became within a few months a fashionable lounge and regular calling place for Edinburgh society. Here coffee and claret were served, and here the more persistent purchasers were offered whisky-and-water on the house. On the mornings when the lots were laid out for viewing the gallery was frequented by many of the well-known names of the city, with personalities from the theatre, book collectors, lovers of the bizarre, artists, writers, and mere bargain hunters, all crowded round the goods on display, with wee Johnny Ballantyne flitting from one group to another, extolling the virtues of the various pieces with a conviction that put pounds on their ultimate value.

The eminently respectable church-going existence that James Ballantyne led, coupled with a mock majesty of walk and gesture, was in striking contrast to the wild activities of his younger brother. He still occupied the bachelor apartments in St John Street that he had moved into soon after leaving Kelso, and his elderly parents, to whom he gave every appearance of being devoted, had a room there also. Despite the fact that he was now forty-two years of age, his mother, who acted as his house-keeper, insisted on fussing around him, spoiling him as one would a little boy and warding off the attentions of any designing female who might happen to cross his path. She went far to encourage the one besetting sin which he was powerless to resist: James was a gourmand; a positive glutton when a well-cooked meal was set before him, eating and drinking until he sometimes had difficulty in rising from the table. For this gross over-indulgence in one of the sins of the flesh the little printer had already paid part of the penalty by becoming as stout as his brother John was thin. He disliked eating alone and was pleased to be known as a generous host who owned one of the best stocked wine cellars in Edinburgh. As a theatre critic whose column appeared regularly in the *Edinburgh Evening Courant*, and as a patron of music and the arts, James soon had a wide circle of friends with similar tastes to his own. His rooms became a meeting place for literary, theatrical and concert hall personalities, and he could be relied upon to give a party for the principal members of the cast after the first night of any major production on the Edinburgh stage. He numbered amongst his friends such darlings of the age as Sarah Siddons, a lady whose talents he so admired that he commemorated her various appearances in the city by recording them, complete with critical dissertations, in the form of a privately printed little booklet for distribution amongst her friends.[1] John Kemble, Edmund Kean, Daniel Terry and John Liston were other supper-party companions at St John Street, while from the world of music there was Braham, Salomon, and a dozen other top flight singers and instrumentalists.

These affairs disguised the fact that James was continually hard up; but this was not due to his having squandered large sums in gambling, womanizing, or riotous living. The reason for him falling deeper into debt with every passing year can be found in his having to renew or pay back the loans he had contracted in the early days of the Ballantyne Press. These he had been forced to make in order to keep his capital in the enterprise on a par with Walter Scott's; or to find money to invest in John

[1] *Dramatic Characters by Mrs Siddons*, Edinburgh, privately printed (1818).

Ballantyne & Company; and to try and equal the advances made by his partner when debts accumulated and funds were urgently needed. His house in St John Street he had now made over to Sir William Forbes & Company, the Edinburgh bankers, to raise £1,200 so that certain pressing debts at the printing house could be met. He had previously borrowed £1,000 from his brother Sandy in order to pay his own share and John's, each of £500, when the publishing company was first formed, all of which they had lost. Sandy had advanced the money in 1808, and it was supposed to be repayable in five years' time, bearing interest at five per cent; but when it became due for payment in 1813, James was in no position to find the money. Sandy agreed to wait another year, despite the fact that he had a growing family and had been repeatedly told by his wife that they badly needed a larger house. On being approached again in the summer of 1814, James offered to make over the title-deeds of his St John Street home to his brother, as they were not at that time pledged to the bank, so that he could mortgage the property. But Scott no sooner heard of the proposed arrangement than he let his partner know, in no uncertain terms, that Sandy was not to receive preferential treatment, and must be prepared to queue like the rest of their creditors. James broke this news to his brother:

Edinburgh 23d. Sept. 1814

My Dear Sandy,

I had a letter from Mr Scott, in which he expresses himself as unprepared to agree to the transfer of the house to you, saying—

'I own I think it questionable how far money borrowed for the advantage of a partner ought to be guaranteed by the company. As it stands, Mr B must take the chance of the rest of the creditors. I cannot think of sanctioning any arrangement which would dispose of your house in his favour, and to the prejudice of the others; and, if you will consider it in this point of view, you must be sensible it would be an improper transaction. The matter may lie over till we meet.'

Well, I suppose you are quite willing to *take the chance of the other creditors*? You *have* the bills of James Ballantyne and Company; and cannot lose. I shall answer Scott's letter triumphantly. He talks of it as 'an improper transaction.' Why, sir, he has, at this moment, an obligation from us in his possession, binding us to give *his* brother security over the printing-office, for money advanced as part of *his* stock, for which he regularly received 15 per cent. That plain tale should put him down, methinks. For here, he receives this enormous interest as a partner, *running all risks*; and he takes an obligation for a security which would prevent the possibility of *his running any risk*. How that should be a wrong transaction applied to *my* brother, which he thought a right one when applied to *his* brother, my blunt intellects cannot see. So, no more of this.

I rest here that you cannot lose in the long run. You have as above said, the bills of the *company*; and the company can pay. Most assuredly, you can draw interest at only 5 per cent. We have too well got over the bond transaction, to renew the same difficulty with the bills. They are *new* securities, untainted by the vice of their predecessor, and must be kept so.

In haste, Yours,
J.[ames] B.[allantyne][1]

Sandy was far from pleased, for he had to placate his wife, but he wrote back to say that he obviously had no alternative but to agree to his brother's request, and a few weeks later a grateful James visited him at Kelso to explain his position more fully and to thank him for his help. But several small creditors back in Edinburgh had become tired of waiting for their money and, during his absence, a distraint for debt was enforced against him. He hurried back immediately with a draft from his long-suffering youngest brother to put the matter right, but to his dismay he was too late to stop the news of his embarrassment becoming widely known. The tidings finally reached the ears of an irate Walter Scott who was anything but pleased, believing, quite rightly, that the credit of the printing establishment had been injured to some extent by this poinding (as the distraint was called) having been issued against one of the partners. In high dudgeon he wrote to John to complain about his brother's conduct.

17th October 1814

Dear John,

I received your letter with the astonishing news of James's utter *disregard to his own credit*. He promised to let me have accounts of his prospects, and consult me upon the management of his cash affairs, but *he has kept his word but lamely*. He is even worse than you, for you generally give a day or two's notice at least of the chance of dishonour, and this poinding is little better. His Kelso expedition has proved a fine one...

[1] *Reply to Mr Lockhart's Pamphlet*, p. 92 of the appendix.

Meanwhile John had been plodding from one bank to another in the vain hope of raising sufficient to meet bills of Scott's which were shortly due for payment. On the 15th October he wrote despairingly to Constable telling him of his lack of success: 'Can you stead us, therefore, in this £310 by a part loan in cash till the end of the month and acceptance (for us to retire when due) for the balance or otherwise as you incline?'[1]

Arrangements were made just in time to prevent disaster, but only after Scott had written a personal letter to Cadell asking him to transfer part of the credit due to him on three bills which had been issued in payment for the *Works of Swift*. Neither Scott nor the Ballantynes had any idea that the firm of Archibald Constable & Company was now itself in a very precarious position financially, all three being at that time under the impression that the company had vast resources its partners could draw upon. In fact when Scott wrote, Constable was in London doing his best to raise funds by the sale of the firm's stock at reduced prices, besides bringing Longmans in once more to support the *Edinburgh Review*, and vainly seeking a sharer in the cost of producing his *Encyclopaedia Britannica*. His bankers had warned him that he was seriously overdrawing his credit, and had hinted that unless he pulled in his horns he might have the greatest difficulty in obtaining funds to continue to trade.

All of them, Constable, Cadell, the Ballantynes, and Scott himself, were doing their utmost to keep the bubble of credit intact until the start of the new year. For by then Scott had promised that two new works would be completed, and upon the success of these they now based all their hopes.

[1] *Archibald Constable and his Literary Correspondents*, Edinburgh, 1873, Vol. III.

JOHN BALLANTYNE WAS held in the highest esteem by Scott when it came to driving a hard bargain with the publishing houses and the author still entrusted him with the task of marketing each of his works, allowing him an agent's percentage for doing so. In December, 1814, the auctioneer caused the following advertisement to appear in the *Scots Magazine and Edinburgh Literary Miscellany*, a monthly paper that carried news of forthcoming publications.

MR SCOTT'S POEM OF *The Lord of the Isles* WILL APPEAR EARLY IN JANUARY. THE AUTHOR OF *Waverley* IS ABOUT TO AMUSE THE PUBLIC WITH A NEW NOVEL, IN THREE VOLUMES, ENTITLED *Guy Mannering*.

The first edition of 1,800 quarto copies of Scott's last major poetical work duly appeared as promised, and a few days later the author asked James to call on him at Castle Street. When Ballantyne arrived he found Scott in his study intent on finishing the third volume of his latest novel. 'Well, James,' he greeted the printer, looking up from the manuscript, 'I have given you a week—what are people saying about *The Lord of the Isles?*' Ballantyne hesitated and then tried to change the subject. 'Come, speak out, my good fellow; what has put it into your head to be on so much ceremony *with me* all of a sudden?' Scott exclaimed impatiently. But when Ballantyne still kept silent he searched his face for a moment with his eyes and then said resignedly: 'But I see how it is. The result is given in one word—*Disappointment*.' James's downcast expression confirmed that this was so, and Scott's face clouded for a moment as he muttered something about being surprised that his poetical popularity should have lasted so long. At this Ballantyne turned in some embarrassment to take his leave, but the author, appearing to shrug the thought of failure from his mind, roused himself to his usual cheerfulness and added: 'Well, well, James, so be it. But you know we must not droop, for we can't afford to give over. Since one line has failed, we must just stick to something else.' And, as he bade the printer goodbye, he turned and took up his quill to resume work on his book.[1] Just over a month after this meeting *Guy Mannering* was published[2] and its instant success established once and for all the future course of his literary career. With its appearance Walter Scott became the first of the best-selling novelists, and on a scale that would entitle him to be so called even in the present day.

The future George IV, to whom Scott had sent a copy of *The Lord of the Isles*, expressed a particular wish to meet him and royally entertained him not once, but twice, at Carlton House. Scott had good reason to be in the best of spirits. He was also immensely cheered by the news from France. Napoleon had been vanquished and banished to Elba. The flags were out in London, and to provide a final flourish to the bright prospect before him, Scott soon discovered that he was treated everywhere as a very famous man. And Charlotte told him with delight that the two recent novels by the Author of *Waverley* were to be seen in every drawing-room she visited.

Not long after Scott's return to Abbotsford the victory at Waterloo finally put paid to Napoleon's ambitions. The author's patriotic feelings were aroused to such an extent by the reports he read about the battle that he became determined to visit the scene as soon as his duties in court permitted him. With an eye to business he had managed to conclude a profitable engagement with Constable, Longman and Murray for a series of letters from the continent which he proposed calling *Paul's Letters to His Kinsfolk*. This was to be an autobiographical account of his tour of the battlefield and of his life in Paris and elsewhere during the first months of occupation by allied troops, and by selling the work he more than paid the expenses of the trip. John Scott of Gala, Alexander Pringle of Whytbank, and Robert Bruce, an Edinburgh advocate, were the three young men who accompanied him on the stage-coach to the south, embarking at Harwich on the 3rd August. The captain of the packet, himself an avid reader of both poetry and prose, discovered the identity of his distinguished passenger and toasted his health in such frequent tumblers of whisky-toddy that the four considered themselves lucky to arrive safely at Ostend.

[1] *Life of Scott*, Vol. III.
[2] The first edition consisted of 2,000 copies, each of three volumes.

In Paris Scott for the first time met his idol and hero, the Duke of Wellington. It was suggested to him later that perhaps the Duke himself felt honoured by having been privileged to meet a great poet and novelist, but Scott professed himself shocked at the very idea. 'What would the Duke of Wellington think of a few bits of novels,' he said, 'which perhaps he had never read, and for which the strong probability is that he would not care sixpence if he had?' This trait of character which was strongly in evidence throughout his life—a feeling of humility when in the company of those whom he considered his social superiors—was an absurd weakness that Scott never overcame. Dukes, marquesses, lords and ladies, he loved them all and they seemingly impressed him by their very rank. He dedicated a number of his major works to them (not the novels for these were issued anonymously) and, as a right-wing Tory of the old school, defended their privileges in a manner which brought him their very grateful thanks.

He had a gay time in the French capital, attending numerous banquets and parties to celebrate the allied victory; watching with other distinguished guests the long march-pasts of troops for review by the Commander-in-Chief; being introduced to the Czar of Russia and General Blücher; and seldom managing to escape to his bed before the early hours of the morning. 'I am quite a Frenchman in eating and drinking, and turn up my nose at roast beef and port wine: fricassees and champagne are much better,' he wrote to Charlotte. 'After all, it is a delicious country, if the people would be but quiet, which I fear they never will.' He finally left Paris on the 9th September and returned via Dieppe to spend a few days in London, where he had his last meeting with Byron. By the afternoon of the 24th he was back in Abbotsford.

Besides the series of letters he sent home, to be edited into *Paul's Letters to His Kinsfolk*, he completed two poems on his return. 'The Dance of Death' was a minor piece of versifying, published in the still struggling *Edinburgh Annual Register* for 1815/16, and telling of the thoughts and actions of a soldier the night before the battle. There was also *The Field of Waterloo*, a most unhappy venture on the poet's part, the profits of the first edition of which, as in the case of *Don Roderick*, he donated to the dependents of the slain.

> *On Waterloo's ensanguined plain*
> *Full many a gallant man was slain,*
> *But none by sabre or by shot,*
> *Fell half so flat as Walter Scott.*

So wrote a contemporary critic, and these lines of doggerel verse give a fair indication of the reception the poem was accorded by the public. The unfortunate Archibald Constable had contracted to publish it and burned his fingers once again.

The author's letters to the Ballantynes at this period are full of money-raising schemes, for he was desperately eager to purchase further tracts of land which he had heard were shortly coming on the market. 'Mr Constable proposes 6000 of *Waterloo* to which I have no objection: the price he proposes to be 5/–. If so settled I presume I should have something handsome to draw for, which will help out matters well. I pray you push on Paul,' he wrote to John. 'Taking the edition at 6000 [at] 12/– & deducting £300 already received, there will be £800 & upwards to draw which will do much to clear next month.' It can be seen by this letter, written early in October, 1815, that they were still living hand to mouth and were only just able to meet their bills as they fell due. But at the same time, even while forcing the pace at the printing works to enable him to have funds to draw upon, he was able to write to Lady Louisa Stuart, whom he considered one of his most trusted and closest friends: 'I have been tempted to write for fame, and there have been periods when I have been compelled to write for money. Neither of these motives now exists.'[1]

It is quite obvious now, as it must have been then, that the second of these motives certainly did exist: the whips of financial necessity were the compelling reason why he drove himself to write ceaselessly in every spare moment he could snatch from his work in court and the social engagements that pressed increasingly upon him. Whether he wished to lull his friends, as well as himself, into a false sense of the soundness of his financial standing, is a matter for speculation. Scott could close his mind to the realities of his pecuniary affairs by the simple expedient of ignoring unpleasant facts. Those who knew the true state of his commitments, such as the Ballantynes and to some extent Archibald Constable and Robert Cadell, were amazed at his temerity

[1] Dated from Abbotsford, 2nd November, 1815.

97

in purchasing that most expensive of luxuries, acres of unimproved scrub and marsh land to add to his estate, at a time when there was still thousands of pounds to be found to settle the debts of the publishing house. He could be extremely stubborn once he had decided upon a course of action, and if he had set his heart on acquiring a new possession, be it antiques he could well have done without, or tracts of land he certainly could not afford, nothing satisfied him until the bargain was concluded and he had become the owner of this fresh embellishment for the ever growing Abbotsford. His innate benevolence and generosity of feelings towards any that he called his friends, could not disguise the fact that he was also capable of letting all and sundry feel 'the violence of his irritable and most ungovernable mind', as one of his companions in his days before his marriage described his temperament.[1] This is often revealed in his letters. Crossed in his purpose, or wounded by an imagined slight, he could react harshly and unfairly, as Douglas Stewart, James Ballantyne, and Archibald Constable all found to their cost. He was, after all, only human, and if he had his faults, he was also gifted with many compensating qualities.

By the end of the year he was hard at work on his next novel, *The Antiquary*, begun and finished in the space of little over four months and published by Constable in May, 1816. The money from its sale was badly needed, for a fresh influx of builders had invaded Abbotsford and further extensive additions and alterations had been commenced at a cost of several thousands of pounds. If the house was growing, so was the estate to surround it. In the autumn of 1815 he had written to John Ballantyne: 'I have thoughts of entering into a transaction for a farm lying contiguous to Abbotsford. It is very extensive & may be had cheap &, as the owner wishes the money to remain in my hands, will occasion no demand but for the interest & will not therefore interfere with the redemption of the £4000.[2] It may cost from £3000 to £4000 & I think in five or six years by judicious outlay I could double its value. It marches with Abbotsford & would add greatly to the value of this place which I think I may now hope to enjoy in peace. Let me know what you think I should do in this matter.' What John really thought

---

[1] *Sir Walter Scott, Bart.*, H. J. C. Grierson, Constable, 1938. Chapter II.
[2] This is a reference to the bond of £4,000 guaranteed by the Duke of Buccleuch, which was not finally redeemed until 1818.

is perhaps best shown by the comment he penned on the outside of this letter, which simply states 'More land!!!'

Scott's personal income at this time, and in the succeeding years, excluding his literary earnings, never exceeded £2,000 a year, the majority of which had to be used to pay the interest charges on the mounting debts his colossal expenditure was continually adding to. The writing was already on the wall, plain for all to see, but for the time being expedients of various kinds kept the Laird of Abbotsford afloat and his dependent crew with him.

In the autumn of 1815, stout little James Ballantyne, now in his forty-fourth year, fell heavily and emphatically in love with a young lady many years his junior. She was the daughter of a wealthy farmer from Scremerston in Berwickshire, Robert Hogarth by name, whose son George, an accountant and Writer to the Signet, had heard rumours that all was not well with James's financial affairs. He had hinted strongly to the printer that his father's consent to the marriage, coupled with what might be a handsome dowry, would not be forthcoming unless clear proof was presented to the old man that James was free from debt and that his future prospects were reasonably bright. Early in November, Ballantyne wrote in considerable ánxiety to Scott, asking that he should receive his discharge from the liabilities of the publishing house on condition that he allowed the author to officially assume the ownership of James Ballantyne & Company, with his own services retained as manager.

The terms of the discharge were agreed, James acknowledging that the proportion of debts incurred on his behalf by the publishing house, plus his liabilities to the Ballantyne Press, amounted in all to £3,000. This was transferred as a credit to Walter Scott to be drawn by him as circumstances permitted from the funds of the printing business. In the meantime, Ballantyne was to be employed as manager of the business drawing a salary of £400 a year; Scott becoming sole proprietor and being responsible for the company's debts but drawing full profits instead of only fifty per cent as previously.

All being settled between them, the Hogarths signified that the marriage arrangements would proceed and, on the 1st February, 1816, James Ballantyne and Christina Hogarth became man and wife. By all accounts, she was a good-looking young lady, and

James's interest in the affair was certainly not solely pecuniary. Later events proved how much he cared for his attractive wife and how happy they both were in their marriage. On their return from their honeymoon, he and Christina settled in the newly decorated and refurnished house in St John Street, the rotund little printer bumbling contentedly around his pet and thoroughly spoiling her with his constant attentions and endearments. The dowry which the new Mrs Ballantyne brought with her amounted to about £3,000,[1] but it was not forthcoming for nearly eighteen months after the ceremony took place, Robert Hogarth first having to sell a strip of land which he had provisionally bequeathed to his daughter as a marriage portion some years before. This delay occasioned considerable embarrassment to James. He still owed his brother Sandy £500 and had promised on several different dates that it would be repaid. Sandy and his wife now had five children, and were still living in a tiny house in Belmont Place, Kelso; an overcrowded home which Mrs Randall Ballantyne resented having to put up with. On her insistence, her husband once again approached his eldest brother with a request that the loan should be repaid, and with this in mind James went to see Walter Scott at Abbotsford in the hope that he would permit a draft to be drawn on the company until such time as his expected windfall from Robert Hogarth came to hand. The author was in no mood to be accommodating, and not only refused Ballantyne's request, but insisted that Sandy should give up the securities of James Ballantyne & Company and accept his brother's personal bills until such time as the debt could be extinguished.

With James assuming personal responsibility for the loan made to him by his brother, the only debts now outstanding against the publishing house were those contracted by Walter Scott himself, and as owner he could manipulate the firm's finances in any way he chose. In justice to James, it should be remembered that the £1,000 borrowed from his brother had been invested in the company as part of his stock at a time when funds of any sort were desperately needed. He had pledged the security of the company to cover this loan, but Scott had done the same on his

[1] According to Ballantyne family legend, this was the amount which James eventually received from the Hogarths. Although confirmation of this figure has not been obtainable elsewhere (Lockhart states he thought the sum not more than £1,500) the amount given above accords well with the facts of Ballantyne's subsequent expenditure and seems to be substantially correct.

own behalf on several occasions when the two men were still partners. And on the sums Scott had borrowed from his brother to invest in the firm, he had drawn interest at fifteen per cent for several years. But now he was master of the enterprise he was determined to see that he retained full control of its finances in a way which would leave his manager in no doubt about his subordinate position.

The Antiquary soon proved itself an even more popular novel than its predecessors, and had the added distinction of being the author's personal favourite amongst his prose works. The charm of the book lies largely in the character of the antiquary, Jonathan Oldbuck, laird of Monkbarns, a learned and garrulous man in which one can easily recognize a portrait or caricature of Scott himself. The story recalled incidents in his early life, and the tales he had heard from George Constable, an old friend of his father's, and the man who first aroused in the writer his passionate interest in Scottish history and the works of William Shakespeare. Within a few months of publication, several thousand copies had been sold, and this time Constable had nothing to complain of in the bargain he had made. But his refusal to purchase any more of the Hanover Street stock had annoyed Scott. Thousands of pounds' worth of books and printed sheets were still lying there, and now that he was sole owner of what was left of the publishing company, every guinea's worth he could clear reduced its remaining debts or went straight into his own pocket. His first priority was to liquidate the remainder of this stock even if this meant finding another publisher. He determined to offer his next novel elsewhere and devised a scheme that appealed to his love of secrecy and would, he hoped, attract a fresh influx of ready money into the hands of 'The Author of *Waverley*'. But that well-known phrase was not to be allowed to appear on the title-pages. Too many people had now guessed the name of the writer of the series of Scotch novels and he was hopeful that his new plan would help to confuse the issue. The difficulties in keeping the knowledge of the author's identity from the workpeople in the printing establishment was one of the causes of leaks of information: the sheets of the original manuscript were always copied out by Sandy Ballantyne or occasionally by John, but clues were sometimes easy to pick up. Sandy Tofts, a machinist at Paul's Works, had discovered that Walter Scott was the author before the second of his novels was published.

> I had just begun to a new sheet of *Guy Mannering*, one night a little after twelve—we were working late in the press-room at that time—and all the compositors had left, when in comes Mr Ballantyne himself, with a letter in his hand and a lot of types. 'I am just going to make a small alteration, Sandy,' he said. 'Just unlock the forme, will you? I'll not keep you many minutes.'
> Well, I did as I was bidden, and Mr B, looking at the letter, altered three lines on one page and one line on another. 'That will do now, I think, Sandy,' were his words, 'but first pull a sheet till I see.' The master then looked carefully over the two pages and said, 'Bring me the printed sheets—they'll have to be destroyed.' And off he went, never thinking that he had left the letter lying on my bank. I had barely time to get a glimpse of it, when back came Mr Ballantyne, but I kent the hand weel, and the signature, and it was 'Walter Scott.'[1]

The fact that Archibald Constable & Company were so closely identified in the public's mind with the works of The Great Unknown, was one of the reasons why Scott decided to offer his new novel to another publishing house. However, a far more important justification for the change from the author's point of view was that their bills had lately become increasingly difficult to negotiate. Even at generous discounts brokers hummed and ha'd before accepting them, for the credit of the firm was now stretched to the limit and their difficulties had become known throughout the trade. 'I had some conversation with young Smith of Glasgow about Constable's business,' Scott wrote to James Ballantyne on the 23rd July. 'The young man seemed to consider him as rather *too* enterprising—these are hints which are seldom dropped without reason. But he added that he was very clever & had many resources.'[2] What Scott needed was spot cash before delivery, or the equivalent in easily negotiable bills-of-exchange. He was not prepared to wait for payment while Constable's bills were hawked from one bank to another with the inevitable loss of large amounts in discounts when they were finally accepted.

He was forced to use James for the negotiations with the new

[1] *Memoirs of Books and Authors*, James Bertram, 1893.
[2] *Letters of Sir Walter Scott*, Vol. I.

publishing house for his brother John had made arrangements for a visit to Paris in search of *objets d'art*, French furniture, antiquarian books, pictures, and any other saleable items for his now thriving auction rooms. Many of the valuable art treasures looted by the allied troops and the retreating French after Waterloo, were reappearing in the back streets of Paris and Brussels at prices that were most attractive if they could once be shipped safely over to London or Edinburgh. Business-wise, John had a most successful trip, but managed to further undermine his now precarious health by a mad round of dissipation in the tawdry but nevertheless expensive drinking clubs, gambling houses and brothels of both capitals. Another reason for using James was no doubt the author's knowledge of the close identification of John Ballantyne by the publishing trade with any negotiations regarding the marketing of the works of the Author of *Waverley*; this new work was, as Scott put it, 'totally different in stile and structure from the others—a new cast, in short, of the net which has hitherto made miraculous draughts.'[1] But before long James had succeeded in misinterpreting several of the instructions he had received for the bargain with the new publishers, and was forced to entirely redraft the agreement before Scott would accept the conditions. 'Having only authority from me to promise 6000 copies, he proposes they shall have the copy-right *for ever*,' the author wrote to John, regarding his brother. 'I will see their noses cheese first....He talks of volumes being put into the publishers hands to consider & decide on. No such thing—a bare perusal at St John Street only.' And there was more in the same vein. Things were finally straightened out to Scott's satisfaction and the new novel went to the London firm of John Murray, acting through their Edinburgh agents, William Blackwood & Company. James had offered them a four-volume romance purporting to be by a rising new author of Scottish descent, entitled *Tales of My Landlord*, which was to be issued under the pseudonym of 'Jedediah Cleishbotham—Schoolmaster and Parish-Clerk of Gandercleuch'. It was stipulated that the work was to be printed by James Ballantyne & Company; it was to be published on a half-profits basis; they were to pay the unknown author £750 for the right of marketing the first edition of 6,000 copies, plus extra for any subsequent editions; and they were to purchase a minimum of £600 worth

[1] *Ibid.*, Vol. I. Appendix.

of the stock of books at Hanover Street. All these conditions were agreed to by the publishers, and on the 23rd August Blackwood was able to announce to Murray the arrival of the manuscript and his intense enjoyment of the opening chapters of *The Black Dwarf*.

The four-volume work contained two separate stories: *Old Mortality*, the latter of the two, was a masterpiece of descriptive writing and more than made up for the tame and disappointing ending to *The Black Dwarf*. Blackwood's initial enthusiasm soon evaporated when he perused the final chapters of the first tale and he sent this portion of the manuscript to William Gifford, editor of the *Quarterly Review*, who came to the same conclusion as himself, namely, that at least part of *The Black Dwarf* ought to be rewritten. This information was duly passed on to Walter Scott by James Ballantyne, who, as soon as he heard of Blackwood's unpardonable liberty in showing his manuscript to Gifford, wrote back in an extremely angry mood.

> Dear James
> My respects to the Booksellers & I belong to the Death-head Hussars of literature who neither *take* nor *give* criticism. I know no business they had to show my work to Gifford, nor would I cancel a leaf to please all the critics of Edinburgh & London: and so let that be as it is. I never heard of such impudence in my life. Do they think I don't know when I am writing ill as well as Gifford can tell me? It is good enough for them, and they had better make up the £200 they propose to swindle me out of than trouble themselves about the contents...
> John's plans seem rational and soberminded. He is an excellent little fellow and if he will but be cautious may do capitally. I beg there may be no more communications with critics. These *born idiots* do not know the mischief they do to me & themselves. I DO by God.
> Yours truly
> W.S.[1]
> *Thursday* [3rd October, 1816]

It is amusing to compare the answer James then sent to Blackwood with the original letter printed above. He toned down the phraseology considerably, but the general sense of Scott's retort remains the same and Ballantyne's editing doubtless prevented a complete estrangement between the publisher and the author.

[1] *Letters of Sir Walter Scott*, Vol. IV.

My Dear Sir,

Our application to the author of *Tales of my Landlord* has been anything but successful; and in order to explain you the reason why I must decline to address him in this way in future, I shall copy his answer *verbatim*.

'My respects to our friends the Booksellers. I belong to the Death-head Hussars of Literature, who neither *take* nor *give* criticism. I am extremely sorry they showed my work to Gifford, nor would I cancel a leaf to please all the critics of Edinburgh and London; and so let that be as it is: They are mistaken if they think I don't know when I am writing ill, as well as Gifford can tell me. I beg there be no more communications with critics.'

Observe—that I shall at all times be ready to convey anything from you to the author in written form, but I do not feel warranted to interfere further.

Yours very truly,

J. Ballantyne

We shall be discussing Walter Scott's biographer and son-in-law, John Gibson Lockhart, at length later in this volume, but it is worthwhile giving an example here of the way he altered and changed the text of certain letters, both to and from his illustrious father-in-law. His motives for doing this were usually to discredit the Ballantynes, and by changes of emphasis, the omission of phrases, or the simple expedient of changing the text, he managed to convey whatever impression he wished his readers to receive. His version of Scott's letter runs as follows:

Dear James,

I have received Blackwood's impudent letter. G——d d——n his soul! Tell him and his coadjutor that I belong to the Black Hussars of Literature, who neither give nor receive criticism. I'll be cursed but this is the most impudent proposal that ever was made.

W.S.[1]

Lockhart was quick to point out to his readers in his *Life of Scott* that Ballantyne's version of the author's letter was a travesty of the original. But if James altered the 'verbatim' version he conveyed to Blackwood, Lockhart most certainly grossly manipulated his own, as he was so fond of doing in his massive

[1] *Life of Scott*, Vol. IV.

biography. In the first edition of the *Life* he makes the text of this letter read: 'I have received Blackwood's impudent *letter*.' Some time later he discovered to his embarrassment that Blackwood had not complained to James in writing. When the second edition of the *Life* was printed, he was therefore compelled to alter the word '*letter*' to '*proposal*'; thus proving that he manufactured the text to suit his own ends, and was not quoting from another version that Scott might have written and then laid aside.

Blackwood and Murray guessed almost immediately the true identity of the author of *Tales of My Landlord*. It would have been quite unthinkable for them to agree to such expensive terms for a novel by anyone else, much less from the pen of an untried and unknown author. In fact, Murray wrote to Scott on the 14th December, just after the work had appeared: 'Although I dare not address you as the author of certain Tales—which must have been written by Walter Scott or the devil—yet nothing can restrain me from thinking that it is to your influence with the author of them that I am indebted for the honour of being one of their publishers.' He went on to say that those who had read the novel were absolutely delighted with it, and that when he asked Lord Holland his opinion, the old man had replied: 'Opinion! We did not go to bed all night, and nothing slept but my gout!'

Neither Constable nor Cadell were sure of the reason that made Scott offer his last work elsewhere, but both were determined to renew their firm's old relationship with the author as soon as they possibly could. They had gone to considerable trouble and expense to keep the writer in a friendly state of mind towards their company and had continued to market his pet project, the *Edinburgh Annual Register* long after it had become obvious that the periodical would never pay its way. Scott himself was conscious of having let them down rather badly; he liked Robert Cadell and considered him straightforward and businesslike, although Archibald Constable had never appealed to him either as a man or a business acquaintance. Nevertheless, the way he had assisted both Scott and the Ballantynes during the worst of their business difficulties, sometimes at considerable expense to himself, was something no just and fair-minded person could overlook. The amounts Scott had received from Murray had helped ease his financial problems for the time being, and he was now in receipt of a legacy of some £3,000 left him by his brother Major John Scott who died in May, 1816,[1] so he could afford to be generous to his old publishers. But only in the sense of allowing them first refusal of the terms he had drawn up with the help of John Ballantyne for the publication rights of his next novel: he was certainly not going to allow sentimental considerations to hurt his pocket.

With the expiration of the fourth edition of *Tales of My Landlord*, Scott withdrew the book from Blackwood and transferred the rights to Constable and his London agents, Longman & Company; they had offered the best terms and that settled the matter. Author and publisher were once again reconciled and business was resumed on the old footing. By the 7th May, 1817, the Edinburgh publishing house were able to write to Longman that 'an agreement for a new work by the Author of *Waverley*' had been signed; 'it is to be entitled *Rob Roy* in 3 vols. and published in September.' Constable and John Bailantyne had met Scott at Abbotsford on the 5th May, and when at last their long meeting broke up John was able to announce excitedly to his elder brother: 'Wish me joy. I shall gain above £600 — Constable taking my share of stock also — The title is *Rob Roy* — by *the Author of Waverley*.' John was more than pleased that Scott had agreed that this pseudonym should once again appear on the title-pages, knowing that the words whetted the public's appetite with memories of the previous excellent fare they had enjoyed, and that this well-known phrase was probably worth the sale of several thousand extra copies. For the privilege of marketing six thousand sets of the new work, the publishers had been forced to agree that they would buy £600 of old stock from Hanover Street. In addition, they had to pay the author £1,700 by May the same year, the manuscript to be in their hands for publication by September. But it was not until the 31st December, 1817, that the work finally appeared in the bookshops, Scott having been stricken with an excruciating attack of intestinal pain while giving a dinner party at Castle Street earlier in the year.

[1] Half of the £4,000 which Scott paid for the original farm at Abbotsford was loaned him by his brother the Major.

BEFORE THIS SUDDEN and severe attack occurred, Scott had been troubled for several months by stabs of pain low down on his right side. He had dosed himself with medicine, drunk copious draughts of hot water, applied hot fomentations and tried numerous other proven remedies in an effort to relieve the symptoms of his internal disorder. His doctors diagnosed the malady as stomach cramp, but there can be little doubt that his intensely painful series of attacks of biliary colic were caused by gall-stones being forced through his bile duct into his intestine. This process always results in the most excruciating agony for the unfortunate sufferer, but today morphia quickly takes the edge off the pain while modern surgery has no difficulty in dealing with the cause of the condition. No such remedies were available in the nineteenth century, and the unlucky patient was forced to bear the spasms as best he could with the help of large doses of laudanum.

It was on the 5th March, 1817, while the Scotts were giving a dinner party for a few friends in their Edinburgh home, that the first really severe attack manifested itself. One moment the host seemed to his wife and guests to be in the best of health, and the next he had collapsed at the table moaning in agony, before staggering from the room to his bed 'roaring like a bull-calf'. About a fortnight later, when he had recovered somewhat, he wrote to John Morritt telling him that the pain he had suffered had even out-devilled the doctors' torturing proscriptions and restrictions. 'Even heated salt, which was applied in such a state that it burnd my shirt to rags, I hardly felt when applied to my stomach,' he told his friend. 'At length the symptoms became inflammatory and dangerously so, the seat being the diaphragm: they gave way only to very profuse bleeding and blistering which, under higher assistance, saved my life.' His recovery from this first attack was slow and tedious, and he was to suffer numerous others during the next few months. Despite his illness, one of the obvious symptoms of which was a badly jaundiced complexion, he continued in the intervals when the pain left him to work at his novel and other literary affairs. Friends who had not seen him for some time were shocked at his appearance, and, by the end of the summer, having been dieted for months and bled a dozen times, he was almost unrecognizable. R. P. Gillies wrote[1] that: 'He was worn almost to a skeleton, sat slanting on his horse, as if unable to hold himself upright: his dress was threadbare and disordered; and his countenance, instead of its usual healthy colour, was of an olive-brown—I might almost say, black tinge.... "The physicians tell me," said he, "that mere pain cannot kill; but I am very sure that no man would, for over three months, encounter the same pain I have suffered, and live. However, I have resolved to take thankfully whatever drugs they proscribe, and follow their advice as long as I can. Set a stout heart to a stey brae, is a grand rule in this world." '

In the course of the last two years he had been tireless in his efforts to turn out the maximum possible amount of literary work. *Paul's Letters, The Antiquary, The Black Dwarf, Old Mortality, Harold the Dauntless,* the start of *Rob Roy,* and lengthy histories of the years 1814 and 1815 for two issues of the *Edinburgh Annual Register,* besides several items of minor work, had all issued from his pen. All this had been accomplished during a period when he was often a very sick man and while he was spending several hours of each day during six months of the year, attending his legal duties at the Court of Session in Edinburgh. In addition, he had been involved in protracted negotiations through John Ballantyne regarding publication rights for his books; had been called upon to make a multitude of decisions about the rebuilding of Abbotsford; while with the help of James Ballantyne, he had corrected several hundred sheets of proofs while his work was passing through the press. Notwithstanding the inroads all these affairs made on his time, he still managed to conduct a voluminous correspondence with his ever widening circle of friends, and a host of others were entertained at either Castle Street or Abbotsford. Washington Irving, in whose writings Scott found much to admire, gave an intimate picture of the author and his family when the two writers met for the first time in August, 1817. The American had been given a letter of introduction to the laird by Thomas Campbell, and while on a

[1] *Recollections of Sir Walter Scott, Bart.*, R. P. Gillies, London, 1837.

visit to Scotland he interrupted a trip to the ruins of Melrose Abbey in order to halt his chaise on the high-road above Abbotsford while the coachman took in his card.

The noise of my chaise [wrote Irving] had disturbed the quiet of the establishment. Out sallied the warder of the castle, a black greyhound, and leaping on one of the blocks of stone, began a furious barking. This alarm brought out the whole garrison of dogs, all open-mouthed and vociferous. In a little while, the lord of the castle himself made his appearance. I knew him at once, by the likenesses that had been published of him. He came limping up the gravel walk, aiding himself by a stout walking-staff, but moving rapidly and with vigour. By his side jogged along a large iron-grey staghound, of most grave demeanour, who took no part in the clamour of the canine rabble, but seemed to consider himself bound, for the dignity of the house, to give me a courteous reception.

Before Scott reached the gate, he called out in a hearty tone, welcoming me to Abbotsford and asking news of Campbell. Arriving at the door of the chaise, he grasped me warmly by the hand: 'Come, drive down, drive down to the house,' said he; 'ye're just in time for breakfast, and afterwards ye shall see all the wonders of the Abbey.'

I would have excused myself on the plea of having already made my breakfast. 'Hut, man,' cried he, 'a ride in the morning in the keen air of the Scotch hills is warrant enough for a second breakfast.'

Meaning to make the visit one of just a few hours, Irving soon found himself persuaded to stay several days. There was only the family at home, and while his hostess hurried off to arrange about his breakfast, Irving was introduced to the children.

...Sophia, then a fine girl about seventeen; Miss Ann Scott, two or three years younger; Walter, a well-grown stripling; and Charles, a lively boy, eleven or twelve years of age.

I soon felt myself quite at home, and my heart in a glow, with the cordial welcome I experienced. I had thought to make a mere morning visit, but found I was not to be let off so lightly. 'You must not think our neighbourhood is to be read in a morning like a newspaper,' said Scott; 'it takes several days of study for an observant traveller, that has a relish for auld-world trumpery. After breakfast you shall make your visit to Melrose Abbey...When you come back, I'll take you on a ramble about our neighbourhood. Tomorrow we will take a look at the Yarrow, and the next day we will drive over to Dryburgh Abbey, which is a fine old ruin, well worth your seeing.'

As we sallied forth, every dog in the establishment turned out to attend us. There was the old staghound, Maida, that I have already mentioned, a noble animal, and Hamlet, the black grey-hound, a wild, thoughtless youngster, not yet arrived at the years of discretion; and Finette, a beautiful setter, with soft, silken hair, long pendant ears, and a mild eye—the parlour favourite. When in front of the house, we were joined by a superannuated greyhound, who came from the kitchen wagging his tail; and was cheered by Scott as an old friend and comrade. In our walks, he would frequently pause in conversation, to notice his dogs, and speak to them as if rational companions...

Our ramble took us on the hills commanding an extensive prospect. 'Now,' said Scott, 'I have brought you, like the pilgrim in the Pilgrim's Progress, to the top of the Delectable Mountains, that I may show you all the goodly regions hereabouts. Yonder is Lammermuir, and Smailholme; and there you have Galashiels, and Torwoodlee, and Gala Water; and in that direction you see Teviotdale and the Braes of Yarrow, and Ettrick stream winding along like a silver thread, to throw itself into the Tweed.' He went on thus to call over names celebrated in Scottish song, and most of which had recently received a romantic interest from his own pen. In fact, I saw a great part of the Border country spread out before me, and could trace the scenes of those poems and romances which had in a manner bewitched the world.

I gazed about me for a time with mute surprise, I may almost say, with disappointment. I beheld a mere succession of grey waving hills, line beyond line, as far as my eye could reach, mono-tonous in their aspect, and so destitute of trees, that one could almost see a stout fly walking along their profile; and the far-famed Tweed appeared a naked stream, flowing between bare hills, without a tree or thicket on its banks; and yet such had been the magic web of poetry and romance thrown over the whole, that it had a greater charm for me than the richest scenery I had beheld in England. I could not help giving utterance to my thoughts. Scott hummed for a moment to himself, and looked grave; he had no idea of having his muse complimented at the expense of his native hills.

'It may be pertinacity,' said he at length; 'but to my eye, these grey hills, and all this wild border country, have beauties peculiar to themselves. I like the very nakedness of the land; it has some-thing bold, and stern, and solitary about it. When I have been for some time in the rich scenery about Edinburgh, which is like ornamented garden land, I begin to wish myself back again among my own honest grey hills; and if I did not see the heather at least once a year, *I think I should die!*' The last words were said with an honest warmth, accompanied by a thump on the ground with his staff, by way of emphasis, that showed his heart was in his speech.

We had not walked much further, before we saw the two Miss Scotts advancing along the hillside to meet us. The morning's studies being over, they had set off to take a ramble on the hills, and gather heather blossoms with which to decorate their hair for dinner, and as they approached the dogs all sprang forward and gambolled around them.

From the vantage point where he had conducted Irving, Scott was able to view his entire domain. Later that autumn he climbed the hill again in order to savour, with eyes full of rich contentment, his latest (and to date his most expensive) addition to the bounds of his estate. 'I have closed with Usher for his beautiful patrimony, which makes me a great laird,' he wrote to John Ballantyne in October. 'I am afraid the people will take me up for coining. Indeed, these novels, while their attractions last, are something like it.' They certainly needed to be, for he had promised to pay his neighbour £10,000 for his Toftfield estate, thus making himself master of hundreds more acres of Border land. Included in the purchase price was a well-built little house set amongst the ferns and heather which the new owner renamed 'Huntly Burn'. This he shortly let to his old college friend Adam Ferguson[1] who had recently retired from the army on half-pay. Ferguson's admiration for his poetry had once led him to read passages of *The Lady of the Lake* to his men as he crouched with them while under heavy fire from the French guns at Torres Vedras during the Peninsular Campaign; 'to keep up their morale' as he later informed the author.

What the Ballantyne brothers secretly thought of this latest purchase of land can only be imagined: they could not, of course, voice any criticism no matter how foolish they believed this vast expenditure on his estate and buildings may have been under the circumstances then prevailing. They had enough troubles of their own to occupy them. James was depressed by the fact that he owed the author nearly £3,000 and still had other debts to

---

[1] It was due to Scott's influence that Adam Ferguson was appointed Keeper of the Regalia of Scotland in 1818. During the royal visit to Edinburgh in 1822, he was knighted by George IV.

clear. Unlike his younger brother, he always looked on the black side of any problem. Currently he was obsessed with the idea, that in the event of his own sudden death, he might well leave his wife and newly arrived family of children completely destitute. This fear was quite illogical, for her parents were wealthy enough to give them all a home in the event of such an unlikely catastrophe occurring, while the long-awaited dowry would soon be available to clear most of his personal obligations to his friends and relations. 'I am sorry to see James so down in the mouth about his own affairs and ours,' Scott wrote to John. 'He seems more overwhelmd than ever & surely has no reason since he has a good income & with exertion might easily work off his debt. Had everyone abandoned themselves to that senseless sort of despair *where* should we have been just now?' But once his father-in-law had paid over the tocher, James's spirits immediately revived. He cleared all the fresh debts his marriage had brought him plus several others of old standing, while the amount Scott was drawing from the paper profits of the printing works was gradually reducing his commitment in that direction also. Before many months had passed he had entered into partnership with his brother-in-law George Hogarth, in order to purchase the *Edinburgh Weekly Journal*, a newspaper whose owner had recently died. For this they paid nearly £3,000, Hogarth and Ballantyne contributing three-eighths of the purchase money each, while Walter Scott stood guarantor for the other quarter share.[1] It proved one of their most profitable speculations, and, as it was printed at the Ballantyne Press, gave James ample opportunity to supervise its affairs without interfering with his management of the printing office. He assumed the editorship himself, drawing a salary of £200 a year, while the services of his brother John were retained as musical and dramatic critic, at which tasks he proved himself surprisingly adept. Under Ballantyne's guidance the paper rapidly increased its circulation, its production giving work for his presses at moments when they might otherwise be standing idle, while Hogarth saw to it that the profits were ploughed back into the business for several years.

---

[1] Scott acted as 'cautioner' for the sum of £720, representing a quarter share of the capital. (See his letter to John Ballantyne, quoted in *Letters of Sir Walter Scott* edited by H. J. C. Grierson, 1933, Volume V, pp. 463–4).

Money always burned a hole in John's pocket and, after a second successful purchasing trip to the continent, the rise in his standard of living more than kept pace with the increasing profits he was making from his auction rooms and the quite considerable sums he earned as agent for Walter Scott in the marketing of his works. His love of speculation and his egotistical desire to prove himself as sharp and astute as any London financier, had led him to entrust nearly a thousand pounds of his own and James's money to a broker by the name of Ainslie, a gentleman who had held out glowing promises of the quick profits to be made by backing bills which the banks would not touch. But upon his return from the continent, he soon discovered that Ainslie was a man of straw and that the money he had entrusted to him had disappeared. So had Mr Ainslie, and for several weeks an increasingly agitated Ballantyne sought news of his whereabouts in the capital and elsewhere in the hope of retrieving at least part of the sum he had handed over to him. Scott had written to James in September, chiding him for his foolishness in backing John in his hair-brained financial schemes: 'I own that it surprizes me that knowing John as you do know him you should again plunge deep into his bill-transactions. Assuredly you will destroy your own credit if you continue this conduct & that will not be very just to those already connected with you. I will assist John myself & have done so in all feasible matters, but *not* with credit & I assure you it will do him no good. The only chance I see of your getting out of the scrape is to keep hold of his share of R.R.[1] for I suspect that between Ainslie and these misadventures John will have a bad account of his affairs when he comes home. He is an unlucky wight.'[2]

Despite his illness, Scott had worked in every free moment to finish his long-awaited novel *Rob Roy*; a tale he later described as 'smelling of the cramp' and which shows several signs of having been brought to a hasty conclusion. His courage and tenacity in continuing writing while being racked with pain calls for the highest praise, and now that we know from his letters how much he suffered, his fortitude can only be applauded. On one occasion, when James called to see him, he was dismayed to find the author sitting at his desk with a blank sheet before him at a time when the printer had expected to see a sheaf of manuscript ready for

[1] *Rob Roy.*
[2] *The Letters of Sir Walter Scott*, Vol. IV.

collection. 'Ay, ay, Jemmy,' growled Scott, on being asked if he was finding difficulty in finishing the tale, ' 'tis easy for you to bid me to get on, but how the deuce can I make Rob Roy's wife speak with such a curmurring in my guts?' Nevertheless, he finished the novel and by the start of the new year *Rob Roy* was at last in the bookshops. Constable and Cadell, who had waited nervously for its public reception, were delighted as an increasing spate of orders poured in for the first edition, while a quick check at the end of the first fortnight revealed that nearly ten thousand copies had already been sold.

The money Scott had borrowed from his personal friends had by this time all been repaid, and his main anxiety now was to clear off the bond for £4,000 which the Duke of Buccleuch had backed for him in the dark days of 1813. For no matter how much ready money came his way, the demands of Abbotsford and his ever increasing living expenses seemed to swallow it up immediately, while bills issued in past years and kept floating by renewals had a habit of falling due for payment at the most inconvenient moments. He found it quite impossible to save money, despite the thousands his writings were earning him. Negotiations to raise sufficient cash to be able to free the Duke of any further responsibility for his overdraft had been started by the author some time in August, 1817, but on the 6th September he had written to John, informing him that his brother James 'tells me that nothing can be done in London respecting the money to pay off the Bond, owing to Rees's absence. I must therefore enter into treaty with Constable (so soon as R.R. is out) for the continuation *Tales of my L[andlord]d* 4 vols. which will make £4000 forthcoming, especially if I change the publishers of the first four volumes.' Once again we have an instance of Scott overcoming his dislike of having dealings with Constable so as to be able to avail himself of the inviting amounts the Edinburgh publisher was willing to offer for the privilege of marketing his works; and we can also perceive with what little compunction he threw overboard Murray and Blackwood whom he had discovered to be far less liberal in their terms than the 'great Swab who is supple as a glove' as the author privately referred to the wily Archibald.[1] As an added inducement for his old publisher to offer the maximum possible amount for the new series of *Tales of My Landlord*, the author was prepared to allow

[1] Letter to John Ballantyne, now in the National Library of Scotland.

him to take over the first series of this work, despite the energetic protests of Murray and Blackwood and their half-hearted threat of legal action to prevent the transference. The tremendous success of *Rob Roy* had made Constable and Cadell more eager than ever to secure any future works from Scott's pen, and their jealousy of other publishing houses, especially Blackwoods who had recently started a right-wing magazine in direct opposition to their *Edinburgh Review*, led them to take risks to have him once more solely to themselves which the shaky financial structure of their business certainly did not warrant.

The senior partner's method of securing for his firm the manuscript of an author of worth was to rush in with an offer of such generous proportions as to take the wind out of his competitors' sails completely. These storming tactics had paid him well in the past, but their success depended on his having sufficient capital to fulfil any promises made, without at the same time straining the credit of the company to a degree that engendered a loss of confidence in its financial standing amongst the bankers of Edinburgh and London. As far back as 1803, soon after he had been asked to act as publisher of the *Edinburgh Review*, he had astounded his rivals in the same field, and secured for himself the most talented of the contemporary writers, by raising to twenty guineas the price he was prepared to pay for a single sheet of copy. This rate of remuneration was unprecedented, but the publicity the news gave to the recently founded magazine more than compensated him for the extra cash that made its way into his authors' pockets. 'Abandoning the old timid and grudging system,' wrote Lord Cockburn,[1] 'he stood out as the general patron and payer of all promising publications, and confounded not merely his rivals in trade, but his very authors, by his unheard of prices.' With those writers whose services he was especially keen to secure, he held out another inducement—that of payment in advance of copy. This was the bait, more than any other, that Scott was unable to resist. The tempting lure of one, two, or even three thousand guineas, for the mere promise of a work to be produced at some time within the foreseeable future, was far too tempting to be refused. But the acceptance of these cash-in-advance terms eventually made him just as dependent on the firm of Archibald Constable & Company as the publishing house was on him: they caused each

[1] *Memorials of His Time*, Henry Cockburn, Edinburgh, 1856.

freshly conceived literary idea to be mortgaged to the hilt months before a word had been committed to paper and the tiresome verbosity exhibited in many of his novels was undoubtedly due to his need to spin out the tale to the length stipulated in his contract.

Soon after the death of Scott's pet aversion, the 'iniquitous' A. G. Hunter, in 1811, Constable formed a business alliance with Robert Cathcart, and, on the strength of the fresh capital he brought into the firm, bought the *Encylopaedia Britannica*, with the idea of enlarging it by producing a supplement. The tremendous sums he offered in order to induce the most famous names to contribute articles (Dugald Stewart was paid no less than £1,700 for a few pages of long since forgotten dissertations) were backed by Cathcart's substantial assets. Constable had also allowed his chief clerk, Robert Cadell, to enter into partnership, and this ambitious young man applied himself with vigour to furthering the fortunes of the publishing house. Then, within twelve months of entering the business, Cathcart died, and every penny he had brought with him had to be returned to his family. The firm was almost immediately plunged into the greatest financial difficulties; the heavy burden of supporting the *Britannica* became intolerable, and Constable could see bankruptcy staring him in the face. 'I have not acted dishonestly to any one in my dealings,' he wrote to Cadell on the 18th October, 1814. 'If I have embarked largely in Bookselling[1] have I not been encouraged to do so? I have, it is true, been most unfortunate in following many plans more for the benefit of my connections than that of myself.' Only the unprecedented success of *Waverley*, of which four editions were quickly sold out, saved them from ruin during the months that followed, but the firm's financial recovery was never more than partial. Cadell was now Constable's sole partner and it was not long before his influence in the company's affairs began to exert an increasing effect. In 1817, at the age of twenty-nine, he married his erstwhile master's daughter, the unfortunate young lady dying in childbed within twelve months of this event.[2] His position within the firm was now secure and he quickly proved to his father-in-law that he was capable of handling a business deal to their mutual advantage as efficiently

[1] The term 'bookseller' was synonymous with 'publisher' in the early part of the nineteenth century.
[2] Cadell married a second time in 1821.

as the great 'Czar of publishers' himself. Despite his comparative youth, Cadell quickly became as grasping and as coolly calculating as any man in the trade, displaying none of the extravagant traits of character for which Constable was justly famous, yet having a keen appreciation that the goodwill of Walter Scott was a prize they must retain at almost any price.

From their first meeting, he showed an active dislike for both James and John Ballantyne, urging his senior partner to find a way of dealing directly with Scott. 'I am quite clear,' he wrote to Constable on one occasion, 'that the way to manage Mr Scott is to attack him in person, apart from the Ballantynes, and speak to him in a plain, business-like manner. I am sure he likes it better than diffidence...he likes candour and openness.' But John and his brother were far too useful to Scott for him to allow them to be brushed aside. Using the pseudonym of 'The Author of Waverley' meant that he must have agents through whom he could deal, and John in particular had proved several times in the past that he was astute enough to secure terms even better than the writer had stipulated in his original instructions. As an inducement to him to obtain the maximum possible advantage, Scott saw to it that both he and James had a slice of the cake in the form of a fractional financial interest in each of his published works. This share, although only small in comparison with his own, often amounted to a considerable sum when the printing of a novel ran into many thousands of copies, thus ensuring that they exerted themselves wholeheartedly on his behalf.

For the vast majority of the novels after *Waverley* the terms agreed with the publishers were similar in detail. Scott would sell them the right to print two-thirds of the first impression, amounting usually to some ten or twelve thousand copies. For this privilege they would pay him from £2,500 to £3,000, in advance of publication, by means of bills-of-exchange. These the author was able to cash almost immediately by allowing the broker a discount. The remaining one-third of this first printing was registered in the name of James Ballantyne, but one-half of this portion also belonged to Scott, James acting merely as his trustee. The other half of this third share the author allowed to be divided equally between James and John for acting as his agents; John being in charge of the business negotiations while James corrected the proofs, saw the book through the press, and gave the author the benefit of his textual criticism. This latter service was one on which Scott came to rely more and more heavily; he often wrote extremely carelessly and, but for Ballantyne's eagle eye, a host of grammatical errors, mis-statements of facts, and errata of all kinds would have littered the pages of his books.

When the time came to negotiate for the second series of *Tales of My Landlord* Constable was determined to have them at any price, Cadell urging caution and finally persuading his partner to allow him to deal with Ballantyne himself. He was worried about the state of Scott's health and had made up his mind that there should be a loophole in the contract to enable them to recover their advance in the event of his death before the manuscript was completed. To issue bills for £4,000, for a work which might never appear, he considered foolhardy in the extreme, and he hedged the agreement with safeguards that would have enabled them to withdraw in the circumstance of the writer being unable to complete his part of the bargain. He and Constable at first believed that Longmans would take a quarter share, thus relieving them of having to find the entire amount, but the London publishers eventually withdrew, much to Cadell's disappointment. He, more than anyone, knew the true state of his firm's finances and how much this latest deal would stretch their slim resources. They were backing everything they had on the venture and a rapid sale of a record number of copies would be needed to ensure success. With Longman's fighting shy of the terms the author demanded, Cadell adroitly managed to persuade John Ballantyne to stand in their place, promising him a one-fourth share in the profits of the speculation in addition to that which the author allowed him as a right. Whether in fact John had so much to command is doubtful. Had Ainslie paid up, as he kept hoping he would, he might have been able to foot the bill and eventually make a handsome profit, but as it was he had later to sell back to the publishers his holding in the work without reaping any benefit from the deal. Cadell had succeeded in beating him at his own game, but he was bargaining with a Ballantyne who was noticeably unwell and whose gay optimism and zest for life had become increasingly tarnished during the last few months.

'It gives me pleasure to tell you—but no one else *knows it*—that I have at last got Walter Scott managed,' Cadell wrote to his partner on the 25th November, 1817. Whether or not they knew it at that time, Mr Scott had also got Messrs Archibald Constable and Robert Cadell managed to his own entire satisfaction. He had all along insisted that the name of their company should appear on the title-pages of the second series of *Tales* only if they agreed to purchase the whole of the remaining stock of books still lying in his warehouse. To the astonishment of the rest of the trade, the partners were in the end obliged to accept this condition, hoping apparently to dispose of them quickly at cost or a little below. And thus, at a single sweep, as Lockhart wrote later, the author 'cleared the Augean stable in Hanover Street of unsaleable rubbish to the amount of £5270!' The mark of exclamation was well merited, for it is known that the majority of these books remained in the hands of Constable and his partner until they were finally obliged to dispose of them for only a third of what they had cost. If John Ballantyne's calculations are to be trusted, Scott, as the result of this most advantageous deal, had now fully recovered all the capital he had invested in his ill-fated publishing concern, and in fact was the gainer by something approaching a thousand pounds. Certainly, he came out of the business far better than he could ever have imagined possible, and must have been extremely happy to be able to extricate himself from a financial catastrophe that was almost entirely of his own making.

The second series of *Tales of My Landlord* provide a classical instance of the way the quality of Scott's writing was affected by his being forced to regulate his output to give himself the greatest possible financial return. His original intention was for the four-volume work to contain two separate tales in the same way as the first of the series. But the composition of *The Heart of Midlothian* so engrossed him that he had written enough to fill three volumes almost before he was aware of the fact. The story had been brought to a conclusion at this point; there was nothing else he needed to say and he could have placed the final full-stop and quite happily written the word 'Finish'. Critics have without exception profoundly wished he had done so. Even before the book was printed, Robert Cadell was writing to him to suggest that 'three volumes now and three in the autumn would very much increase the interest', realizing that to extend the story any further was quite unnecessary and would almost surely result in him boring his readers. But Scott had contracted to supply only a four-volume work, not two tales each of three volumes, and he made it quite plain that a fresh novel would have to be the subject of another bargain involving the payment of several thousand pounds in advance of delivery of the manuscript. He would see to it that *The Heart of Midlothian* was stretched and padded until he had brought it to the stipulated number of words. He had promised that the work was to be one of four volumes and four volumes the publishers would most certainly have.

The work appeared in the middle of July, 1818, and several critics at once pounced on the fact that the tale showed obvious signs of having been artificially extended to the required length. In August, the reviewer in *Blackwood's Magazine* wrote: 'We rather suspect that our good friend Mr Constable wished a fourth volume in the way of trade, that he might, with more show of justice, charge the exorbitant price of £1 12s. for a book which in former times would have been sold for little more than half that price.' Any student of Scott's works who has been forced to plough through reams of flat and uninteresting prose in the final volume would endorse the strictures levelled by Thomas Seccombe, in his 'Scott Centenary Articles', published in 1932. 'In this book, perhaps his greatest, the fissure is first plainly seen in the mountain of Scott's fame. The artist in Scott was not dead but lulled to sleep when he proceeded to add five hundred pages of sheer padding to his noblest story. The contract was for four volumes—the material barely filled three. But Constable had to be placated....Already Scott, artist, castellan of Abbotsford, was hag-ridden by the necessity of selling nothing as something, and to sweeten the bargain he gave of his best—but too much. Cruel necessity! Uncanny insight of Craigenputtock!'

Notwithstanding the manifest faults of construction which had been pointed out to them by the reviewers, the public flocked eagerly to buy copies. Seldom had a book been received in such rapturous terms by his readers in general and his countrymen in particular. Whatever they thought of the final volume, they were satisfied that they had received more than their money's worth by the contents of the first three, in which Scott had revealed himself not only as a talented novelist standing higher than any of his contemporaries but as a social historian as well. His graphic descriptions of the Edinburgh riots, during which the mob dragged the reprieved Captain Porteous from his cell and lynched him in the street outside the prison, received unaminous praise; while in his pure and virtuous heroine, the too-good-to-be-true Jeanie Deans, he portrayed a Scottish lass whom the strictest Calvinists among the congregation of Old Greyfriars would have been proud to call their own. He had succeeded once again in producing a work which set the whole publishing trade on edge for a chance of bidding for the next manuscript to issue from his hand. The receipts from its sale lifted the chins of Constable and Cadell above the flood of debts which threatened to engulf them, restored their credit with the banks, and whetted their appetites for something new. They could afford to be high-handed with their agents and rivals in the London trade, and when they discovered that Longman & Company had handled a spurious imitation of Scott's *Tales*, masquerading under the title of *Pontefract Castle*, they severed all connection with them and turned to Hurst, Robinson & Company instead. This, as later events were to prove, was a fatal move, bringing not only their own destruction nearer, but that of the author on whom their fortunes depended.

8

IN THE EARLY summer of 1818 Scott was a guest at a private dinner party and found himself sitting next to a sharp-featured, dark-haired young man who was introduced to him as John Gibson Lockhart, barrister-at-law. This was the author's first meeting with the pale and fastidiously attired bachelor who was destined to become his son-in-law, and who would one day write the massive seven-volume biography of his life; a biography in which fact and fiction are sometimes inextricably mixed, but which nevertheless still retains its place as one of the most outstanding works of its kind in the history of English literature. Lockhart was not yet twenty-four years of age but already was establishing himself as a hard-hitting right-wing journalist whose aptitude for invective and biting sarcasm endeared him to those of his own political persuasion, while making him heartily detested by those who were not. Although shaking his head at some of the writer's coarser sallies, Scott had nevertheless applauded as loudly as the rest of the Scottish Tories the attacks this shining new Sir Galahad was making on the Whigs, and he now paid him the compliment of remaining in conversation with him for most of the evening. In the absence of legal work Lockhart had applied his talents to literature in general and journalism in particular as a means of making his living, and, until the older man had served his purpose, was an inseparable companion of John Wilson, the 'Christopher North' of later years. Both were briefless advocates with little love for the Bar, and fervent advocates of the Tory cause. Both prided themselves on being merciless in dealing with those they considered their political opponents, but whereas Wilson admitted regretting the fact that he had often hurt and injured friends that he otherwise respected, Lockhart seemed implacable in his hatred of the liberal cause and the personalities of those who espoused it.

It was not long before an opportunity presented itself for them to show the world that they were capable of demolishing Whigs,

Radicals and reformers with blasts of invective so biting in satire that their opponents could only squirm under their ridicule and, so they hoped, be silenced for ever with shame. In this enterprise they were joined by James Hogg, the oldest of the triumvirate but one only too eager to lend all the assistance he could in so laudable a cause. All three had cultivated the acquaintance of William Blackwood, whose Edinburgh publishing house had developed into a most prosperous business and who was now looking around for fresh fields to conquer. Blackwood had the coarse, pushing shrewdness of a recently self-made man, and his burning ambition was now centred on ousting Archibald Constable from his position as the leading Scottish publisher so that he might usurp the crown for himself. Like many another *nouveau riche* commercial speculator who had come up the hard way, he had embraced the Tory cause with a fervour that he believed would not go unnoticed by those he considered his social superiors and whose company he now found so desirable. The elegant acerbity and rapier-like witticisms of the leading contributors to the *Review* irritated him beyond measure, and he set himself the task of holding them up to ridicule and exposing these astute advocates of a wider franchise for the political tricksters he believed them to be. With this object in mind, in April 1817, he produced the first number of the *Edinburgh Monthly Magazine*, entrusting its fortunes to the editorship of two crippled literary veterans, Cleghorn and Pringle, both of whom could only move with the aid of crutches. The first few numbers soon revealed the new publication to be as painfully pedestrian as these two well-meaning journalists, whose unrivalled capacity for stodgy dullness rendered the magazine all but unreadable. Within six months, with the circulation falling with each issue, Blackwood had had more than enough and he succeeded in dismissing them both on payment of £125 to secure their share of the copyright. He was in two minds as to whether to close the project down and cut short his losses, but his determination that 'ma Maga', as he came to fondly call the renamed *Blackwood's Edinburgh Magazine*, should eventually topple the *Edinburgh Review* from public favour by capturing the largest part of its readership, made him risk his capital in another attempt to establish the paper on a really firm footing. With himself as editor, he took the chance of allowing a free hand to several of the younger Tory intellectuals of Edinburgh and the gamble paid off in a way that not only astonished the proprietor but came close to causing fights in the streets of the capital.

The next issue of the magazine, and the first under its new name, was the seventh, due for publication in October, and under Blackwood's direction Lockhart, Wilson and Hogg worked far into the night with whetted knives, reshaping the paper to their own design and preparing an onslaught on the Whigs of a fury that would make it impossible for them to ignore. At all costs they were determined to make a startling impact on the reading public, and, as events transpired, they succeeded in a fashion they could hardly have imagined possible.

The October issue had not been in the hands of the booksellers for many hours when the first violent reactions began to make themselves felt from those leading citizens of the town who discovered themselves to be libelled and held up to ridicule. The magazine contained a long article, written in the style and phraseology of the Old Testament and purporting to be an ancient Chaldee manuscript which the erudite and well-read sub-editors of *Blackwood's* had succeeded in transcribing. In reality the article turned out to be a venomous attack, not only on the publisher of the *Edinburgh Review* and his leading contributors, but on most of the leading citizens of the town who were thought to have Whiggish sympathies. Even the two recently dismissed editors of their own magazine were not spared, Lockhart drawing attention to their deformities by describing them as 'skipping about on staves'. A glowing picture of the present editor of *Blackwood's Magazine* was painted, as might be expected, and the paper's future prospects and the issues yet to come were presented in a dazzling light. James Hogg claimed the credit for propounding the original idea of the Chaldee MS, but there is no doubt that much of the article was from the pens of Lockhart and Wilson. All three had done their best to ensure that the widest publicity would follow its publication, for some of the outrageous remarks contained in its pages were so insulting to the persons singled out for attack that tongues were wagging in every drawing-room in the city for days and weeks after the paper first appeared. Although many leading Scottish Presbyterians proclaimed themselves scandalized by the apparent profanity shown by this parody of Holy Writ, they obviously relished the satirical references to many of Edinburgh's best known personalities and hurried to purchase extra copies to present to their friends. Within a few days the October issue was sold out and it became necessary to print a second edition. But the threat of libel actions and the mounting anger of so large a section of the town amongst whom were many he could ill-afford to offend, finally persuaded Blackwood that the article might rebound in a way that would be a source of potential harm to his business interests. When the second edition appeared the Chaldee MS was missing from its pages. But the outcry, which at first had seemed to threaten the extinction of the magazine, was in fact, as is usually the case, the best possible stimulant to its success. The name of *Blackwood's* was now on everyone's lips and the editor and his anonymous staff of contributors were delighted to find the paper thriving, with its circulation increasing at each new issue.

But the damage its attacks caused to the reputations of any writer or poet whom Lockhart and his colleagues believed to hold different political opinions to themselves was incalculable. Charles Lamb, William Hazlitt, Samuel Coleridge, Leigh Hunt, John Keats, and many others, principally the members of what Lockhart designated as the 'Cockney School of Literature', all suffered to a greater or lesser degree at their hands. All of this mud-slinging and vilification was carried out while its originators carefully sheltered behind pseudonyms or remained discreetly anonymous. Literary worth or poetical excellence were completely disregarded if the writer concerned was suspected of holding unorthodox religious opinions or was known to have liberal Whiggish sympathies. The praises of such solidly respectable right-wingers as Southey, Wordsworth, or Walter Scott himself were sung time and again, while any associates of that execrable mocker of the Monarchy, the abominable Leigh Hunt, were hounded without mercy. In the words of Carlyle, Hunt himself suffered 'obloquy and calumny through the Tory Press—perhaps a greater quantity of baseness, persevering, implacable calumny, than any other living writer has undergone.'

The fact that Carlyle in no way exaggerated the vitriolic nature of the attacks Hunt was forced to endure can be perceived by reading Lockhart's review of *The Story of Rimini*, a long poetical work based on the story of Paolo and Francesca which Hunt gave to the world in 1816. The review can only be described as incredible, coming as it did from a man who was at pains to impress those with whom he came in contact with his cultured outlook and gentlemanly demeanour. Little of what Lockhart said had any bearing on the quality of Hunt's verse, neither did he give his readers a critical appraisal of the poem's worth from the literary standpoint. It was the man himself he attacked throughout the review. After informing the world at large that he felt 'disgust at the idea of opening *Rimini*', and describing the verse as akin to 'the sounds of a paltry piano-forte,' he turned his attention to the poet himself. 'His poetry', he informed his readers, 'is that of a man who has kept company with kept-mistresses. He talks indelicately like a tea-sipping milliner-girl. Some excuses for him there might have been had he been hurried away by imagination of passion. But with him indecency is a disease, and he speaks unclean things with perfect inanition. The very concubine of so impure a wretch as Leigh Hunt would to be pitied, but alas! for the wife of such a husband. For him there is no charm in simple seduction; and he gloats over it only when accompanied by adultery and incest.'

Hunt's shoulders were broad and he fought back with a vehemence that made Lockhart thankful that he was sheltering under a pseudonym. But there were others from whom he knew he had nothing to fear in the way of bodily violence. One of these was Keats. The sneering depreciation of his *Endymion*, which appeared in the August, 1818, issue of *Blackwood's*, once more came from Lockhart's pen. 'To witness the disease of human understanding, however feeble, is distressing,' Lockhart wrote in mock sympathy, 'but the spectacle of an able mind reduced to a state of insanity is ten times more afflicting. It is with such sorrow as this we have contemplated the case of Mr John Keats. This young man appears to have received from Nature talents of an excellent, perhaps even of a superior order—talents which rendered him a respectable if not an eminent citizen....But all has been undone by a sudden attack of the malady to which we have already alluded. Whether Mr John has been sent home with a diuretic or composing draught to some patient far gone in the poetic mania we have not heard. This much is certain, that he has caught the infection and caught it thoroughly. The phrenzy of the *Poems* was bad enough in its way; but it did not alarm us half as seriously as the calm, settled, imperturbable drivelling idiocy of *Endymion*....Mr Hunt is a small poet, but he is a clever man. Mr Keats is a still smaller poet, and he is only a boy of pretty abilities which he has done everything in his power to spoil....We venture to make one small prophecy, that his bookseller will not a second time venture £50 upon anything he can write. It is better and a wiser thing to be a starved apothecary than a starved poet. So back to the shop, Mr John Keats, back to "plaisters, pills and ointment-boxes"...But for Heaven's sake, young Sangrado, be a little more sparing of extenuatives and soporifics in your practice than you have been in your poetry.'

The biting satire Lockhart habitually employed from behind his cloak of anonymity when not using vulgar abuse, too often had a needlessly cruel twist to the thrust. He was an expert at making enemies and seemed to revel in precipitating those he could call his friends into situations from which they could extricate themselves only with considerable loss of dignity or even physical or financial harm. One particularly disgraceful episode resulted in the death of one young man and the arrest of others. The affair started when John Scott of London, who was no relation of his northern namesake, became incensed at the attacks made in *Blackwood's* on Coleridge and other poets of the day, and published in the *London Magazine* three articles attacking the anonymous reviewers in general and Lockhart in particular. He accused Lockhart, with some truth as we know now, of forging testimonials to his own publication and of being responsible for the savage attack on Coleridge's *Biographia Literaria*, for which it is possible John Wilson was to blame. He resolutely refused to believe Lockhart's denial of these charges, and the reviewer eventually came to London in the hope, so he put it, of receiving satisfaction from Scott. Through two young London friends named Christie and Traill, Lockhart issued a challenge to Scott to meet him in a duel, at the same time being careful that Christie should convey the message that they considered Scott a liar and a coward. No challenge followed and Lockhart published a statement declaring that, although he was a contributor to *Blackwood's* he played no part in its editorship. By some mysterious circumstance, yet to be explained, the only printed copy to lack this definite assertion was the one Christie delivered to John Scott. In the meantime Lockhart had disappeared to Edinburgh, leaving Christie to do any explaining that might be necessary. On reading the communication Scott immediately noticed the discrepancy between what Christie was saying and the statement in his hand and was not long in pointing out that he considered Christie a liar. A challenge was instantly made and accepted, and the unfortunate Christie found himself facing John Scott at ten paces distant at dawn a few days later. Scott fired first and missed, either deliberately or accidently, we will never know. Christie then deliberately fired into the air, but his seconds prevailed upon him to aim once more at the target before him. The second ball passed through Scott and he fell mortally wounded. He was carried to an inn near Chalk Farm where the duel had taken place, but despite a surgeon being sent for he died a few days later. The two seconds, Traill and Patmore, and Christie himself, were subsequently declared guilty of murder at a coroner's inquest, but at their trial at the Old Bailey were acquitted. John Gibson Lockhart was the only individual to escape unscathed.

Attempts have been made to excuse Lockhart's use of the tactics employed by gutter journalists, by the plea that his youth and lack of means forced him to attempt to make a name for himself by shocking the public into an awareness of his existence. More than one of his contemporaries, including Walter Scott himself, advanced this in mitigation of his scurrilous attacks on those without means of answering back, wishing to forgive an obviously intelligent young man the worst of his excesses in the hope that age and experience would mature and mellow his personality. Against this argument it can be stated that, some fifteen years later, when he was firmly established as the well-paid editor of one of London's leading magazines, he permitted his paper to print a brutally unjust and completely damning review of a newly issued volume of poems by the then struggling Alfred Tennyson, the severity of which wounded the future poet laureate to an extent that silenced him for the following ten years. Scott sometimes professed himself unhappy at Lockhart's more disgraceful outbursts, but he made no bones about admiring the spirit which prompted the young writer to harpoon his political opponents so effectively.

The journalist was careful to cultivate the illustrious author's acquaintance at every available opportunity and with the calculated ingratiation of one whose eyes were ever open for chances of financial or social advancement, he became an increasingly frequent visitor at both Castle Street and Abbotsford. It was not long before his air of ineffable superiority to the world in general, coupled with his dryly humorous conversation, to say nothing of his attractive good looks, had swept Scott's eldest daughter

Sophia off her feet and made him a readily acceptable suitor for her hand. They were married in April, 1820, the father of the bride writing eupepticly to his friend Lord Melville: 'She might have made a wealthier marriage but could scarce have found a more accomplished & honourable man. He is besides of my own cast every way, a sound friend of king and country, and possessed of qualifications which, with prudence & the assistance of friends, must raise him high one day.'

Whatever may have been the bridegroom's feelings towards his bride-to-be before their marriage it is certain that he came to love her deeply, and he was to become a devoted father to his children, cherishing them with a fervour that embarrassed those not of the family who watched him fondle and pet them with an almost feminine show of affection. When his son fell ill, he would walk for hours with the wasted infant in his arms, pacing the bedroom floor throughout much of the night in an effort to comfort the boy and relieve his pain. Yet he could subscribe to the hanging of a score or more fathers of families, the unfortunate scapegoats for a few hundred weavers desperate enough to shake their fists at their masters by calling for a wage they could live on; and applaud the judge's decision to 'make an example of you men', by welcoming the verdict with his pen. Throughout his life he appeared to be completely insensitive to the sufferings of those less fortunate than himself, unless they happened to be members of his immediate family. In literature and the arts, the unknown writer struggling to make a name or the poet hopefully presenting his first stanzas to the world, should they by word or example let it be known that their political views were anything less than hard-right of centre, then they could expect no mercy notwithstanding the quality of their work. With those whose names were established, or who had influence to wield, his views and criticisms were more balanced. About such as these he was more inclined to tell the truth.

The first glimpse Lockhart gives us of Scott and himself alone together, is during a visit the former made to Castle Street in the summer of 1818. He had arrived to discuss an article he was preparing for the historical section of the *Edinburgh Annual Register*, and found the author in his study with his massive wolfhound, Maida, and Hinse, his favourite cat. The scene Lockhart paints so vividly is given to us in an excellent piece of descriptive writing, the type of literary accomplishment at which the journalist-turned-biographer eventually became a past master.

[Scott] at this time occupied as his *den* a square small room, behind the dining parlour at Castle Street. It had but a single Venetian window, opening on a patch of turf not much larger than itself, and the aspect of the place was on the whole sombrous. The walls were entirely clothed with books; most of them folios and quartos, and all in that complete state of repair which at a glance reveals a tinge of bibliomania. A dozen volumes or so, needful for immediate purposes of reference, were placed close by him on a small movable frame—something like a dumb-waiter. All the rest were in their proper niches, and wherever a volume had been lent, its room was occupied by a wooden block on the same size, having a card with the name of the borrower and date of the loan, tacked on its front. The old bindings had obviously been retouched and regilt in the most approved manner; the new, when the books were of any mark, were rich but never gaudy—a large proportion of blue morocco—all stamped with his *device* of the portcullis, and its motto *clausus tutus ero*—being an anagram of his name in Latin. Every case and shelf was accurately lettered, and the works arranged systematically; history and biography on one side—poetry and the drama on another—law books and dictionaries behind his own chair. The only table was a massive piece of furniture which he had constructed on the model of one at Rokeby; with a desk and all its appurtenances on either side, that an amanuensis might work opposite to him when he chose; and with small tiers of drawers, reaching all round to the floor. The top displayed a goodly array of session papers, and on the desk below were, besides the MS at which he was working, sundry parcels of letters, proof-sheets, and so forth, all neatly done up with red tape. His own writing apparatus was a very handsome old box, richly carved, lined with crimson velvet, and containing ink-bottles, taper-stand, &c. in silver—the whole in such order that it might have come from the silversmith's window half an hour before. Besides his own huge elbow chair, there were but two others in the room, and one of these seemed, from its position, to be reserved exclusively for the amanuensis. I observed, during the first evening I spent with him in this *sanctum*, that while he talked, his hands were hardly ever idle. Sometimes he folded letter-covers—sometimes he twisted paper into matches, performing both tasks with great mechanical expertness and nicety; and when there was no loose paper fit to be so dealt with, he snapped his fingers, and the noble Maida aroused himself from his lair on the hearth-rug, and laid his head across his master's knees, to be caressed and fondled.

The room had no space for pictures except one, an original portrait of Claverhouse, which hung over the chimneypiece, with a Highland target on either side, and broadswords and dirks (each having its own story), disposed star-fashion round them. A few green tin-boxes, such as solicitors keep title-deeds in, were piled over each other on one side of the window; and on the top of these lay a fox's tail, mounted on an antique silver handle, wherewith, as often as he had occasion to take down a book, he gently brushed the dust off the upper leaves before opening it. I think I have mentioned all the furniture in the room except a sort of ladder, low, broad, well-carpeted, and strongly guarded with oaken rails, by which he helped himself to books from his higher shelves. On the top step of this convenience, Hinse of Hinsfeldt,—(so called from one of the German *Kinder-märchen*)—a venerable tom-cat, fat and sleek, and no longer very locomotive, usually lay watching the proceedings of his master and Maida with an air of dignified equanimity; but when Maida by thumping the door with his huge paw, as violently as ever a fashionable footman handled a knocker in Grosvenor Square; the Sheriff rose and opened it for him with courteous alacrity,—and then Hinse came down purring from his perch, and mounted guard by the foot-stool, *vice* Maida absent upon furlough. Whatever discourse might be passing was broken, every now and then, by some affectionate apostrophe to these four-footed friends. He said they understood every thing he said to them, and I believe they did understand a great deal of it. But at all events, dogs and cats, like children, have some infallible tact for discovering at once who is, and who is not, really fond of their company; and I venture to say, Scott was never five minutes in any room before the little pets of the family, whether dumb or lisping, had found out his kindness for all their generation.[1]

At the end of November, 1818, Charlotte was delighted to be informed by her husband that the Prince Regent had been graciously pleased to offer him a baronetcy. He was showered with congratulations from every quarter as soon as the news became generally known and his happiness was only marred by the death of Charles, Duke of Buccleuch, the most aristocratic of his many noble friends, and the fact that he was himself suffering from a renewed series of excruciatingly painful attacks of gall-stones. This latest onslaught, which continued inter-mittently until the end of 1819, happily proved to be the last

[1] *Life of Scott*, Vol. IV.

he had to endure. But he had not come through the long illness unscathed: it had aged him terribly and he had lost forever much of the vigour that had characterized him in earlier days.

It was during the intervals when the pain was less severe, that Scott dictated, either to John Ballantyne or William Laidlaw, the third series of his *Tales of My Landlord*, containing *The Bride of Lammermoor* and *A Legend of Montrose*. These two stories appeared in June and provided an astonishing example of how a man, strong in spirit and determined that his bodily weakness should not reflect itself in the quality of his writing, was able to disguise from his readers the fact that he had been physically afflicted during the period of their composition. Yet he stated later that he could remember little or nothing of *The Bride*, and listened while it was read over to him with the curiosity of one hearing the story for the first time, the pain he had suffered while dictating it having erased nearly all he had invented from his mind.

As the weeks went by and some of his former strength returned, he settled with a fierce determination to catch up with unfinished work, writing with a speed that rendered his already difficult hand almost impossible to decipher. Even before the latest series of the *Tales* had finished printing he had mapped out the plot of a fresh novel, remaining at his desk for hours on end in order to complete it in good time to catch the Christmas trade. That December saw *Ivanhoe* take its place beside the other *Waverley* imprints, the three volume romance being received with greater delight by both young and old than any of its predecessors in the same field. It still firmly retains its place among the required reading of the schoolboys of Britain, as it did for their Victorian and Edwardian counterparts, perhaps being one of the reasons why it is said that everyone has read Scott as a youth, but precious few adults now read him for pleasure.

Speculation about the fortune Scott was supposed to be making from the sales of his novels was rife in Edinburgh in the early 1820's and did much to inspire confidence in commercial circles as to his ability to meet the expensive commitments he so light-heartedly entered into. The public's seemingly insatiable appetite for fresh editions of his works, plus the record sums he received for titles yet to be written, resulted in his income from literary sources regularly exceeding £6,000 a year at the height of his popularity as an author. If one adds to this sum the salaries he derived from his sheriffdom, his clerkship of the Court of Session, and his income from private sources, one can increase this amount by nearly £1,800 annually. One may therefore accept that he was in receipt of a total of from seven to eight thousand pounds a year, a most handsome income for a landed gentleman in the first quarter of the nineteenth century, and one that would allow him to maintain a standard of living equal to the wealthiest of any of his friends. But Scott knew he was in no position to let his literary output diminish: payment of interest charges on loans raised in the past was a serious drain on his resources; massive debts had still to be repaid; while his ever increasing personal expenses and capital expenditure more than accounted for what was left. He was meticulously careful with his personal book-keeping, for beneath the surface of the poet and dreamer lurked the practical man of business, the secret backer of commercial enterprises, and the gambler who was eager to invest in land or any other commodity if he believed he might one day reap financial advantage from it. A man who was careful enough to note down even the trivial amounts he paid in sixpences to pass through toll-gates and turnpikes on his journeys around the countryside, and who kept track of the smallest items of domestic expenditure, was unlikely to be unaware of how much Abbotsford and its estate was costing him. His letters to the Ballantynes contain numerous references to debts, large and small, which he or other members of his family had incurred with Edinburgh tradesmen and which he wished checked, altered, or settled; and he knew, almost from the day he moved in there, exactly what his Tweedside home and the ever increasing acreage which surrounded it now amounted to in terms of hard cash. In the spring of 1819, years before his estate had reached its ultimate dimensions, he wrote to Stephen Barber in London: 'I am to pay for an addition bit of land here in the beginning of the month which will make about £35,000 which I have bought & found out of the booksellers pockets—or rather out of the public & made a very nice estate.'[1] And this figure of £35,000 referred only to his purchases of land, taking no account whatsoever of the vast sums the noble edifice of the half-completed Abbotsford had cost him. But still his builder, John Smith

[1] This letter of Scott's to Stephen Barber of 72, Cornhill, London, appeared for sale in catalogue 899 of Messrs Maggs Bros Ltd, of London, the antiquarian booksellers, in November, 1965.

of Darnick, laboured with his small army of workmen to add new wings, erect a castellated tower, and raise, in the place of the original humble cottage and farm buildings, a country mansion worthy to be the residence not only of a county sheriff and Border laird, but one of which a baronet and his lady could be justly proud.

In August, 1820, the freshly dubbed Sir Walter Scott entered upon his fiftieth year of life feeling better in health than for longer than he cared to remember. The popularity of *Ivanhoe*, the first edition of which was oversold in less than a week, was an added spur to further literary endeavour, for he had returned from kissing the hands of the recently proclaimed George IV in London, full of grandiose schemes for making Abbotsford the show place of the Borders if not of the whole of Scotland. Expensive antiques were now purchased by the roomful; suits of armour, shelves of books, oil paintings, chandeliers, bric-à-brac and ornaments, oriental carpets and rugs, and a host of other impedimenta arrived by the cartload; skilled woodcarvers pared and chipped at the staircases and overmantels; artists in plasterwork laboured to embellish the ceilings; while the finest in household furnishings were bought in Edinburgh and London by John Ballantyne and Daniel Terry in order to clothe its interior with the richness its master thought it deserved. Money was poured out in all directions. No sooner had the builders finished work in one section of the mansion than Scott commissioned fresh sets of plans from his architects which called for further suites of rooms to be constructed in a style even more sumptuous than those erected previously. The whole building was to be lit by gas manufactured on the premises; an innovation practically unheard of for a private house in those days, but one which Sir Walter delighted to show off to astonished visitors, although his wife much preferred candle- or lamp-light as being more flattering to the complexion of a lady.

The money necessary to pay for all this luxury he hoped would come from the profits of novels as yet unwritten, and he spent every spare minute he could snatch from his other duties writing at his desks in either Castle Street or Abbotsford. Before the end of March, when his baronetcy was officially gazetted, Constable & Company, in conjunction with Longmans of

London, had published *The Monastery*. In the introductory epistle, which occupied a quarter of volume one, the author for the first time referred to John Ballantyne as 'my jocund friend', a phrase that gave the little man a great deal of pleasure. On the strength of the small share he owned of the work as the author's agent, Ballantyne saw to it that his name appeared on the title-pages, followed by the words: 'Bookseller to His Majesty the King', an honour entitling him to supply copies of books published in Scotland if ordered by the Royal Librarian. Sir Walter's recommendation had been sought as to the most worthy candidate to fill this post and John Ballantyne's name had been approved without demur; a fact which placed him under a further obligation to his influential friend but gave him the great satisfaction of having beaten the rest of the trade in securing the honour.

The Monastery had been dashed off at a speed which made it almost inevitable that the manuscript would have to undergo considerable revision before the work was sent to the printers. Nothing of this kind was done, however, and the book as it eventually appeared shows us Scott at his most slip-shod and boring. The tale lacked interest, was commonplace in its characters, deficient in its plot, and had a stale sameness about the incidents he sought to portray. Only the magic words 'By the Author of Waverley', persuaded the booksellers to purchase as many copies as they did, for the reviewers received it coldly and many critics condemned the tale as being pedestrian and slow-moving and far beneath what the public were entitled to expect from an author of the calibre of The Great Unknown. But its successor, *The Abbot*, was out by September, retrieving much of his lost reputation and selling on a scale that made his publishers forget their previous disappointment as the orders poured in for extra copies. Robert Cadell was amazed at the speed with which Scott was able to churn out a novel, especially as he knew that he was tied to his desk in the Court of Session for a large part of the day for at least five months of the year. When Lockhart asked him later why he thought Scott laboured so assiduously to complete the manuscripts in record time, Cadell replied: 'December 1819 saw the completion of *Ivanhoe* — March 20 of *The Monastery*, *The Abbot* in September and *Kenilworth* in the January following....Scott still depended on the appearance of each new novel for the bills it was to produce.' Even with payment in advance for four full-length novels in a space of little over twelve months, the author still found that the money he received (much of it in what he described as 'Longmans beautiful & dutiful bills') was only just sufficient to save him once again from serious financial embarrassment. 'My own powers of helping, unless in very hard pinch, are not great just now, being pretty deep in all my Banks,' he wrote to James Ballantyne in August, 1820, referring to the difficulty John Ballantyne was in to find sufficient cash to retire bills incurred on his (Scott's) behalf and shortly due for payment; adding, 'It is whimsical enough to be pressed with £8000 certain in three weeks time.' It is hardly surprising that he should have found himself hard pressed, for as fast as he received a negotiable bill he immediately cashed it at a discount, the proceeds being swallowed up by fresh expenditure almost as soon as they were paid into his bank account. Land was bought at prices that must have caused his name to be toasted in bumpers by every small farmer and 'cock-laird' whose fields adjoined his own, the spending he indulged in at this period making inevitable the constant renewal of loans at punishing rates of interest, thus mortgaging his future and sowing the seeds of the coming financial disaster.

In December, 1818, Charlotte had been very distressed to hear that her brother Charles had died on the 4th June at Salem, when on his way home from India. She had not seen him for some twenty years or more, but he had been her only living relative other than her immediate family and, as such, was often in her thoughts. By the terms of his will the fortune he had made out East was life-rented to his widow, but at her death was to be equally divided among the children of Walter and Charlotte. 'There is upwards of £30,000 safe in the British funds,' Scott wrote to the Duke of Buccleuch shortly after hearing the news, 'and about £10,000 more or less still in India, which he was in the act of realizing in order to return here, when it pleased God to cut him short after a very few days illness. The eventual fortune thus secured to my young people leaves the fruits of my labour much at my own disposal & makes my mind very easy upon futurity.' But, as later letters show, the actual amount of Charles Carpenter's fortune was much less than Scott had calculated, and his widow perversely lived on until 1863, by which time Scott and his wife and all their children were long since in their graves. The fact that he considered that, come what may, his children were now well provided for, coloured his thinking regarding the financial provision he ought to make for them, and seemingly freed him from any pangs of conscience about not putting aside in their interest any of the money he spent on his hobby of making Abbotsford the showplace of the north. His eldest son had decided he would gratify his father's ambition by making the army his profession, and Scott was soon to discover what an expensive business the purchase of a commission and the military outfitting this entailed could be. In all, he had to find nearly £1,500 to set up Cornet Walter Scott as an officer in the 18th Hussars, and it was not long before the young man, now stationed at Cork in Ireland, was receiving anxious letters from his father, counselling prudence in the spending of his yearly allowance of £250, and warning him of the pitfalls into which one fresh in the service was liable to fall. 'You will not be hasty in forming intimacies with any of your brother officers untill you observe which of them are most generally respected and like to prove most creditable friends,' he wrote his son in August, 1819. 'I shall be most glad to hear you are fitted with a good servant. Most of the Irish of that class are scapegraces & drink, steal and lie like the devil. If you could pick up a canny Scotsman it would do well. Let me know your mess-habits when you learn them. To drink wine is none of your habits but even drinking what is called a certain quantity every day hurts the stomach and by hereditary descent yours is delicate. The poor Duke of Buccleuch laid the foundation of that disease which occasioned his premature death in the excesses of Villars regiment and, I am sorry and ashamed to say for your warning, that the habit of drinking wine, so much practised when I was a young man, occasioned I am convinced many of my cruel stomach complaints. You had better drink a bottle of wine on any particular occasion than sit and soak and tipple at an English pint every day.' And a few days later he wrote: 'I beg you will keep an accot. of money received and paid. Buy a little book ruled for the purpose for pounds, shillings and pence and keep an accompt of cash received and expended. The balance ought to be cash in purse if the book is regularly kept. But any very small expenses you can enter as "Sundries £0: 3: 6" which saves trouble.'

Bearing in mind these strictures from his father regarding thrift, one can imagine what the tall and lanky eighteen year old youth thought of his parent's plan, detailed in a letter to him dated a month later, for purchasing the nearby estate of Faldonside for no less than £30,000. 'I am trying a sort of bargain with neighbour Nicol Milne at present.' Sir Walter wrote to him: 'He is very desirous of parting with his estate of Faldonside and if he will be contented with a reasonable price I am equally desirous to be the purchaser. I conceive it will come to about £30,000 at least. I will not agree to give a penny more and I think that sum is probably £2000 and more above its actual marketable value. But then it is extremely convenient for us and would, joined to Abbotsford, make a very gentlemanlike property worth at least £1800 or £2000 a year. I can command about £10,000 of my own, to which, in case of Mrs Carpenters demise, you could add the same sum, and if I be spared life and health, I should not fear rubbing off the rest of the price as Nicol is in no hurry for payment.' He went on to detail the improvements he proposed to carry out if he acquired the estate, and finished by saying: 'Such are my present plans, my dear boy, having as much your future welfare and profit in view as the immediate gratification of my own wishes.' The widow Carpenter, however, had no intention of dying for many years to come, and the baronet's scheme for persuading his son to invest his inheritance in Nicol Milne's estate had to hang fire indefinitely. He contented himself with spending a thousand or two in buying a small portion of Milne's land, then turned his attention to the fresh pastures that were being dangled before him by his other eager neighbours.

If at this point in time Scott had concentrated his efforts towards clearing himself of debt, and had halted all further capital expenditure until his personal affairs, and those of the printing business on whose credit he drew so heavily, were restored to a solvent state, then there might have been a happy ending to this story. But he continued on a path which was bound to lead to a financial situation from which it would be impossible to extricate himself. Every month he paid out hundreds of pounds in order to satisfy the demands made on him for wages and salaries for his servants and estate workers; to meet the cost of planting, improving and maintaining his lands at Abbotsford, nearly all of which were wholly unproductive; to pay interest charges on loans; and to keep up at his town and country houses a standard of living and the lavish hospitality he believed accorded with his position in society. These day-to-day expenses cost him well over £5,000 a year; and in addition to this he indulged in further expenditure of more than £10,000 in an average year on land, buildings, and the purchase of trees, shrubs, livestock, agricultural implements, furniture and antiques, and a multitude of minor luxuries that went with them. The total amount he must have spent is signified by the immense sum at which Abbotsford and its estate was valued six years later, and this took no account of all the treasures he housed within its walls. To spend on this scale while still heavily encumbered with uncleared debts, on an income which he himself assessed as having reached a maximum of 'from £5,000 to £10,000 a year,'[1] was to court inevitable disaster. He and his business associates may have assumed, during the early 1820s, that they were in the process of clearing their feet of the debts that had held them back for so long, but their chronic lack of capital meant that they had to borrow funds to launch each new enterprise, the profits from which were largely swallowed up in payment of interest charges. The tide of paper promises-to-pay, I.O.U.s, accommodation notes, and long dated bills, that flowed from Constable to his London agents, then back again to James Ballantyne & Company and Sir Walter Scott, increased in amount with each passing year, loans being renewed at higher and higher rates of interest and fresh ones entered into to clear those they were forced to meet. One person who had no illusions about how things actually stood financially, despite the huge sums that came Scott's way and the vast number of volumes that Constable & Company contrived to sell, was little Johnny Ballantyne. He had not been well for some time and was at present making a partial recovery from what he preferred to call 'congestion of the lungs'. From his sick bed he wrote to Archibald Constable: 'I was thinking, if you and I were to pop off at this crisis, what a fine "redd up" they would have to set about.' Although a little premature, his words were to prove themselves prophetic.

[1] Scott's Journal — 18th December, 1825.

9

SOON AFTER RETURNING from the continent in 1817, John Ballantyne had experienced increasing discomfort from pains in his back and chest accompanied by fits of coughing and difficulty in breathing. For a considerable time he had concealed even from his closest friends the fact that he was unwell, hoping that the symptoms would clear up of their own accord. That year, amongst his other activities, he had started a weekly magazine called *The Sale Room*, to which Scott and many notable literary figures were persuaded to contribute. The articles which appeared in it were of a far higher standard than those commonly found in similar periodicals, but nevertheless, after some twenty-eight numbers it languished and died and John was forced to concentrate his talents in writing his column of musical and dramatic criticism for the *Weekly Journal*. His notices were widely read and gained him a considerable reputation, a circumstance which resulted in his receiving a continual flow of invitations to parties and musical evenings, few of which, according to his long suffering wife, he ever refused

He liked to be noticed, and appeared at even the most formal functions dressed in silks and satins that would have startled the most blasé bucks of London's West End. On the hunting field, John could be relied upon to jog into sight wearing his latest and most resplendent attire, what he lacked in inches being masked by the dazzle of his coats and breeches. John Morrison recalled one occasion when they were out with Scott hare hunting:[1] 'Miss Scott rode Queen Mab, a little pony; John Ballantyne was mounted on Old Mortality, an old gaunt white horse. He was dressed in a green coat, the buttons of which were in mother-of-pearl, silver and gold — with, if I remember well, a precious stone in the centre of each, and altogether he presented a most harlequin and piebald figure. Sir Walter appeared to laugh and amuse

[1] 'Random Recollections of Scott and the Ettrick Shepherd', by John Morrison, in *Tait's Magazine*, 1843.

himself with his grotesque appearance. I admired the buttons. "And well you may," said Sir Walter. "Those buttons, sir, belonged to the Great Montrose, and were cut, by our friend John, from an old coat belonging to the Marquis..." '

The description Lockhart gives us of the life John led at this period is undoubtedly coloured by his intense dislike of the whole Ballantyne family, prompted by his desire to make them the scapegoats for Scott's subsequent downfall and ruin. So many of the biographer's statements have subsequently been proved to be untrue that any tale he tells, unless confirmed from other sources, must be viewed with the greatest suspicion. He wished to paint a picture showing that the Ballantynes in general, and John in particular, scattered Scott's hard earned wealth in riotous living on a scale far above what they could reasonably have been expected to afford from their share of the profits of the *Waverley* novels and from their other legitimate sources of income. After his *Life of Sir Walter Scott* was published, many distinguished figures came forward to testify that much of what he had written about James and John varied considerably from their recollection of what took place during the years preceding the final catastrophe, and the arguments advanced on both sides will be given in a later chapter. However, Lockhart was an intimate of Scott and the Ballantynes for the whole of this period and his testimony is given as he printed it:

[John] in those days retained, I think, no private apartments attached to his auction-rooms in Hanover Street, over the door of which he still kept emblazoned 'John Ballantyne and Company, Booksellers.' At any rate, such of his entertainments as I ever saw Scott partake of, were given at his villa near to the Firth of Forth, by Trinity; a retreat which the little man had named 'Harmony Hall,' and invested with an air of dainty voluptuous finery, contrasting strikingly enough with the substantial citizen-like snugness of his elder brother's domestic appointments. His house was surrounded by gardens so contrived as to seem of considerable extent, having many a shady tuft, trellised alley, and mysterious alcove, interspersed among their bright parterres. It was a fairy-like labyrinth, and there was no want of pretty Armidas, such as they might be, to glide half-seen among its mazes. The sitting-rooms opened upon gay and perfumed conservatories, and John's professional excursions to Paris and Brussels in quest of objects of *virtu*, had supplied both the temptation and the means to set forth the interior in a fashion that might have satisfied the most fastidious *petite maitresse* of Norwood or St Denis. John too was a married man: he had, however, erected for himself, a private wing, the accesses to which, whether from the main building or the bosquet, were so narrow that it was physically impossible for the handsome and portly lady who bore his name to force her person through any one of them. His dinners were in all respects Parisian, for his wasted palate disdained such John Bull luxuries as were all in all with James. The piquant pasty of Strasburg or Perigord was never to seek; and even the *piece de resistance* was probably a boar's head from Coblentz, or a turkey ready stuffed with truffles from the Palais Royal. The pictures scattered among John's innumerable mirrors, were chiefly of theatrical subjects—many of them portraits of beautiful actresses—the same Peg Woffingtons, Bellamys, Kitty Clives, and so forth, that found their way in the sequel to Charles Mathews's gallery at Highgate. Here that exquisite comedian's own mimicries and parodies were the life and soul of many a festival, and here, too, he gathered from his facetious host not a few of the richest materials for his *at homes* and *monopolylogues*. But, indeed, whatever actor or singer of eminence visited Edinburgh, of the evenings when he did not perform several were sure to be reserved for Trinity. Here Braham quavered, and here Liston drolled his best—here Johnstone, and Murray, and Yates, mixed jest and stave—here Kean revelled and rioted—and here Roman Kemble often played the Greek from sunset to dawn. Nor did the popular *cantatrice* or *danseuse* of the time disdain to freshen her roses, after a laborious week, amidst these Paphian arbours of Harmony Hall.[1]

By February, 1819, this same gallant, gay Lothario was writing despondently in his diary: 'Miserably ill to-day. Scarce able to stand upright: what can be the cause? Unless it is that I have wholly destroyed my naturally good constitution.' Either his doctor was unable to diagnose what was wrong with him, or he did not wish to depress his patient by informing him that he was in the steadily tightening grip of pulmonary consumption, for Ballantyne was ignorant of the precise nature of his complaint until the end. Dr Dick prescribed a course of pills containing mercury, and on the days when he felt particularly unwell John dosed himself with double and treble the recommended amount of this highly dangerous compound, thus poisoning his system and suffering much additional discomfort from the side-effects the drug produced. Scott credited this same doctor with his own relief from the pain caused by gall-stones and biliary colic. The extended use of mercury, taken in small doses in the form of

[1] *Life of Scott*, Vol. IV.

calomel, had been the prescription in his case also, and this seems to have been Dick's specific for any complaint that refused to give way to purging. As might be expected, it had absolutely no effect on the tubercle bacilli with which Ballantyne's lungs were now heavily infected, the disease continuing to weaken him further with each passing month. The increasing effort it took him to accomplish even the lightest of tasks, coupled with a painful shortage of breath, finally frightened him into more abstemious habits: he cut down on the amount of wine and whisky he drank, switching his attention to ale and punch; he gave up cigars entirely, and often felt so utterly worn out in the evenings that he was obliged to retire to bed before nine o'clock. He missed the ministering attentions of Hermione, for they had parted again some time before the onset of his illness and he was now being cared for by a young woman who answered to the same Christian name as his estranged wife. Miss Hermione Roberton was the attractive daughter of William Roberton, a farmer of Friars near Kelso, on whose land John often coursed hares with his greyhounds. Unfortunately for her husband, Mrs Ballantyne had discovered that hares were not the only things he coursed on his visits to the country, and after a stand-up row she had stalked out of Harmony Hall, vowing never to return. John's latest (and last) mistress remained with him until his final return to Edinburgh, and he acknowledged her services by leaving her the sum of £100 in his will. He was as generous hearted when dying as when he stood, a gay auctioneer, on his rostrum in Hanover Street. Scott related that at one sale he attended he overheard Ballantyne say to a thin and wretched looking student of divinity who was eyeing the books about to be auctioned with the dejection of one with no hope of possession, that he believed him to be in a poor state of health. The young man assented with a sigh and made to move away. 'Come,' said John, 'I think I ken the secret of the sort of draft that will relieve you — particularly,' he added, handing the incredulous student a cheque for five pounds — 'particularly, my dear, if taken on an empty stomach.'

By the end of 1820 the already painfully thin little man had lost so much additional weight as to make it quite obvious that he would be lucky to survive another twelve months. Until his health finally gave way, he continued to conduct his auction sales, and financially he was better off than he had ever been before in his life. On the days he had the strength to go to town he was kept busy negotiating with Constable and others, in order to extract from them the best possible terms for publishing Scott's novels. A voluminous correspondence could be quoted to show how much Scott relied upon John's knowledge of the intricacies of the financial market to supply him with cash on the most favourable terms whenever he needed it, and letters and instructions flowed constantly between Abbotsford and Harmony Hall regarding the methods Ballantyne should employ to raise the maximum amount of money in the shortest possible time. The author's main worry was that his ailing friend would be unable to carry out his duties in Edinburgh, for although he considered James an excellent printer and an honest manager of his company's affairs, he had less faith in the eldest Ballantyne brother's ability to cope successfully with the wily Constable and the hard-headed Cadell. 'By no means *overstrain* your kind exertions,' Scott wrote to John in May that year. 'Get your good health again! Be cautious of it and we shall all be exceeding well.'[1] He flattered the little man with his attentions, frequently asking him to dine at Castle Street or Abbotsford and often going out of his way to call on him at Harmony Hall at times when he was least expected. 'This ought to be the proudest day of my life,' John wrote exultingly in his dairy on the 28th April, 1820,[2] 'Sir Walter Scott returned from London last night, full of fame and dignity, & made his *first* call upon me this morning at Trinity Grove. Plain, simple & unaffected as ever: his friendship "like an elder brother's love" (and how much more effectual) was balm to my heart. What ought I *not* to do for this man!' Three days later Scott called again, but this time to ask a favour. He had written to Ballantyne the previous day: 'Of course it would be highly agreeable to me if the Bond for £2100 could be cashed because I shall have £1000 to give a family occasion and other exigencies....'[3] Ballantyne noted in his diary that night: 'Sir Walter & James down on business. Agreed to buy his bond— [£]2100.' Perhaps, after all, Scott's immediate visit to his ailing friend on his return from London was not without a deeper motive than that of unaffected friendship.

[1] This letter of Scott's is in my own collection.
[2] The portion of John Ballantyne's diary covering the period from December 1814 to December 1816 is now in the National Library of Scotland. The Pierpont Morgan Library of New York has the section covering the period from February 1819 until his death.
[3] This letter is in my own collection.

All that summer John did his best to carry on with his duties as the author's agent, but the damp of a chill autumn played havoc with what was left of his lungs and he was forced to spend weeks at a time in bed. In October he collapsed while trying to conduct a sale, and the following month he threw in his hand and accepted an offer for his auctioneer's business as a going concern made to him by a Mr Cameron. At all costs he knew he had to leave the confined atmosphere of smoky Edinburgh and, no sooner was the deal completed, than he and his mistress packed their bags and drove by gig to a country cottage he had rented at Boroughmuir Head. Scott was extremely displeased when he learned from James that his brother had deserted his post in town and had expressed the intention of living permanently in the country. Next morning he had his horse saddled and rode over to demand an explanation. Hating to convey unwelcome news in any form, John as usual prevaricated. He made a pretence to the irate Sir Walter that the arrangement was merely a temporary one, and that his previously stated intention of buying a house and settling at Kelso had been abandoned as being unsuited to his financial circumstances. But after the somewhat placated author had returned to Abbotsford, Ballantyne revealed his real feelings about the matter by writing in his diary: 'Sir W. Scott called and...disapproves of my retiring to the country. Hard, but I cannot help it. I *must* go.' However, the cold dry air of a hard winter checked for a time the progress of his complaint and allowed him to convince himself that he might at last be on the mend. Coupled with a persuasive offer from Scott, this was enough to induce him to return to his brother's house in St John Street; Harmony Hall by this time having been let on a long lease to another tenant.

For several months Ballantyne had been toying with the idea of publishing a series of volumes under the general title of 'Ballantyne's Novelists' Library', reprinting the most popular romances and fictional tales by well-known authors of the past at prices the general public would be able to afford. He had mentioned to Scott that this was a scheme on which he might one day embark, but he had discussed it only in the most general terms, the whole idea remaining a somewhat nebulous dream that lack of capital would almost certainly prevent being translated into practical effect. In the form in which he had first proposed it to them, the publishers displayed little interest, and to finance the project himself was far beyond his means; so there the matter had been allowed to rest. However, a few days after his previous visit to Boroughmuir Head, Scott rode over there again, this time accompanied by Lockhart.[1] The two men stayed only a short time, and, as John insisted that he should accompany them for a mile or so on their homeward journey, they waited while he saddled Old Mortality and then rode off together at a slow walking pace in order that the invalid should not be left behind. Before they had proceeded very far, Scott broached the subject of the 'Novelists' Library', and, to John's surprise and delight, offered to write short biographies of the authors featured in the series for Ballantyne to prefix to each volume. Needless to say, this offer was most eagerly embraced by the editor-to-be, for he knew that, with such a distinguished name on the title-pages, the series could hardly fail to be a commercial success. To edit the work, read the proofs, and see each volume through the press, meant that John would be forced to return to Edinburgh, and as he envisaged the series ultimately extending to some forty volumes, all thought of making a permanent home any distance from the city would have to be abandoned. There is no means of ascertaining whether Scott made his unexpected offer secure in the knowledge that by so doing his agent would once more be at hand in Edinburgh to handle his financial affairs; or whether it was merely a disinterested attempt on his part to help a friend of long standing. One can only speculate on the fortuitous timing of the proposal from Sir Walter's point of view, for it is doubtful if any other inducement would have persuaded the ailing John to risk losing what strength still remained to him by braving once again the smoke and fogs of the city.

John's diary for the next few weeks was full of details of the financial manipulations he carried out in Edinburgh on behalf of Scott, together with the terms of the agreements reached with Constable & Company for the marketing of new editions of the

[1] Lockhart, for reasons of his own, translates this whole incident to Kelso, at a time when 'Walton Hall' was apparently half way to being completed. He dates the happening as 'One fine day this autumn...' (i.e. the autumn of 1820); and goes on to say that he and Scott watched with John the building of his new 'corps de logis behind, which included a handsome entrance hall...' etc., etc. The whole of Lockhart's tale is plainly a figment of his imagination. John did not purchase the ground on which Walton Hall was destined to be built until March, 1821, and he was dead long before the builders had completed its foundations.

novels of 'The Author of *Waverley*'. References occur relating to the latest three-volume work promised by Sir Walter: *The Buccaneer* as Ballantyne calls it, although it was actually issued under the name of *The Pirate*. For this as yet unwritten work, John saw to it that the author received bills-of-exchange totalling £4,500 for the publisher's half-share of the profits, a bargain with which his elated friend professed himself well pleased. In addition to these activities, Ballantyne spent hours in the printing works supervising the publication of the first two novels in his 'Novelists' Library', works of Smollett and Fielding, and for which Scott had written short biographies.[1] Both works appeared in February, 1821, but before their publication Ballantyne was once again prostrated by a severe attack of what he preferred to call 'asthma'. For several days he could hardly breathe and at one time thought he was about to expire, the symptoms so alarming him that he vowed, come what may, that he would quit the city for ever if he once regained sufficient strength to travel. He had rented a small holiday home at Kirklands, not far from Earlston, meaning to go there for the summer and as soon as he was able to stand he ordered his gig to be brought round to James's front door, made his way unsteadily down the steps and was driven off there wrapped in blankets.

He was now firmly determined not to return to Edinburgh under any circumstances, and had set his heart on finding a permanent home in his birthplace of Kelso. In January an advertisement had appeared in the *Kelso Mail*, which his brother, the editor, had cut out and sent to him. It gave details of some property in the town that was to be offered for sale by auction in the spring, and as soon as he had settled in at Kirklands, John went over to make a careful inspection of the site in the company of Sandy. The entries in his diary regarding his health had become more and more ominous with the passage of time, and it seems that he must have at last realized that only a miracle could enable him to survive another winter. 'This day made a *proper* Will, & signed it at Melrose,' he wrote on the 17th February; and three weeks later there is the entry: 'Ill; first suspicion of spitting blood. God forbid!' Nevertheless, as Lockhart put it, 'his spirits continued...to be in general as high as ever; nay, it is now, after his maladies had taken a very serious

[1] According to the Cambridge Bibliography of English Literature, only four volumes of 'Ballantyne's Novelists' Library' were published.

shape, and it was hardly possible to look on him without anticipating a speedy termination of his career, that the gay, hopeful spirit of the shattered and trembling invalid led him to plunge into a new stream of costly indulgence. It was an amiable point in his character that he had always retained a tender fondness for his native place. He had now taken up the ambition of rivalling his illustrious friend, in some sort, by providing himself with a summer retirement amidst the scenery of his boyhood; and it need not be doubted, at the same time, that in erecting a villa at Kelso, he anticipated and calculated on substantial advantages from its vicinity to Abbotsford.' How ridiculous this last remark of Lockhart's was, can be perceived by Scott's reaction to John's intended move.

On the 14th March, Ballantyne finally committed himself to the life of a country gentleman of insubstantial means, by bidding £420 at the Kelso sale for an adjoining pair of old thatched-roofed houses which had been advertised as being part of the unentailed property of the late Duke of Roxburgh. They stood on gently sloping ground overlooking the river, their front gardens skirting the road leading to the heavy iron gates that guarded the present Duke's magnificent estate and the castle of Floors. Their back windows commanded a particularly fine view of the surrounding landscape, the wide expanse of the salmon-stocked Tweed flowed past the far end of the lawn, and it was in every way a delightful spot for a retired gentleman of sporting habits to reside. John was driven back to Kirklands that night well pleased with at last having a place to call his own in the town where he had spent his boyhood and youth, and he immediately set about drawing up plans for a modern residence to replace the two old houses. Within three weeks he had reached agreement with a local builder, and had commissioned him, at a cost of £715, to erect his new home. He ordered, amongst other things, that it was to have a spacious marble hall, a large drawing-room with a circular bay-window overlooking the Tweed, and stabling extensive enough to house a couple of hunters as well as his horse and chaise. It says much for his boundless optimism that he should still have sufficient confidence in his own future prospects to approve plans for a house that might well take a year to build, when there was every indication that the disease from which he suffered was becoming every day more malignant. He named his home-to-be Walton Hall in memory of the immortal Izaak, for he and his two brothers had been devoted to the angler's art ever since their childhood.

As soon as James learned from Sandy of John's action, he sat down and wrote him an angry letter, warning him that Scott would be furious to learn of his impending move, and that if he persisted in his declared intention of residing in Kelso he would undoubtedly cause the great man the most extreme annoyance. The result could well be that their business relationship with him would suffer harm at a time when they could look forward to reaping the benefits of a somewhat easier financial climate. His haughty strictures as to his younger brother's future conduct went unheeded by John who seems to have ignored James's letter altogether. Receiving no reply to his note of warning, the printer washed his hands of his wayward brother's affairs and informed Scott of all that had transpired. The news seems to have decided Sir Walter that the time had now come to replace persuasion and cajolery with a threat of disciplinary action of the type that was likely to hurt John the hardest, and he wrote immediately to the Kirkland cottage to let him know his views:

My dear John,
I assure you my objections to your establishing yourself at Kelso are not capricious but arise out of the nature of our connection. I asked you at Borough M[uir] Head whether you had not some intentions of this kind and as you then disclaimed them, adding that it would not suit your circumstances which would just do to carry you on comfortably but no more—I said nothing further.

I would otherwise have told you, as I do now, that to maintain the necessary confidence betwixt us, frequent & personal intercourse was necessary, for which cause your chief residence must be at or near Edinr. I am aware that while things are so easy in the money market this may be less necessary for immediate provision, but we all know, by experience which I shall never forget, how suddenly all this may change. And it is not merely your interference in raising money that is wanted but your advice upon many points, as well as explanations of accots. etc, which I am slow in understanding by the pen. I am therefore under the necessity of repeating what I said to James—that I consider this Kelso scheme as a virtual resignation of the agency if persisted in.

I am besides certain I am doing you a good turn in stopping your proceedings, if they are stopped. You have mortgaged one pretty place[1] for the sake of buying & building elsewhere—this must be

[1] Harmony Hall.

always imprudent in the eye of the world and of monied men who know the movements of their customers full well; and assure yourself it makes muttering even amongst such as wish you well. It appears to me you go to the most unhealthy place in Scotland with a broken constitution, for I never knew Kelso without rheumatic fevers. Besides, it abounds with those temptations to too much exercise & too much society which a busy man may resist but an idle one seldom can.

All these, however, are circumstances for your own consideration, but I have thought the matter over & over as it is likely to affect me & have been necessarily led to the conclusion I have mentioned...I do assure you that I have your interests as much in my view as my own in the subject of this letter and that there are few in which I have ever made up my mind more satisfactorily.

Yours very truly,
W.S.

Abbotsford 28 April[1]

Although the genuine affection he had always entertained for the little man had caused him to soften the tone of his remarks somewhat, it was a cruel choice to set before one desperate to find some sort of relief from the symptoms that made his life a misery. Scott knew quite well that John could ill afford to lose the several hundred pounds which the agency brought him in every year. To return to the city Ballantyne considered little less than suicide. But whereas he was still quite capable of making short visits to Edinburgh to finalize details of any agreements reached and could carry on other negotiations by letter, he knew quite well that what Scott really needed him for was the day-to-day discounting of bills, money-changing, and loan-raising—activities the author now considered essential for the maintenance of his increasingly expensive way of life.

Ballantyne was convinced he now had no alternative but to stand his ground, come what may, and Scott's threats failed in their intended effect. The ex-publisher, ex-auctioneer, and now ex-author's agent, had made up his mind to live out what little time remained to him enjoying the country air and the rural surroundings he wished he had never left. But on the 31st May, a few weeks after his forty-seventh birthday, he foolishly attended a dinner party with some friends in Kelso, noting that he 'drank some claret & felt *unusually* well at night'. Next morning he was

---

[1] This letter is assigned to 1819 in the collection in the Writers to the Signet Library. John Ballantyne's diary shows clearly that it was written to him in 1821.

in such a pitiful state that he was forced to dictate an urgent note to his eldest brother requesting his help. James lost no time; as soon as he read its contents he left immediately for Kirklands to bring him back.

John's wife had been informed by James of the serious condition her husband was in and she hurried over to St John Street to await his arrival from Kirklands. There he was instantly put to bed after his brother had helped him upstairs, Hermione being in constant attendance from that time onwards, nursing him, cooking what little food he ate, and seeing to it that his doctor's instructions were carried out to the letter. A day or two after Ballantyne's return to Edinburgh, Scott and his son-in-law went to the bedside of the emaciated, bright-eyed little man that either could now have lifted with one hand. They stood while he plucked at the papers which strewed his bed, seeing the pleasure shining from his flushed face as he gasped his thanks for their arrival. Lockhart described the scene as being the last time he and Scott saw John alive. 'We sat with him for perhaps an hour, and I think half that space was occupied with his predictions of a speedy end, and details of his last Will, which he had just been executing, and which lay on his coverlid; the other half being given, five minutes or so at a time, to questions and remarks, which intimated that the hope of life still flickered before him—nay, that his interest in all its concerns remained eager. The proof-sheets of a volume of his Novelists' Library lay also by his pillow; and he passed from them to his Will, and then back to them, as by jerks and starts the unwonted veil of gloom closed upon his imagination, or was withdrawn again. He had, as he said, left his great friend and patron £2000 towards the completion of the new Library at Abbotsford—and the spirit of the auctioneer virtuoso flashed up as he began to describe what would, he thought, be the best style and arrangement of the book-shelves. He was interrupted by an agony of asthma, which left him with hardly any signs of life....Scott was visibly and profoundly shaken by this scene and its sequel.'

At half-past eight on the morning of the 16th June, John Ballantyne died peacefully in the comforting warmth of his wife's buxom arms, and a few days later Sir Walter Scott and a large concourse of the dead man's relatives and friends followed his diminutive coffin to its last resting place in Canongate Churchyard. Among the crowd who thronged the graveside were many who had travelled considerable distances to pay their last respects to the now extinguished spark that had been his endearing personality; the number of mourners who attended, drawn from all walks of life, giving an indication of the esteem in which he had been held. 'As we stood together...while they were smoothing the turf over John's remains in Canongate Churchyard,' reported Lockhart in his usual detail, 'the heavens, which had been dark and slaty, cleared up suddenly, and the midsummer sun shone forth in his strength. Scott, ever awake to the "skiey influences," cast his eye along the over-hanging line of the Calton Hill, with its gleaming walls and towers, and then turning to the grave again, "I feel," he whispered in my ear, "I feel as if there would be less sunshine for me from this day forth." ' A few days later the author wrote to his son in Ireland to acquaint him with the news. 'I have had a great loss in poor John Ballantyne who is gone after a very long illness,' he told him. 'He persisted to the very last in endeavouring to take exercise in which he was often imprudent, and was up and dressed the very morning before his death. In his Will the grateful creature has left me a legacy of £2000, life-rented however, by his wife. The rest of his little fortune goes betwixt his two brothers. I shall miss him very much, both in business and as an easy and lively companion who was eternally active and obliging in whatever I had to do.' Scott's final testimony to John was contained in some lines he inserted in the long introductory epistle prefixed to *The Fortunes of Nigel*, published the following year. 'I now miss the social and warm-hearted welcome of the quick-witted and kindly friend who first introduced me to the public,' he told his readers, '[a man] who had more original wit than would have set up a dozen of professed sayers of good things, and more racy humour than would have made the fortune of as many more.'

Lockhart, with his usual disregard for the truth in any instance where it was possible for him to injure the reputation of the Ballantyne brothers, stated categorically that John 'died as he had lived, ignorant of the situation of his affairs, and deep in debt'. This penniless spendthrift, he implied, did not even realize that he was insolvent! Was this the sort of man that Scott should have trusted to handle his financial affairs and advise him regarding business matters and the money market? 'A more reckless, thoughtless, improvident adventurer never rushed into the serious responsibilities of business,' he declared with

153

solemnity, and went on to make clear to his readers that the fact that Ballantyne died 'deep in debt', while apparently under the impression that he was able to leave his friends and relations bequests amounting to several thousands of pounds, only confirmed how utterly he was out of touch with financial reality. 'The day that brought John into pecuniary connexion with him (Scott) was the blackest in his calendar.' Lockhart thundered with the fervour aroused by unrequited expectations; yet even he was forced to pay tribute to the loyalty of the Ballantynes towards their illustrious patron, and at no time was he able to cast any reflection on their honesty in their conduct of his affairs. 'They both entertained him; they both loved and revered him; and I believe would have shed their heart's blood in his service,' he wrote on one occasion, there being too many of their friends and contemporaries still alive to allow him to say otherwise. So he attacked James and John on the score that they were little better than half-wits in business and complete fools when it came to their conduct of the author's commercial concerns.

Characterization of this sort needed bolstering with instances of their stupidity and John's death allowed Scott's son-in-law to hold up to the world a picture of an improvident pauper masquerading as the benefactor of the man his policies had helped on the road to ruin. But in fact Ballantyne was very far from being a fool when it came to concluding a bargain, assessing a balance sheet, or deciding the soundness or otherwise of a financial proposition. Would Scott, with his delight in behind-the-scenes manipulation, have been so keen to retain his services if he had thought him anything less than efficient? John was let down on more than one occasion when he invested his personal capital with friends he thought honourable men; the business propositions they advanced were sound in themselves, but the fact that one of the partners disappeared with a large proportion of the firm's assets put an entirely different complexion on the matter. It was Ballantyne's money which was lost, not that of Scott; he trusted associates that on two occasions turned out to be rogues and thus burned his fingers badly. John was generous to a fault, and his extravagance when he had money to spend frequently brought him fair-weather companions out for an easy touch. But there is no evidence that he deluded himself into believing that he had funds at his command when in fact he was deep in debt. He most certainly did not die leaving a horde of creditors to besiege his wife's door, as Lockhart led his readers to believe. On the 3rd January, at a time when his continuing ill-health had made him realize that he ought to make legal provision for his wife, so that, in the event of his death, she would not be left too long without funds, he totalled his resources and then noted in his diary: 'I am now worth at least seven thousand pounds, & of course independent.' On the 17th February, he drove over from Kirklands to his solicitor's office at Melrose and there made a fresh will. After his death in June, this was read in the presence of his trustees (his two brothers and Sir Walter Scott among them) and the box which John had indicated would contain deeds and personal papers was opened by George Hogarth who, as a Writer to the Signet, had been appointed to administer the estate. Inside, the trustees discovered receipts from Ballantyne's bankers showing that he had deposited with them, shortly before his death, sums amounting to £2,900; there was also £346 in banknotes, plus a post-dated cheque made out in John's favour for a further £200. His will revealed that he had left £1,000 to each of his brothers and £2,000 to Scott; but that his wife was to have the benefit of the interest brought in by the sum realized by his estate during her lifetime, the other beneficiaries having to wait until after her death before they could claim the sums bequeathed to them. The only exceptions to this proviso were a few small bequests that were to be paid immediately (including £10 to each of the trustees to purchase mourning dress for the funeral) and the sum of £100 he left to his mistress—'my said wife' as he called her.[1]

There are strong reasons for doubting the accuracy of Ballantyne's estimate that his estate was worth in the region of seven thousand pounds, although it is difficult to understand why he should wish to deceive himself by making a grossly inaccurate entry in his private diary. Hermione was successful in secreting from the Trustees a considerable sum in ready cash and was not above pleading poverty and writing begging letters whenever it suited her purpose. Nevertheless, there is mystery surrounding the amount John actually left. The freehold house he owned at Kirklands was valued at £450 (according to a note made in James Ballantyne's hand); Harmony Hall, although mortgaged to the

[1] John's mistress, Hermione Roberton, to whom he left the £100, in 1831 was married to William Duke of Alicante, Spain.

extent of part of its value, managed at its sale to bring in a balance of several hundred pounds after this loan had been repaid. The site in Kelso on which Walton Hall was intended to be erected was purchased by Sandy at its market value of £420, the builders being instructed to continue with their work in accordance with the plan drawn up by the late owner. John's personal effects, his livestock (he kept three horses and two brace of greyhounds) plus his furniture, antiques, pictures and books, more than cleared by their sale the few debts of a personal nature he had left outstanding. The balance, added to the sum realized by the sale of his part interest in the last two *Waverley* novels, was a nest egg which his widow concealed to an extent that totally deceived his Trustees. As she revealed in 1837 (the letter is quoted in full in a later chapter) wee Johnny Ballantyne, had contrived to die 'in easy circumstances', leaving his 'legal' wife, if not well off, at least with enough capital to allow her an adequate living for the next few years; certainly sufficient to permit a childless widow to exist in comfort if she avoided extravagance. Hermione often sighed for the little luxuries she had known in the old days, and Sir Walter Scott was in receipt of more than one begging letter, and was persuaded on occasions to put his hand in his pocket in answer to her pleas. Despite her size, or perhaps because of the round lump sum she had pre-served as bait, on the 17th September, 1828, she once again walked up the aisle, this time to emerge as the new Mrs John Glover of Kendal. Her second marriage was unfortunately fraught with as many financial difficulties as her first, and in 1830 we find her and her husband in the sanctuary of the Isle of Man, where Mr Glover had fled to escape his creditors. Hermione wrote to Duncan Cowan, Scott's fellow trustee, telling him she was living in poverty on an income of £44 a year, having to support her second husband, now insolvent, and ekeing out a precarious existence by giving lessons in French and music. The money she once had was long since spent, and the one thing of value she still possessed was the original manuscript of *The Lady of the Lake*. This literary treasure Robert Cadell managed to prise from her grasp for as little as £10; but later he and the Ballantyne family, assisted by Scott, managed to secure for her a joint annuity amounting to £40 per annum. On this and her income from teaching, Hermione survived until 1854, dying peacefully on the 23rd March at Belhaven near Dunbar.

10

In 1821 SCOTT received the latest set of plans prepared by his London architect Mr Blore, giving details needed for the final phase of the building of Abbotsford. With these to hand, Smith of Darnick instructed his men to commence digging the foundations of the last of its many wings, while others started work on the outside embellishments and carvings and the beautiful open screenworks of stone connecting the house with its gardens. The main construction of the noble edifice had now been completed, and already there were sufficient sumptuously furnished reception rooms in commission to allow the laird to act as host to his constant procession of guests on a scale that had seldom if ever been heard of in the county before. But he was far from neglecting his writing. After breakfast, no matter how distinguished a visitor he was entertaining, he would disappear to a dressing-room upstairs, there to stay undisturbed while he finished a chapter of *The Pirate*. He worked incessantly, and hardly had James Ballantyne finished supervising the printing of the last pages of halting narrative and interminable padding that comprised so much of this book, than the first manuscript sheets of *The Fortunes of Nigel* started to arrive at Paul's Works.

This novel, which turned out to be one of the most popular works the author wrote, was finished in the early spring of 1822 and published in May of the same year. A delighted Archibald Constable, who had gone to London to be on hand at Hurst, Robinson & Company, his agents there, wrote jubilantly to his partner that no less than seven thousand copies had been disposed of in the capital before noon on the first day of issue; and that he had bumped into a number of people in the street with their heads buried in the novel as he had made his way back to his hotel. 'Our most productive culture is the Author of Waverley,' Cadell replied. 'Let us stick to him, let us dig on and dig on at that extraordinary quarry.'

This seemingly inexhaustible fountain of prose on which he

drew enabled Scott to churn out thousands of words every week, but he was now having qualms of conscience regarding the speed with which each new work from his pen was rushed through the presses and foisted upon an as yet uncomplaining public. Since the publication of *Ivanhoe* early in 1820, it had become increasingly noticeable how often a skimped and poorly written novel followed hard on the tail of one of real interest and literary worth. Certain critics were quick to point this out, and others had the temerity to advise the Author of *Waverley* that he ought to give full value to his readers for money received by restricting his output. It was obvious that he had insufficient time to revise (and if necessary rewrite) each work before it was placed, raw and untrimmed, before the public. Hints were dropped that his constant preoccupation was the amassing of the maximum amount of copy-money in the shortest possible time, a charge that was near enough to the truth to sting Scott into making a reply. He prefixed the story of *The Fortunes of Nigel* with a long 'introductory epistle', and used this as a means of answering the charges levelled against him. 'The critics, they have their business, and I mine,' he retorted with some heat, 'as the nursery proverb goes:

The children of Holland take pleasure in making,
What the children of England take pleasure in breaking.

I am their humble jackall; too busy in providing food for them, to have time for considering whether they swallow or reject it... A man should strike while the iron is hot, and hoist sail while the wind is fair. If a successful author keeps not the stage, another instantly takes his ground.' And to the charge that he was supposed 'to work merely for the lucre of gain,' he replied: 'Supposing that I did permit the great advantages which must be derived from success in literature, to join with other motives in inducing me to come more frequently before the public, — that emolument is the voluntary tax which the public pays for a certain species of literary amusement — it is extorted from no one, and paid, I presume, by those only who can afford it, and who receive gratification in proportion to the expense... For myself,' he went on, 'I am not displeased to find the game a winning one; yet while I pleased the public, I should probably continue it merely for the pleasure of playing; for I have felt as strongly as most folks that love of composition, which is perhaps the strongest of all instincts, driving the author to the pen, the painter to the palette, often without either the chance of fame or the prospect of reward. Perhaps I have said too much of this. I might perhaps, with as much truth as most people, exculpate myself from the charge of being either of a greedy or mercenary disposition; but I am not, therefore, hypocrite enough to disclaim the ordinary motives, on account of which the whole world around me is toiling unremittingly, to the sacrifice of ease, comfort, health, and life.'

Some months before writing this (in fact as soon as it became obvious that John Ballantyne was unlikely to recover from his illness) Scott had started to make tentative arrangements to promote James from the position he held as manager of the printing business to that of his personal agent and partner. A few days after he and Lockhart had visited the dying man, he wrote James what he termed a 'missive letter', setting out the details of the new co-partnership he proposed between them. As an added inducement he also informed the printer that he was increasing his salary from £400 to £500 per annum forthwith. 'It is proper to set out by reminding you,' he wrote him on the 15th June, the day before John's death, 'that upon the affairs of the printing-house being in difficulties about the term of Whitsunday 1816, I assumed the total responsibility for its expenditure and its debts, including a salary of £400 to you as manager; and on condition of my doing so, you agreed that I should draw the full profits. Under this management, the business is to continue down to the term of Whitsunday next, being 1822, when I, considering myself as fully indemnified for my risk and advances, am willing and desirous that this management shall terminate, and that you shall be admitted to a just participation of the profits which shall arise after that period....It appears from the transactions on our former copartnery, that you were personally indebted to me in the year 1816 in the sum of £3000, of which you have already paid me £1200, by assigning to me your share in the profits of certain novels; and as there still remains due at this term of Whitsunday the sum of £1800, I am content to receive in payment thereof the profits of three novels, now contracted for, to be published after this date of Whitsunday 1821. It may be proper to mention, that no interest is imputed on this principal sum of £3000; because I account it compensated by the profits of the printing-office, which I have drawn for my exclusive use since 1816.' After enumerating various minor points that had to be settled between them before the agreement could be signed, Scott pointed out to James that, as from Whitsunday 1822, 'as I will remain liable personally for such bills of the Company as are then current...I shall retain my exclusive right of property to all the several funds of the Company, book debts, money, bills, or balances of money, and bills in bankers' hands, for retiring the said current bills, and indemnifying me for my advances; and we are upon these terms to grant each other a mutual and effectual discharge of all claims whatsoever arising out of our former contract, or out of any of the transactions which have followed thereupon, excepting as to the two sums of £1800 and £1287 10s due by you to me as above mentioned.'

Since Scott assumed sole ownership of the printing business in 1816, he had drawn heavily of the resources which its credit facilities opened to him, with the inevitable result that the amount of bills outstanding against the firm had increased with each passing year. By May 1822, the Company's debts amounted to over £36,000. Sundry trade debtors and the amount due from James Ballantyne personally (to clear which he made over to the business an endowment policy he had taken out) came to approximately £9,000, leaving a balance outstanding of some £27,000. As we have seen, Scott accepted full personal responsibility for this sum; he also considered himself, as he put it, 'fully indemnified' for the capital he had previously advanced and any risks he might have run 'because I account it compensated by the profits of the printing-office, which I have drawn for my exclusive use since 1816.' But he had drawn a great deal more than the mere amount of yearly profit the business had made, with the result that there was now a millstone of debt round the firm's neck to the tune of an extra £27,000. To James, it is true, he acknowledged this was his personal responsibility, but to the outside world this was a debt contracted by the firm, for the secret of the author's ownership of the business had not been shared with the bankers and finance houses with whom their ability to obtain backing for their bills ultimately rested. The fact that the business had been hampered from its inception by being so grossly under-capitalized made the granting of credit facilities of paramount importance if it was to be able to pay its way and also compete successfully with the increasing opposition it encountered from other printing houses. As owner, Scott was entitled to manipulate the company's financial affairs in any way he thought fit, but to encumber it, as he had, with debts of these proportions, even though the interest on the loans was debited to his personal account, meant that its ability to borrow money to finance its trading activities was curtailed to an extent that made them almost non-existent. As security for the £27,000 the lands and estate of Abbotsford gave James confidence that there was more than sufficient collateral to see them safely through any emergency, and he therefore signed the partnership agreement with a light heart in the full expectation that a few more years might see the Ballantyne Press once more in a position to expand its activities. On the 12th May 1822, the partnership agreement, drawn up by George Hogarth, was signed by Scott and Ballantyne, and James was once again part owner of the firm. By this act he made himself liable, not only for a share of its profits, but also for a proportion of its debts, a fact he was bitterly to regret within the course of a few more years.

Now that he was once again to be admitted into partnership with the Author of *Waverley*, James sought a means of lightening the amount of work which the management of the printing business, the editorship of the *Edinburgh Weekly Journal*, and proof-reading each new novel of Scott's imposed upon him. With the end of the war against France there had started a progressive decline in the circulation of the *Kelso Mail*, and also in the turnover of the local printing and publishing business which his brother Sandy conducted from the Kelso newspaper office, so James seized the opportunity which Sandy's worries about his future prospects presented to write and ask him to join him in Edinburgh.

With business as bad as it was, at any other time Sandy would probably have accepted his brother's offer by return of post; but he was now pledged to continue the building of Walton Hall into which his wife Randall and his family were eager to move. They had lived since their marriage in a small and overcrowded house in Belmount Place, Kelso, a tiny villa that appeared quite large enough for their requirements when there were only the two of them, but was now bursting at the seams with the pressures caused by an active and growing family of seven children. At the auction sale where John had purchased the site to erect the Hall, Sandy had bought a patch of ground large enough to allow him to have a house built that would accommodate his family in comfort, giving them an extra room so that Randall could have a living-in servant to act as nursemaid to their younger children. They had called their new home-to-be Seven Elms Cottage after the trees that flanked its garden, and the foundations were already dug and the building materials had arrived at the site when Sandy was informed of John's death in Edinburgh. This news completely changed the situation: the proposed Walton Hall was to occupy a far more desirable situation overlooking the Tweed than the one Sandy's new house commanded, and he immediately wrote to his late brother's trustees asking them if he could be allowed to take over the site and complete the building. Permission was granted to him to do this, and by the time that James's letter arrived the structure was being roofed and the garden landscaped.

In later and less fortunate years, the Ballantynes looked back on the short period when they were able to afford the upkeep of Walton Hall as being some of the happiest months of their married life. In order to be able to stay on in the town where he was bred and born, Sandy employed every device he could think of to revive the flagging circulation of the *Kelso Mail*, but in vain. In the summer of 1824 he threw in his hand and made arrangements to dispose of the paper. He informed his wife, who loved Kelso and had no desire to move, that he had now no alternative but to agree with Scott's request, and sorrowfully and with many regrets, they packed up their belongings and despatched them to a house they had rented at 25 Comley Bank. A few months later they moved again, this time to Ann Street, a thoroughfare situated in one of the most desirable districts in the capital, where the following April their eighth surviving child, Robert Michael Ballantyne, was born. This boy was later to become the author of *The Coral Island* and one of the most famous writers of books for young people that the Victorian era produced.

The end of 1824 saw Sandy in charge of the office at Paul's Works, combining this duty with the task of editing the *Weekly Journal*. James's name continued to appear as editor, but he confined his services to supplying a column of dramatic criticism and an occasional article upon the political affairs of the day. Sandy took no part in the frequent discussions that took place between his brother and Sir Walter Scott concerning the commercial policies the firm was to pursue; nor, to his relief, was his

John Ballantyne

James Ballantyne

AN

APOLOGY

FOR

TALES OF TERROR

—— A THING OF SHREDS AND PATCHES.
Hamlet.

KELSO:
PRINTED AT THE MAIL OFFICE.

1799.

Ballantyne's first printing commission from Scott

Paul's Works

Wooden press used in printing the *Waverley* novels

Archibald Constable (by Andrew Geddes)

John Gibson Lockhart (by Sir Francis Grant)

One of the many accommodation notes signed by Scott

Abbotsford from the south

Entrance Hall, Abbotsford

Sir Walter Scott and his friends at Abbotsford (by Thomas Faed) (*See key opposite*)

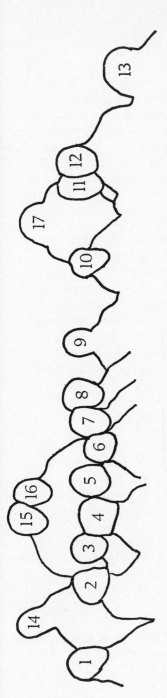

1. Thomas Thomson 2. James Ballantyne 3. A. Constable 4. Thomas Campbell 5. Thomas Moore 6. Adam Ferguson 7. Lord Jeffrey 8. William Wordsworth 9. J. G. Lockhart 10. Rev. George Crabbe 11. Henry Mackenzie 12. Sir Walter Scott 13. James Hogg 14. Sir Humphrey Davey 15. Sir David Wilkie 16. Sir William Allen 17. Prof. John Wilson

advice asked regarding the complicated financial transactions that absorbed the partners' anxious attention as each month's settlement day drew near.

Most of James's time was taken up with the constant proof-reading and correcting that Scott's tremendous output entailed. The author's refusal to alter or rewrite his hastily dashed-off sheets of manuscript before sending them to the printer, meant that more than usual care had to be taken by Ballantyne when he came to revise and correct the original copy. Scott had come to rely upon him more and more in this respect, and Ballantyne's one-sixth share in the half profits of each novel had to be earned by meticulous and painstaking devotion to his duties as reader. Not only was Scott's handwriting little better than an illegible scrawl, but his letters and manuscripts were notorious for their lack of punctuation, faulty syntax, and grammatical errors of all kinds. As the author grew older his hand became even more cramped and difficult to read, advancing from thirty-eight lines to a page for the manuscript of *Waverley*, to nearly sixty by the time he came to write *Ivanhoe*. His scrawl became progressively more difficult to decipher, until finally he was unable to scan a sheet of his own handwriting when James was forced to return it to him for explanation. In his journal entry for 22nd June, 1828, he wrote: 'Had a note from Ballantyne complaining of my manscript, and requesting me to read it over. I would give a £1000 if I could; but it would take me longer to read than to write. I cannot trace my *pieds de mouche* but with great labour and trouble; so e'en take your own share of the burden, my old friend; and, since I cannot read, be thankful I can write.'

It was not just as a corrector of errata that James was so useful; Scott had come to respect his ability as a literary critic to an extent that would have made him consign a new work to the waste-paper basket if Ballantyne had condemned it out of hand. He would readily accept adverse comment if it was levelled at the general construction or make-up of a work, or if a plot was condemned as being far-fetched or ill-conceived: but he was far more sensitive to any disparagement of his literary style. This was set and unalterable and the public would have to like it or lump it.

Lockhart printed in his *Life of Scott* some of the comments which Ballantyne made on the proof-sheets of *The Field of Waterloo*, published by Constable in 1815. These 'animadversions', as the biographer termed them, were liberally sprinkled throughout the stanzas, and reveal that the author was not above accepting the printer's recommendations about even so personal creation as his poetry. Experience had long since convinced him that Ballantyne knew better than the majority of his critics when a work would, or would not, win favour, satisfy taste, and enhance his reputation as a writer. Scott made no secret about his determination to reap the maximum possible financial benefit from his pen, and the fear that haunted him above all others was that he would one day wake to find that his immense popularity was on the wane. To prevent this happening he wrote what he thought the public most wanted to read, and was prepared to take advice, from any quarter he thought knowledgeable, if by so doing he was better able to catch the national mood. 'No one will find me rowing against the stream,' he wrote on one occasion.[1] 'I care not who knows it — I will write for the public amusement; and though I never will aim at popularity by what I think unworthy means, I will not, on the other hand, be pertinacious in the defence of my own errors against the voice of the public.'

When he was not engaged in proof-reading, the rest of Ballantyne's working day was usually spent progressing the printing of the immense number of volumes in all sorts and sizes that passed through the presses at Paul's Works every month. Some idea of the turnover of the printing works can be gained by reading a note that Archibald Constable appended to a letter he wrote to Scott in June, 1822. This gave the author details of the work Ballantyne & Company had in hand for the publisher, and from which Scott would derive direct benefit. 'This is a summary to which I venture to say there will be no rival in our day!' Constable wrote proudly, and few living authors, before or since, can have had so much of their work in production at one and the same time.

A new edition of Sir W. Scott's Poetical Works in 10 vols. (miniature) — 5000 copies	50,000	volumes
Novels and Tales, 12 vols. ditto — 5000 copies	60,000	,,
Historical Romances, 6 vols. ditto — 5000 copies	30,000	,,
Poetry from Waverley, &c. 1 vol. — 5000 copies	5,000	,,
Volumes in production at the Ballantyne Press	145,000	volumes

[1] Introductory epistle to *The Fortunes of Nigel*, Edinburgh, 1822.

The list Constable sent to Scott took no account of the large quantity of printing work for other publishing houses on which the presses of James Ballantyne & Company were continually engaged; or of that undertaken for their many customers who were not directly connected with the publishing trade. Most of the Scottish printing orders for legal stationery and official documents also came their way, thanks to the influence of the senior partner; while their larger presses had more than enough to do by printing the *Weekly Journal* and other newspapers and magazines. The twenty presses that were now in operation at Paul's Works (two of which were of the latest steam-powered type) had sometimes to be kept going night and day in order to satisfy the demands of the trade for speedy delivery; much of the credit for the way the wheels were kept turning being due to the work's foreman, John Hughes, who had been James's right-hand man since his earliest days as a printer in Kelso.

There is little wonder that James was keen to be once again admitted into partnership, for he knew better than anyone that the business which bore his name was a flourishing commercial concern with prospects as bright as any printing house in Scotland. Its presses were seldom, if ever, short of work, and, if only capital had been available for expansion, he could probably have doubled its turnover without materially reducing the prices he charged. Competition was brisk at times and had lately become even keener, especially from their principal rivals in Edinburgh, George Ramsay & Company, whom Constable sometimes employed on volumes other than those of Scott (whose works he was forced to have printed by Ballantyne whether he liked it or not). When the typographical excellence of the finished product was the main concern of the customer, rather than how cheaply he could manage to have it produced, then James Ballantyne & Company won the order nearly every time, for there were few firms able to compete with them in the quality of their printing. This had resulted in their having acquired a high reputation in the trade, and the goodwill that went with it, their connections extending from one end of the country to the other, and orders being sent them from as far afield as London and the south of England.

From May, 1822, when Scott inveigled a willing James into signing the new partnership agreement, until January 1826, when the firm was forced to stop further payments, the profits of the company, after all expenses had been paid, averaged approximately £2,000 a year.[1] But this thriving concern, staffed by some of the best technicians that the Scottish printing trade had produced, had for years been milked dry of every penny of liquid capital that could be squeezed out of it. Money that should have been used to retire some of the bills they owed had gone instead to pay the wages of the masons working on Abbotsford; the bills could easily be renewed provided sufficient interest was paid, but the masons could not be kept waiting a day longer than their due. By using the name of the firm to obtain credit, Scott burdened it with an ever increasing millstone of debt, all of which was directly of his own making and for which he accepted full responsibility. As we have seen, when James rejoined the firm in 1822 this amounted to approximately £27,000; but by January 1826, discount charges, stamp duties, and interest, plus further loans incurred by Scott, had caused the figure to soar to £46,500; an increase of £19,500 in three and a half years.

With the builders having at long last reached the point of putting the finishing touches to the castellated magnificence of Abbotsford, Scott proceeded to hold court there in a style that would not have discredited a minor princeling of the Blood Royal. The summer of 1822 had witnessed the arrival in Scotland of the first Hanoverian king ever to set foot there, Scott having persuaded the now almost continually bemused George IV to honour the city of Edinburgh with his presence. From the time that the official notification of the King's acceptance of the invitation arrived in the capital, the author assumed control of the arrangements for his reception by planning a magnificent pipes and tartan entertainment. From soon after dawn to nearly midnight his house in Castle Street was besieged with members of one or other of the legion of committees that had sprung up almost overnight to handle the details of the Royal Visit: quarrels between opposing factions were frequent, friendships of years standing were broken by violent disagree-

[1] This estimate is confirmed by a letter Mr James Glen of Glasgow sent to Sir H. J. C. Grierson, the editor of the definitive edition of *The Letters of Sir Walter Scott*, published in twelve volumes by Constable & Company, 1932–37. Mr Glen had made an exhaustive study of the events leading up to the final collapse of the firm of James Ballantyne & Company, and his long letter is printed in full in Volume One of the above work. He stated, *inter alia*, that 'a full estimate of half the profits would be £3,000' (i.e. for the three years up to January 1826), making a total of approximately £2,000 a year for this period.

ments as to the order of precedence for shaking the Royal Hand, and Scott, sitting in Solomon-like judgement and thoroughly enjoying the experience, was appealed to time and again to settle arguments and smooth tempers ruffled by imagined slights. As the great day drew near, hundreds of kilted Highlanders arrived in the town, each clan with its chief and all seemingly armed to the teeth. These rough and quick-tempered men were placed under Scott's direct command, and to prevent old scores being settled during drunken back-street fights, he kept the whole mob of plaided, dirk-carrying Highlanders continually piping their different ways through the decorated streets of the city. Pibroch and pennon were out from Leith to the Canongate, and Scott himself, thanks to a right secured from one of his long dead ancestors, was resplendent in Campbell tartan, although wearing trews and not the kilt.

Accompanied by a flotilla of warships, the King's yacht dropped anchor off Leith on 14th August. It was a wet and miserable day with visibility in the Firth obscured by driving rain, but despite the downpour Scott left immediately for the *Royal George*, eager to be amongst the first to greet his sovereign. He had sacrificed a month of his time to make the visit the success he thought such an occasion merited; had written a song in the King's honour, and had planned the entire pageantry. He was undismayed by the sarcastic references to the expense of the whole ostentatious affair that emanated from some of the more radical Scottish sources. Even Lockhart, Tory though he was, jibed that it seemed that 'our fat friend came in the promise and bloom of three-score' to represent Bonny Prince Charlie at Holyrood.

Scott's unswerving loyalty to his monarch was rewarded to a degree that warmed his heart by the King's remark when told that the author's boat had bumped its way alongside: 'What!' he exclaimed, with the uplift that the chance of shedding boredom engendered, 'Sir Walter Scott! The man in Scotland I most wish to see. Let him come up.' The bard was quickly helped aboard, limped his way to the quarterdeck, and there made a gallant little speech he had prepared before presenting, on behalf of the city, a St Andrew's Cross beautifully wrought in silver. The King essayed a few words in reply, handed the cross to his equerry, then moved to more important business by reaching for a whisky bottle and downing a brimming bumper to toast the baronet's health. Not to be outdone, Sir Walter charged his own glass, raised it on high, proposed a health unto His Majesty, then sank the contents at a single swallow. The Royal visit had officially begun.

For the whole of the following fortnight festivities of every sort continued unabated, with banquets and wining taking pride of place. The seldom sober monarch, bare-kneed and kilted beneath a belly that carried all before it, showered his patronage in any way his tail-tugging courtiers requested, while greeting with a genial wave of a chubby and bejewelled hand those of his northern subjects that thronged the streets to see his coach roll by. He granted a petition for the restoration of the Scottish peerages, forfeited after the Jacobite insurrections; knighted Scott's close friend Adam Ferguson and the artist Henry Raeburn; promised that 'Mons Meg', a cannon that had been carted off to London after the Stuart rising, would be returned to Edinburgh Castle; and granted favours and indulgences carefully calculated by his advisers to delight the hearts of loyal Scotsmen.

But for those in his immediate entourage he set a very hot pace indeed. The casualties amongst his favourites, who were forced, night after rollicking night, to hip their unsteady ways to bed, were many and grievous. Scott lasted as long as any, then contracted a form of alcoholic poisoning that resulted in what he termed 'a strong cutaneous eruption' affecting his arms and legs. 'Prickly heat' his doctor called the malady, but the symptoms were such that his patient came to believe that the novel on which he was then working, *Peveril of the Peak*, would, as he put it, 'smell of the apoplexy'. He was ill for several weeks after he had thankfully witnessed the departure of his florid-faced King, but it was during this period that the manuscript of *Peveril* was finished and sent to the printers.

He took some weeks to recover from the self-inflicted wounds sustained during George's visit; admitting, in a letter to John Richardson on the 15th September, that he was still 'rather the worse of my exertions in the Royal Cause'. One wag dubbed the blotches that reddened his skin the King's Evil; but by the late autumn he was back in the saddle and once more acting the generous host to the visitors who came and went so freely at both his houses.

In June 1823, he at last had his long-hoped-for meeting with Maria Edgeworth, a writer whose work had exerted a considerable influence on his fictional romances and whose style he had always admired. After reading *Waverley* she had written to James Ballantyne to say how much she liked the novel and would he convey her congratulations to the author of the work. Through the medium of James's hand, Scott had replied in gallant vein by saying: 'If I could but hit Miss Edgeworth's wonderful power of vivifying all her persons, and making them live as real *beings* in your mind, I should not be afraid.' James forwarded her a copy of *The Lord of the Isles* and there was a further exchange of compliments in which Scott also praised her recently published *Patronage*. Several times he invited her to stay as the guest of himself and Lady Scott at Abbotsford, and in the summer of 1823 Maria arrived in Scotland accompanied by her younger sisters Harriet and Sophy. They had taken rooms at Abercrombie Place, Edinburgh, and there a letter was awaiting them from Lady Scott pressing them to come round the same evening to Castle Street that they might hear a Highlander sing boat-songs. It was after ten when they set off, and Maria described the scene. 'As the coach stopped we saw the hall lighted, and the moment the door opened, heard the joyous sounds of loud singing. "The Miss Edgeworths", called out by three servants, sounded from hall to landing-place and as I paused a moment in the anteroom I heard the first sound of Walter Scott's voice—"The Miss Edgeworths *come!*" The room was lighted by one globe lamp. A circle was singing loud and beating time—all stopped in an instant and Walter Scott in the most cordial and courteous manner stepped forward to welcome us: "Miss Edgeworth this is so kind of you!" '

As soon as the welcomes were finished and they had been shown the various rooms they returned to watch the merry-making taking place below. ' "Will you then join in the circle with us?" Scott asked as he put the end of a silk handkerchief into my hand and others into my sisters. They held by these handkerchiefs all in their circle again, and the boatman began to roar out a Gaelic song to which they all stamped in time and repeated the chorus which, as far as I could hear, sounded like *At an Vam! At an Vam!* frequently repeated with prodigious enthusiasm. In another I could make out no intelligible sound but *Bar! bar! bar!* But the boatman's dark eyes were ready to start out of his head with rapture as he sang and stamped and shook the handkerchief on each side, and the circle imitated. Followed supper at a round table, a family supper, with attention to us just sufficient and no more…Walter Scott is one of the best-bred men I ever saw, with all the exquisite politeness which he knows so well how to describe, which is no particular school or country, but which is of all countries, the politeness which arises from good and quick sense and feeling, which seems to know by instinct the characters of others, to see what will please, and put all his guests at their ease. As I sat beside him at supper I could not believe he was a stranger and forgot he was a great man.'

On the 27th July they all arrived at Abbotsford where the Miss Edgeworths enjoyed a fortnight they remembered all their lives. Lockhart wrote to his friend John Wilson with his usual malicious candour: 'Miss Edgeworth is at Abbotsford…a little dark, bearded, sharp, withered, active, laughing, talking, impudent, fearless, outspoken, honest, Whiggish, unchristian, good-tempered, kindly, ultra-Irish body. I like her one day, and damn her to perdition the next. She is a very queer character. She, Sir Adam, and the Great Unknown are too much for any company.' Anne Scott, who was gifted with a higher intelligence than any of her brothers or sister and was an excellent conversationalist, described Miss Edgeworth as talking a great deal 'and does not care to hear others talk. There was a dreadful scene at parting. The great Maria nearly went into fits; she had taken such a fancy to us all.'

When one realizes the scale on which Scott was forced to entertain (for many of the sometimes distinguished visitors who arrived at Abbotsford with little or no prior warning stayed for days or even weeks), and the numerous invitations he extended to friends he wished to call—one feels sympathy for the Ballantyne family in their efforts to lay a great deal of the blame for the financial collapse of their business on his extravagant mode of living. 'The most wealthy of the English nobility,' Sandy Ballantyne wrote later, 'are accustomed to entertain large parties of guests at their country mansions at certain periods of the year, such as the Christmas holidays or the commencement of the shooting season, for a few days, or a week or two perhaps, at a time; but the halls of Abbotsford, for months and months in succession, were filled with parties of noble and distinguished guests, and crowds of pampered servants, while the stables might at any time have mounted a troop of horse.'[1]

[1] *Reply to Mr Lockhart's Pamphlet*, p. 95–6.

11

By August 1823, Archibald Constable was becoming more and more anxious when he contemplated the mass of bills bearing the name of his firm and that of James Ballantyne & Company that the two concerns were forced to keep floating between the finance houses of London and Edinburgh. The initial sales of *Quentin Durward* had not come up to his expectations, and on the 19th of that month details had been supplied by his chief clerk which showed that current bills issued in the names of the two firms 'amount just now to about £30,000.' The total sum involved actually came to considerably more than this figure, being made up of two distinct kinds of paper promises-to-pay. Firstly, there were the bills issued for actual 'value received' or literary work executed on behalf of the company. In the case of the publishing house, these were Constable's bills for (1) the copyrights purchased outright from the author; (2) shares in *Quentin Durward* and *Peveril* which Scott and Ballantyne had reserved, but which the publisher had since acquired; (3) money they owed the Ballantyne Press for printing undertaken on their behalf, plus sundry items of expenditure of a less important nature. Together, these made up a total of approximately £30,000.

But in addition to this considerable sum, there were the accommodation loans granted by the two firms for which counter bills had been issued. This was a delightfully simple credit raising procedure much used at that time, but one that lent itself to so many abuses that it appears inconceivable that no action was taken by the government to discourage or abolish the practice. Accommodation bills were not issued for any value received or work done, but were merely granted to enable the recipient to obtain cash or credit from his bank for services he had promised to perform for the loan drawer at some future date. Only in the event of this credit not being repaid or renewed on the due date, or the firm or individual to which it had been granted defaulting in any way, would the company who issued the accommodation note be called upon to find the money. Whoever discounted such a bill did so on the basis of the acceptor's reputation. Suppose we imagine that Archibald Constable & Company granted an accommodation note to Scott for, say, £1,000; he would then be able to cash this at a discount for the amount shown or obtain credit for a like amount at his bankers. But to enable Archibald Constable & Company to obtain credit for a similar sum, so that the firm had enough liquid resources for trading, they would expect Scott (under the commercial heading of James Ballantyne & Company) to issue them with a counter-note, also for £1,000. These counter-notes were not always cashed immediately, but were usually held in reserve in case funds were urgently required. If, as actually happened later, Constable was unable to comply with his bargains and the accommodation notes issued by his firm were found to be worthless on the due dates, then Scott, in the case of the £1,000 we are considering, would be called upon by the bank to refund the entire sum he had drawn. Furthermore, if Constable had put the counter-note into circulation, either to obtain credit by depositing it as security, or had cashed it at a discount, then the unfortunate Scott would once again be called upon to pay the amount for which it had been issued. For the £1,000 he had originally received, he would now have to repay a total of £2,000 plus interest charges. In 1823, the stage was rapidly being set for this to happen on a scale that took away all hope of financial survival and left the parties concerned ruined beyond repair.

It was not to be wondered at that Constable was becoming increasingly anxious, for by that year bills of this type, not drawn in payment for actual work done or value received, came to a total of £27,000, in addition to the £30,000 already mentioned. On top of this amount, on Scott's insistence that the works would be forthcoming and to prevent him approaching any other publishing house, Constable & Company had advanced him a total of £11,000 for a series of four novels, not one of which had yet been written. The publisher's obligations towards the author and the Ballantyne Press now came to the staggering total of £68,000. Bills-of-exchange issued in payment for literary work were, of course, eventually recouped, plus profit, as the booksellers paid their accounts for the volumes they had ordered; but the long credit that had to be given by the publisher, and the inevitable time-lag that always occurred before the booksellers paid up, meant that a vast amount of capital was required in order to keep trading. This was the asset that cool, calculating Cadell knew full well they lacked to a degree which made it imperative that not the slightest breath of suspicion regarding the financial soundness of the business should cloud their ability to borrow sufficient cash to pay their way. Above all, no hint of their difficulties must reach Sir Walter's ears, for without him and the confidence inspired by their being known throughout the trade as the publishers of the works of the Author of *Waverley*, the façade of financial well-being they had so carefully erected to deceive the outside world would be exposed as a sham in a matter of months.

Every new work of Scott's they published was a gamble that just *had* to come off, and the fact that the sales of *Quentin Durward* were at first a disappointment was sufficient to thoroughly alarm both the partners and set them at each others throats. 'This has been a labouring concern for twelve years,' Cadell wrote exasperatedly to Constable in London; and again: 'It is the want of capital that is the bane of all our operations...I cannot send Mrs Constable's sum without stating to you explicitly that it is wholly impossible for the concern to afford so much to its partners....I cannot discharge a more proper duty than that of warning you once more against what will in time assuredly sink this concern, that is its expense and the drains of the partners.' Constable, with all his supposed shrewdness, lived in a dream world of grandiose fancyings. He was a speculator who loved to impress his hearers by talking in thousands when they had expected him to say hundreds. He exuded an air of sweltering prosperity that deceived nearly everyone and certainly deceived Scott. 'Constable's business seems unintelligible,' he wrote in his journal after the edifice of cards had collapsed. 'No man thought the house worth less than £150,000. Constable told me when he was making his will that he was worth £80,000. Great profits on almost all the adventures. No bad speculations — yet neither stock nor debt to show.'

Although the junior partner in the enterprise, Cadell was gradually assuming more and more control of the business, his letters to Constable became bolder in tone as his confidence in his own ability to run the affairs of the publishing house single-handed became more sure; he was now completing business deals with only scant reference to his partner. He paid Scott £1,000 for his poem *Halidon Hill*, without having seen the manuscript, knowing that, at all costs, they must not let any work from his pen appear over any other imprint than their own. In January 1823, Cadell wrote again to Constable, stating: 'About the Works of the Author of Waverley—you and I differ so widely on this point. I feel more gratitude to that author than I can express. I know what his works do for us & see what they do for us—& fear nothing so long as the public *buy as they do and he writes as he does....*One other point only and I am done, and it is as to Banks & Bankers. *I am not surprised* at a little miff regarding us from time to time. We have been so long carrying on large transactions, and all the time with an apparent strain & want of money—they may say to themselves—"*are these men never to get easy?* are all these Reviews and Encyds. & books of the Author of Waverley, about all which we have heard of such immense profits being made—are these books never to bring them home?"!!! I have little doubt these feelings shoot often across some minds—such feelings would be soon driven away, were it not for the great, the terrible expense—we are just like two horses with a load, travelling on the same road with two having an empty cart & going downhill—we all the time going up.'[1]

But the alarms and excursions of 1823 died down as the sales of *Quentin Durward* picked up and cash started to roll in from the booksellers of London and the provinces; the printing works was as busy as ever, and at Abbotsford Sir Walter lived the life of a landed gentleman surrounded by a grateful family and a retinue of well-fed and contented servants. 'You will hardly know my premises when you see them again, and I begin to think I have flung away a good deal of money which might have been as well saved,' he wrote to Miss Clephane in January 1824. 'But having all my life certain visions respecting a house, I could not resist the temptation of realizing them, so now, like Christabel's phantom guest, the place is

A thing to dream of—not to tell.'

The late summer witnessed Abbotsford invaded by a posse of painters, varnishers, glaziers, upholsterers, cabinet makers, curtain-hangers, seamstresses and similar tradespeople; closely followed by a horde of local charwomen to scrub and sweep and

[1] Letter in the Constable MSS in the National Library of Scotland.

clean up the mess they left behind them. Except for the mysterious non-arrival of several large mirrors that had disappeared in transit from London, the house was now as fully furnished and complete as its owner could make it. It was over twelve years since the Scotts had first moved into the broken-down farm and cottage that stood at Clarty Hole, but during that period the original site and the countryside for miles around it had been so completely transformed as to be unrecognizable. And now, with the departure of the gilders engaged on burnishing the gold-leaf on the coats-of-arms with which the hall ceiling was heavily encrusted, a peaceful silence at last descended on the mansion. The din of carpenters' hammers and the metallic clanging of the masons' chisels was finally stilled, and late that autumn Sir Walter limped his way through the carpeted and curtained rooms secure in the knowledge that his dreams had at last come true. 'I will not stick my fingers into mortar again while I live,' he wrote to James Ballantyne, adding that, 'as I am rather behind with my pen, I had better ease these affairs by borrowing perhaps for two or three years, the sum of £5000 or £6000 as proposed by Hogarth.'[1]

Redgauntlet was the only novel from his pen to appear that year (*St Ronan's Well* having been published in December, 1823) and neither of these two works met with a particularly warm reception from the public. He had been forced to give a great deal of his time to editing the second edition of his monumental nineteen-volume works of Jonathan Swift, the 1814 edition having been out of print for many months. No sooner had he completed this task than he commenced writing *Tales of the Crusaders*, a four-volume work comprising *The Betrothed* and *The Talisman*. The first of these two stories was so poorly written that, according to Lockhart, Ballantyne and Constable seriously considered consigning the manuscript to the flames. The fact that most of the book was already in print prevented this, but it did not prevent James writing to Scott and telling him that the first of the two stories had little literary merit and must be called a failure; at the same time he recommended alterations to the plot that he thought might help it achieve some modicum of success. 'I am very apprehensive of finding some remedy for the failure which you justly announce,' Scott replied, 'but I greatly doubt your recipe. What has happened may happen

[1] George Hogarth, W. S., James's brother-in-law.

again under the same circumstances. Constable, I fear, had more shrewdness than either of us when he recommended a *fallow*. But we will talk over this. In the meantime, be assured that sincerity is the quality I most value in a friend or critic, and though I think you are sometimes fastidious about trifles, I never fail to consider your opinion as completely authoritative upon general results, especially when, as in this present case, it completely coincides with my own. For you must not think that, as Dorax says to Sebastian:

> *... Thou hast dared*
> *To tell me what I durst not tell myself.'*

But the companion story in the *Tales* saved the day for the ever anxious publishers. *The Talisman* received praise from critics and public alike, and the heroic exploits of a poor but doughty Scottish crusader, known as Sir Kenneth or the Knight of the Leopard, 'dazzled the eyes of the million as to the defects of the twin-story.'

In retrospect, 1824 could be seen as a year of chequered fortunes for the Scott family. At the end of January, their eldest daughter, now Mrs Lockhart, had given birth to a daughter, only to lose the infant a few days later. Sophia's surviving child, little John Hugh (the Hugh Little John of Scott's *Tales of a Grandfather*), although a bright and intelligent boy, had become increasingly unwell of late. He was attacked at intervals by an undulating fever that sometimes prostrated him for days at a time. His father was absolutely devoted to his ailing son and paced the bedroom with the thin and stunted child in his arms, hoping against hope that each fresh attack might be the last he would suffer and that the boy might grow out of them as he approached manhood. The symptoms of Johnnie's illness, as far as we can perceive them today, seem almost certainly to point to the malady from which he suffered being Pott's disease, a tubercular disease of the spine. If this diagnosis is correct it is little wonder that each succeeding year left the lad worse in health, and he finally succumbed to the disease in 1831.

The opening of 1825 was marked by the marriage of Scott's eldest son, young Lieutenant Walter Scott, to Miss Jane Jobson, niece to Sir Adam Ferguson and heiress to an estate at Lochore in Fifeshire, a lady whose husband would find himself the lucky recipient of an income of between £1,500 and £2,000 a year.

Miss Jobson's mother, whom Scott had come to describe over the marriage bargaining as an Old Tartar, had qualms about the match and had made it quite clear, through the medium of her intermediary Sir Adam Ferguson, that she expected Sir Walter to make a financial settlement in favour of his son of a size that would help to balance the amount her daughter was bringing with her. To the Highland lady's grateful astonishment, and, no doubt, to that of the Fergusons, Scott intimated that he had decided to settle the entire estate of Abbotsford upon the affianced couple, subject only to a clause giving him power to raise a mortgage of £10,000 on the property if required, and of his being permitted to enjoy the life-rent until his death. This was an immeasurably more generous settlement than Mrs Jobson had ever imagined possible and with her last doubts and hesitations removed she signed the contract with a light heart. With the law as it stood at that time, Scott had now put the mansion of Abbotsford and its surrounding estate beyond the reach of his creditors, and made his son's position there secure whatever might happen in the future. As a lawyer, he was well aware of the implications of his action, but he wished no mention of what he had done to be allowed to reach the ears of his partner Ballantyne. With this in mind, he made sure that all concerned respected the need for secrecy over the terms of the settlement.

In all his calculations respecting the solvency of the Ballantyne Press, the little printer had never failed to reckon his partner's estate as weighing down the scales on the credit side of the company's ledger—remove it from the balance and their insolvency was plain for all to see. He was well aware, when he re-entered the partnership in 1822, of the vast debts that Sir Walter had run up in the company's name, debts Scott acknowledged to be his personal responsibility and which James had always assumed were backed by the security of his lands and buildings. 'Then add Abbotsford—and there's the head for washing!' was the phrase with which he comforted himself when assessing the soundness or otherwise of the business. This expression was apparently noted without demur by his partner,[1] and was uttered without any suspicion on James's part that the lands and edifice that had consumed such vast sums, could not at any time be invoked as an asset and mortgaged in case of pressing financial necessity. The fact that his friend and con-

[1] *Refutation*, pp. 30 and 50.

fidant did not see fit to divulge to him the news that Abbotsford and its estate had been transferred to the ownership of another man, and that it no longer stood a bastion supporting the tottering walls of the Ballantyne Press, was later to come as a shock that he and his brother Sandy felt very deeply. For the present the two were kept in blissful ignorance of the action the senior partner had taken, but their awakening a few months later was to be a rude and hurtful one.

Although Mrs Jobson still shed an occasional tear at the thought of her daughter having to brave the wilds of County Cork and the austerity of life in the married quarters of an Irish barracks, she was now so far reconciled to the match as to permit the marriage ceremony to be held in her house in Edinburgh. Scott had returned to town to resume his duties at the Court of Session and the rest of the family had moved to Castle Street in order to leave Abbotsford free for the newly-weds to spend their short honeymoon alone. The baronet's wedding present to his son and daughter-in-law was £1,000 in cash, plus an extra £250 'for the purchase of immediate necessities'. On top of this he advanced Walter a further £3,500, which his son was to regard as a loan, in order that he should be able to purchase a captaincy in his regiment. £1,000 of the above came from Archibald Constable & Company for literary work still to be performed, and most of the rest was presumably found out of the loan of £5,000 George Hogarth raised for him, as mentioned in his letter to James Ballantyne. But his insatiable desire to increase the size of his estate was still upon him, and despite the manifold expenses and drains on his capital that his son's marriage had caused, we find him writing to Ballantyne as late as December 1824: 'My occasions for cash this term are £500 more heavy than I expected, owing to my having purchased for that sum three small parks which square my property at Huntly Burn and render it considerably more valuable. You will therefore be so good as to send me two bills payable on London @ £500 each & one for Galashiels.'

The marriage took place in the evening of the 3rd February, and the young couple left immediately afterwards for Abbotsford; being joined there a week later by Sir Walter and Lady Scott and their daughter Anne. They found them 'living very comfortably and quietly as if they had been house-keepers for ten years', and the more Scott came to know his daughter-in-law the more he came to realize that the diminutive Mrs Scott of Lochore (looking especially tiny by the side of her six-foot two-inch husband) was possessed of qualities that endeared her to his heart. A few days later Jane and her husband left for London on the way to rejoin his regiment in Ireland and upon their arrival in Dublin the baronet started a voluminous correspondence with his daughter-in-law that contained some of the happiest letters he ever wrote

for my part, [he wrote her] every morning I wake I think on the verse in Cymbeline:

> *The bird is flown*
> *That we have made so much of.*

The inclosed piece of paper will add a pen-feather to my pretty bird's wing since fly away she must. You have only to put your name on the back and Walter will get the contents for you. I meant to have bought a set of teaplate for you, but perhaps the most convenient, though least genteel, way is to send you the vile Mammon of unrighteousness and leave you to put it to the use most convenient...And here I ought to stop for I have twenty letters to write. But like all old papas I would rather read nonsense to my children than play *genteel, sensible* and *clever* with half the world beside. [And a few days later he wrote to her again, saying]:Believe me, my love, I am VERY grateful for the time you bestow on me and that you cannot give so great happiness to any one as to me by saying you are well and happy. My daughters, who deserve all the affection a father can bestow, are both near me and in safe guardianship; the one under the charge of a most affectionate husband, & the other under the eyes of her parents. And for my sons—I have taught them, and what was more difficult, I have taught myself, the philosophy that for their sake and their necessary advancement in life, their absence from my home must be long and their visits short, and as they are, I hope, able to conduct themselves wisely and honourably. I have learned to be contented to hope the best without making myself or them uneasy by fruitless anxiety. But for YOU, my dear Jane, who have come amongst us with such generous and confiding affection, my Stoicism must excuse me if I am more anxious than becomes either a philosopher or a hackneyed man of the world, who uses, in common cases, to take that world as it goes...I know Walter's care & affection will soften and avert these as [much] as possible, and if there be anything in the power of old papa to assist him in the matter, you will make him most happy by tasking that power to the utmost...Well then—I am the most indulgent papa in the world and so you see I have turned

over a new leaf. The plain sense of all this rambling stuff which escapes from my pen, as it would from my tongue, is that I have visited for a day, with Isaack Bayley, your dominions of Lochore, and was excellently entertained and as happy as I could be where everything was putting me in mind that she was absent whom I could most have wished present; for where everything put me in mind of my child and she was so far distant, the predominant feeling was a sort of quiet melancholy. It felt somehow like an intrusion, and as if it was not quite right that I should be in Jane's house while Jane herself was amongst strangers. This is the sort of false colouring which imagination gives to events and circumstances. Well! But I was much pleased with all I saw, & particularly with the high order Mr Bayley has put everything in. And I climbed Bennarty like a wild goat, and scrambled through the old crags like a wild cat, and pranced through your pastures like a wild buck (fat enough to be in season though) and squattered through your drains like a wild duck, and had nearly lost myself in your morasses like the Ninth Legion, and visited the old Castle (which is not a *stupit place*) and in short wandered from Dan to Beersheba and tired myself as effectually in your dominions as I did you in mine upon a certain walk to the Rhymer's Glen...I trust you will find yourself happy for a few days at Edgeworthstown, where I know you will be received with open arms, for Miss Edgeworth's kindness is equal to her distinguished talents. Meanwhile, here we are till May—that is Lady Scott, Anne and I, for the Lockharts remain in town... *Buona notte amata bene.* Good night, darling, and take good care of yourself. I will always remain, Your affectionate father,
    Walter Scott

By midsummer he could no longer contain his impatience to see his son and daughter-in-law again, and he made arrangements to leave for Ireland in July, his first visit abroad since he was in Paris in 1815. In the ten years which had passed since then he had written no less than eighteen novels, plus *Paul's Letters to his Kinsfolk* and several biographies of leading novelists of the past. In addition, he had contributed lengthy articles to the *Encyclopaedia*, the *Quarterly* and the *Edinburgh Annual Register* and carried on a voluminous correspondence with countless friends, acquaintances and strangers both at home and abroad. Then there was the *Tales of the Crusaders* on which he was still working; but even before these had finished printing, the Great Czar of Literature (as Archibald Constable was dubbed when out of earshot) arrived at Abbotsford with James Ballantyne in attendance to expound a magnificent scheme of literary endeavour that would make them all richer than their wildest dreams.

Lockhart was present while the details of the proposed new venture were being discussed, and he painted a colourful picture of the scene. After dinner was over and the ladies had withdrawn, Scott and Ballantyne sat with Lockhart round the mahogany table in the dining room sipping their whisky and water and listening in growing admiration as the florid-faced publisher, short-winded and asthmatic and his heavy features glistening with the perspiration induced by the recently consumed bottle of claret, excitedly expounded the particulars of this revolutionary plan. 'Constable explained his views in a manner that might well excite admiration, not unmixed with alarm,' Lockhart wrote. '[He] was meditating nothing less than a total revolution in the art and traffic of bookselling; and the exulting and blazing fancy with which he expanded and embellished his visions of success, hitherto undreamt of in the philosophy of the trade, might also have induced serious suspicions of his sanity, but for the curious accumulation of pregnant facts on which he rested his justification....He startled us at the outset by saying: *"Literary genius may, or may not, have done its best; but printing and bookselling, as instruments for enlightening and entertaining mankind, and, of course, for making money, are as yet in mere infancy. Yes, the trade are in their cradle."* Scott eyed the florid bookseller's beaming countenance, and the solemn stare with which the equally portly printer was listening, and, pushing round the bottles with a hearty chuckle, bade me "Give our twa *sonsie babbies* a drap o' mother's milk." Constable sucked in fresh inspiration, and proceeded to say that, wild as we might think him, his new plans had been suggested by, and were in fact mainly grounded upon, a sufficiently prosaic authority—namely the annual schedule of assessed taxes, a copy of which interesting document he drew from his pocket, and substituted for his D'Oyley.'

Within half-an-hour the publisher was well on the way to convincing his audience that his vision of the future, and a not-too-far-distant future at that, enabled him to foresee a time when even the meanest cottage had its shelf of books in the ingle-nook, and the middle-classes, that up to now had relied very largely on the circulating libraries to supply their literary needs, would be buying at least one book a month instead of borrowing them.

By mass-producing titles in sufficient quantities and casing the volumes in the recently introduced cloth bindings instead of the usual boards, he could bring down the price of his publications to a figure even an artisan could afford, 'Troth,' said Scott, 'you are indeed likely to be The Grand Napoleon of the realms of print.' 'If you outlive me,' said Constable with a regal smile, 'I bespeak that line for my tomb-stone; but, in the meantime, may I presume to ask you to be my right-hand man when I open my campaign of Marengo? I have now settled my outline of operations—a three shilling or half-crown volume every month, which must and shall sell, not by thousands or tens of thousands, but by hundreds of thousands—ay, by millions! Twelve volumes in the year, a halfpenny profit upon every copy of which will make me richer than the possession of all the copyrights of all the quartos that ever were, or will be, hot-pressed![1] Twelve volumes, so good that millions must wish to have them, and so cheap that every butcher's callant may have them—if he so pleases to let me tax him sixpence a week!'

Gifted as we now are with hindsight, we can applaud the commercial acumen displayed by the publisher when he conceived the idea of producing *Constable's Miscellany*. Carried to fruition,[2] as it would have been if circumstances had not intervened to prevent its large scale introduction, there seems little doubt that both he and his partners in the enterprise would have found themselves extremely wealthy men in the course of only a few years. Those that came after and copied his idea made themselves fortunes, and by the 'thirties and 'forties Libraries, Cyclopaedias, and Miscellanies were being issued by a dozen different houses. His scheme of producing books for the masses, at prices they could afford, foreshadowed the cheap reissues in handy format that appeared in such publications as Bentley's Standard Novel Series (one hundred and twenty-six titles between 1831–55, at

[1] This was a reference to the quarto volumes, usually of poetry or non-fictional works, produced at that time. They sold for as much as two or even three guineas a copy, putting them far out of the reach of all but the wealthiest purchasers. 'Hot-pressing' was a process used to impart an extra sheen to the printed page, but was usually subject to an added charge.

[2] In January 1827, after his bankruptcy, Constable attempted to promote his Miscellany on a small scale. Hall's *Voyages* (dated 1826) appeared in three volumes in a glazed canvas binding with paper label, priced at three shillings and sixpence a copy. In July the same year the publisher died, but the series was continued, being taken over in 1832 by Whittaker, Treacher & Company. When it finally ceased to appear in 1835, over eighty volumes had been issued.

five shillings a copy), and the 'yellow-backs' of the latter half of the nineteenth century,[1] to say nothing of the millions of paper-backs that cover the counters and shelves of bookshops in the present day. 'Your plan,' Scott told him, 'cannot fail, provided the books be really good...I am willing to do my part in this grand enterprise.' 'This is the cleverest thing that ever came into the head of the cleverest of all bibliopolic heads,' the author wrote to Lockhart ; and so the matter was settled. It was arranged that Constable should pay a visit to his monied friends in the City of London to raise the capital that would set the machinery in motion which would turn out pocket-sized volumes by the million. And it was further proposed that Sir Walter should start the ball rolling forthwith by writing 'the most wonderful book which the world ever read—a book in which every incident shall be incredible, yet strictly true—a book recalling recollections with which the ears of this generation tingled, and which shall be read by our children, with an admiration approaching incredulity. Such shall be the *Life of Napoleon Bonaparte* by the Author of *Waverley*.'

With details of these grandiose money-making schemes filling his imagination, he set out with an excitement he had not felt for many years for his promised holiday in Ireland. On the 14th July he reached Dublin, accompanied by his daughter Anne and his son-in-law Lockhart, and went to stay with Walter (now a Captain) and Jane in their house in St Stephen's Green. No man of letters ever had such a reception in the Irish capital as Sir Walter Scott. From the day of his arrival a constant succession of carriages drew up at his door filled with notable figures from every walk of life. The Lord-Lieutenant, the Archbishop of Dublin, the Attorney-General, the Commander-in-Chief, and a procession of lords and ladies from the city and surrounding counties came in a constant stream to leave their

[1] 'Yellow-backs' first appeared in 1854, with the publication of Maria S. Cummins' *The Lamplighter*. This tale was issued in pictorial paper covered boards, colour printed from wood blocks, using a new process invented by Edmund Evans. It was a cheaply produced but lurid type of cover, designed to catch the eye of travellers on the railways and other readers who might be induced to part with a shilling for the purchase of a book. The first title produced in pictorial paper covers by Edmund Evans' process was Horace Mayhew's *Letters Left at the Pastry Cook's*, published in 1853. This cover had a white paper base, and to lessen the risk of soiling the trade asked for a toned paper. Titles which followed had their covers printed on yellow paper—hence 'yellow-backs'.

cards and wish him well. Before he said goodbye to Dublin the honorary degree of Doctor of Laws was conferred upon him, and life in the capital had resolved itself into attendance at one reception and dinner after the other. Crowds gathered to cheer his carriage in the streets, and when he visited the theatre to see a performance of *Much Ado About Nothing* the play was interrupted by the audience calling upon him to make a speech. Most of those he met respected his wish to keep up the charade regarding the authorship of the Waverley novels; but one university professor put his foot in it by saying: 'I have been so busy that I have not yet read your *Redgauntlet*.' 'I have not happened to fall in with such a work, Doctor,' Scott dryly informed him.

The month-long visit was a continual ovation. 'I well intended to have written from Ireland,' he informed Joanna Baillie after his return. 'But, alas! Hell, as some stern old divine says, is paved with good intentions. There was such a whirl of visiting and laking and boating and wandering and shouting and laughing and carouzing, so much to see and so little time to see it, so much to be heard and only two ears to listen to twenty voices, that upon the whole I grew desperate and gave up all thoughts of doing what was right and proper upon post-days....I have not the pen of our friend Maria Edgeworth, who writes all the while she laughs, talks, eats, drinks, and, I believe, though I do not pretend to be so far in the secret, all the time she sleeps too....We had Lockhart to say clever things, and Walter with his whiskers to overawe postillions and impudent beggars, and Jane to bless herself that the folks had neither houses, clothes nor furniture, and Anne to make fun from morning to night,

And merry folks were we.'

Of course there were bills to pay. 'I was in Ireland last summer and had a most delightful tour.' he wrote in his journal after his return. 'It cost me £500, including £100 left with Walter and Jane, for we travelled a large party and in style.' But he comforted himself with the thought that there was plenty more to be had where this six hundred had come from.

On the 28th August, he was back home at Abbotsford, and the last real holiday he was ever to enjoy was over and done with. He settled down immediately to start work on his *Life of Napoleon* which was to form the first three volumes of the 'Miscellany' and about which Constable had written him that the announcement of the *Memoirs of Napoleon* 'has excited the interest we anticipated. I have already had various applications on the subject of French and German editions.' But he found the task far harder than he had anticipated. 'He read and noted and indexed with the pertinacity of some pale compiler in the British Museum,' Lockhart wrote, 'but rose from such employment, not radiant and buoyant, as after he had been feasting himself among the teeming harvests of Fancy, but with an aching brow, and eyes in which the dimness of years had begun to plant some specks before they were subjected again to that straining over small print and difficult manuscript, which had, no doubt, been familiar to them in the early time when (in Shortreed's phrase) "he was making himself"....It now often made me sorry to catch a glimpse of him, stooping and poring with his spectacles amidst piles of authorities, a little note-book ready in his left hand, that had always used to be at liberty for patting Maida.'

A task of such complexity and length (the work finally filled nine octavo volumes) would have been a full time occupation of several years for a qualified historian; yet Scott, it must be remembered, for nearly six months of every year was tied to his desk in the Court of Session for several hours a day. Not content with the task in hand, he decided to break the monotony of his researches by starting a new novel, and by the 6th November he was writing to James Ballantyne: 'I have begun *Woodstock*— your doubt about the title may be supplied by an additional one.'

What time he had at his country seat was constantly interrupted by his never ending stream of distinguished visitors; 'Lord and Lady Ravensworth and their son Mr Liddell are staying here; they are all very pleasant.' (20th September). 'We have a large houseful just now, Lord and Lady Gifford, Lord Chief Baron and Lady Shepherd, besides two friends of Lord Sidmouth....There is the Solicitor too, by the way...We have the Russells with us for ten days.' (11th October) 'John Richardson has been here....' (12th October) 'We expect the great Mrs Coutts today, bringing in her train the Duke of St Albans and his sister.' (25th October) 'Mrs Coutts, good lady, has taken possession of my home and kicks up a row which would be less troublesome at any other time.' (26th October) 'Thomas Moore is here and in grand feather.' (To James Ballantyne, 6th November). And so it went on, month after month; Sir Walter slipping away for an hour or two's peaceful writing in his study, then reappearing to act the part of host at a crowded dinner table, the sideboards piled with food, and the attentive servants quick to fill the empty glasses of his appreciative guests.

One other visitor must be mentioned; for he helped to influence John Gibson Lockhart's choice of a future career in a way that decided his destiny for many years to come. On the 27th September there appeared unexpectedly 'a sprig of the rod of Aaron, young d'Israeli.' He had brought a message from John Murray, the owner of the right-wing review *The Quarterly*, offering Lockhart the editorship of a daily paper he projected, to be called the *Representative*, at a starting salary of £1,000 a year. Benjamin Disraeli had been sent north by Murray to use his persuasive tongue in an effort to induce Lockhart to accept, for the reputation he had made for himself by his contributions to *Blackwood's Magazine* made him just the sort of man the publisher needed to launch the new enterprise with an impact that would ensure its success.

In his memoirs, Disraeli recalled meeting Archibald Constable there, and described Scott as being a 'rather stately person: with his pile of forehead, sagacious eye, white hair and green shooting-coat....I have seen him sitting in his armchair in his beautiful library...with half-a-dozen terriers about him: in his lap, on his shoulders, at his feet....As I came down to dinner, Sir Walter was walking up and down the hall with a very big, stout, florid man, apparently in earnest conversation. I was introduced to him before dinner as Mr Constable—the famous publisher of the *Edinburgh Review* and the *Waverley Novels*, the authorship not then acknowledged. It struck me that I had never met before such an ostentatious man, or one whose conversation was so braggart. One would think that he had written the *Waverley Novels* himself; and certainly that Abbotsford belonged to him. However, he seemed to worship Scott and to express his adoration....'

In the second week of October, Lockhart and Disraeli travelled up to London together to meet John Murray, the former carrying a letter from Scott to Constable who had been in the capital a week seeking funds with which to launch his Miscellany. Murray's eagerness to secure Lockhart's services enabled the younger man to drive a hard bargain and gain for himself the post he coveted. William Gifford, for many years the editor of

The Quarterly had resigned the post on the grounds of ill-health in 1824, and John Taylor Coleridge, a lawyer and a nephew of the poet, had been appointed to fill the chair. Southey had previously been offered the job but had turned it down, later expressing the hope that, with Coleridge in control, there would be an end 'of that injustice and cruelty (for example) which was shown towards Keats.' Within a few months Murray showed that he had lost faith in the new editor's ability to manage the paper with the success he thought such an important publication deserved, and he started looking around for a suitable replacement. The bargain he concluded with Lockhart is explained by a letter the publisher wrote to Scott on the 15th October: 'I have proposed to Mr Lockhart to come to London as the editor of the *Quarterly* — an appointment which I verily believe is coveted by many of the highest literary characters in the country, and which of itself would entitle its possessor to enter into and mix with the first classes of society. For this, without writing a line, but merely performing the duties of an editor, I shall have the pleasure of allowing him a thousand pounds a year; and this, with contributions of his own, might easily become £1500.' In addition to this Lockhart was given a share in the *Representative*, the profit of which it was hoped would amount to about £1500. Sophia, and all at Abbotsford, were delighted at the good news. and the fact that another member of his immediate family would soon be settled comfortably with a lucrative career before him, enabled Scott to settle back in his favourite chair that night, with the inevitable dram of whisky and choice cigar, pervaded with a contented feeling of rosy euphoria. All was well with his world and it was good to be alive.

12

BUT IN THE heart of Britain's financial empire, the mighty bulk of Archibald Constable was being rudely buffeted as he puffed his ponderous way up the stone steps and through the heavy oak doors of one banking house after the other. His legs swollen by dropsy and one foot bandaged against the gout, he described himself as 'a helpless old fellow, who must take a man-servant along with me' in a letter to J. O. Robinson, of Hurst, Robinson & Company, the firm of London publishers with whom the fortunes of his own business were now so intimately entwined. He had been in the capital only a day or two when he discovered that he had chosen a most unpropitious time to endeavour to raise capital for any new commercial enterprise. The year 1825 had witnessed a mad whirl of speculation sweep through the City of London, the lure of easy profits spreading a wave of get-rich-quick mania that caused uproar on the floor of the Stock Exchange as orders poured in from far and wide to Buy! Buy! Buy! at prices that made brokers believe that the sky was the limit as far as their clients were concerned. 'The people are all mad about joint-stock companies,' Scott had written to Maria Edgeworth in March, 'and the madness which possesses John Bull has caught his speculative brother Sawney.' Then suddenly there came a pause, a flurry of selling, a bankruptcy or two, a scramble to unload by the first to take fright, then a wave of panic selling that brought prices tumbling and a series of suicides amongst those who had held on and now found themselves utterly ruined. There was a run on the banks, made far worse by a credit-squeeze imposed by the Bank of England which was itself embarrassed by the withdrawal of funds on a scale unprecedented. Robinson had speculated over £40,000 in hops, in an effort to corner the market in a commodity in which fortunes had been made in recent years, only to find that the market was glutted and the brewers refused to purchase further supplies. He was forced to sell at rock bottom prices, and the moneylender from whom he had borrowed £30,000 'at an usurious rate of interest', a Mr Green of Enfield, refused to advance another penny and was now demanding the return of his capital. This was the mêlée into which a smiling Archibald Constable innocently limped his way in the expectation of returning to Edinburgh with the promise of sufficient funds to launch his Miscellany. He was not only rudely disappointed but horrified to find that Hurst, Robinson & Company were themselves having the utmost difficulty in meeting their obligations.

Back in Edinburgh, Robert Cadell was startled to discover that instead of the expected drafts from London, the publishers there were suddenly making urgent demands for money to be sent them immediately at whatever rates of interest the lenders liked to demand. 'I write today on account of a letter I have from Robinson about cash,' he wrote anxiously to Constable, 'which has put me completely out of sorts, as I am utterly at a loss what to do. He says, draw £10,000 on Dixon & Co., and £10,000 on Carstairs, *and remit me in course of post*. He might as well say, draw the same sums on the Bank of England. It was only on Wednesday that we increased Carstairs above £2000 for ourselves in consequence of repeated refusals at the various banks. His account is very high (£12,000). As to Brooks & Co., it is higher just now than ever it was (£16,000), and they gave us a growl the other day. It would be madness to do what Robinson says—I mean to the extent: absolute madness. It would utterly demolish our credit...We cannot get one shilling of London from Sandy Smith; if we could, I might have taken £2000 on credit, and got it paid somehow. His want has compelled me to assail Dickinson to meet our bills at Brooks & Co., also Hood's for a small bill. We have to provide Brooks & Co., with £14,700 in November, and God only knows how it is to be got! They have refused us discount just now, but I have asked for a little in November in order to help us.' Next day he despatched another letter in much the same vein: 'There is nothing that I would not do to do Robinson all the good in our power; but at present I see no practicable plan without endangering our own safety. I know well that Robinson and we are one and the same in some points of view, and the mutual credit of both must be maintained; but after what we have done, more, at this moment, is past our power.'

He managed to raise enough to satisfy the needs of the immediate position, but the deeply anxious tone of his partner's letters galvanized Constable into action. As soon as he perceived the rapidly worsening state of affairs at Princes Street, he hurried to seek assistance from some of his monied friends in the City; then on to his bankers, Dixon & Company, to quiet their fears by informing them that his mission in the capital was to liquidate as much of his firm's stock as possible in order to reduce his overdraft. He met with a very cool reception. 'I was in Abchurch Lane today,' he wrote to Cadell on the 31st October. 'Mr Carstairs is at Ramsgate. I saw Mr Cheape, who said the Joint-Stock Companies had done a great deal of mischief, and would do more. On my way I called at Dixon & Co's, where I had hoped, from the amount of your remittances, to find matters improved. I regret to say I found them far from it. Mr D said the amount of the accounts must be reduced — that *their own credit* was at stake — the old drafts not paid when new ones were presented would never do. He said he was just about sending for me to have a conversation on the subject...There is a general *distrust* at the present moment with everybody.' Next day he was summoned to his banker's again and told, in no uncertain terms, that he must forthwith reduce the amount of his firm's indebtedness by at least £2,000 a month until their overdraft was down to £8,000. Constable had no alternative but to agree.

The anxious publisher left London for his home at Polton near Lasswade, about six miles from Edinburgh, on 3rd November, arriving there on the 7th in a completely exhausted physical state. He was an extremely worried man, but he was far too unwell to attend his office and was confined to bed for over a fortnight, Cadell being forced to send out a clerk so that Constable could dictate the letters he was too ill to write. About ten days after the publisher's return to Scotland, Lockhart, now back in Scotland, received a letter from his friend William Wright, a barrister at Lincoln's Inn and at whose rooms he had stayed when in London, to the effect that rumours in the City had it that Archibald Constable had fled from the capital a ruined man due to his banker closing his account and refusing to honour any further cheques drawn upon it. This shattering piece of information Lockhart immediately communicated by letter to Scott, who was then in Edinburgh,[1] and the shocked and

---

[1] In his biography of Scott, Lockhart set out to deliberately mislead his readers by inventing a dramatic tale of Scott being told the news at Abbotsford,

anxious author hastened round to his publisher's office to demand an explanation.

Cadell had gone to considerable trouble during the previous few weeks to ensure that no hint of the mounting financial difficulties confronting Archibald Constable & Company and their London agents should reach his ears. The very last thing either he or his partner wanted was that Scott should lose confidence in the firm and perhaps approach another publishing house for the financial accommodation he so frequently required. Any hint that he had gone elsewhere to market his works would destroy what little remaining confidence the bankers had in their ability to one day clear their debts; for the publication of each succeeding novel was in itself an exceedingly profitable transaction, as the finance houses were well aware. Unfortunately, these gentlemen also knew that the loans raised by the company in the past, and constantly renewed ever since, now carried interest at rates that swallowed these profits and much more besides, and that the weight of debt which encumbered the under-capitalized concern increased with every passing year. Borrowing from Peter to pay Paul was now a pre-occupation in which the partners were constantly engaged, but any breath of suspicion regarding their ability to meet their obligations would slam every banker's door in their faces and leave them stranded in all their nakedness. So far, by advances from London and elsewhere, usually from Hurst, Robinson & Company for the marketing rights of Scott's novels (although Constable had lately been driven to mortgaging his house at Polton to the hilt 'to the

---

ordering his carriage to be brought round to his door, then whipping up the horses for a wild night drive to confront Constable at Polton. The facts are that Constable left London early in November, reaching his home on the 7th. He reported his arrival back in Scotland in a letter to Scott on the 11th; a thing he had no need to do if they had already met since his return. Scott was back in Edinburgh that same day, and it was not until the 18th that he received from Lockhart the letter in which Wright announced having heard that Constable was ruined. He went immediately to see Cadell, who reassured him all was well. That same afternoon Scott wrote to Lockhart: 'Your kind and attentive letter gave me a shock...' etc., and then went on to inform his son-in-law that he found all was well at the publishers and the rumours Wright had heard in London must have been false. Lockhart's tale, that on receiving Wright's letter: 'I rode over to Abbotsford to communicate its contents. I found Sir Walter alone, over his glass of whisky and water and cigar...I gave him Mr Wright's letter to read...', etc., followed by his story of Scott having returned next morning after his all-night journey to Polton and back, is clearly another of his inventions, inserted solely for the dramatic effect it created.

extent that it would not stand another £100'), they had just managed to scrape through unscathed. Bills were somehow met on the due date and their credit-worthiness, although low, had not been entirely destroyed. But let one of their drafts be returned with payment refused, or one bill-of-exchange find no funds to meet it on the due date, and the bubble would burst with an irrepairable POP!

Cadell had seen to it that a bond payable to Scott, which could have been met a little later by taking advantage of the days of grace granted in such cases, was covered by a bill-of-exchange to the full amount of £2,500 on the due date: at the same time, to the surprise of the author's solicitor, John Gibson, they had nonchalantly refused the proffered accommodation note of the same amount saying they had no need to take advantage of this service at the present time. This was a confidence-inspiring manœuvre that impressed Sir Walter and was now to stand them in good stead. Although his sudden visit to the Princes Street offices was totally unexpected, Cadell received him calmly, acting his part confidently and well. He pooh-poohed the story of Constable's flight from London as being too ridiculous to demand any explanation, and produced what he said was documentary proof of their financial soundness in the form of a letter from their London bankers. Sir Walter left him thoroughly reassured and wrote the same evening to Lockhart to put his fears at rest.

I saw Cadell and told him that I had heard from a friendly person towards them and me & by letter from London, that their affairs were in bad order & that Constable had left town in consequence of his Bankers having abruptly closed his accompt. He listened gravely but without the least concern...I mentioned the circumstance of Mr Robinson having been engaged in business out of the bookselling line. Cadell said that more than a year ago he knew that when money was plentiful he had advanced £1000 on a speculation about hops which had brought immense profit, but did not believe he was engaged in any other. He added that Constable had done no business in London except about the Miscellany.

All this, especially the banker's letter, and the fact that they paid to myself within these four days £2500 which they might have retained, and were willing, if I pleased, to pay me as much more since, [has] put the matter entirely at rest, on which I heartily felicitate myself & you...I think the report has originated in the difficulties of the moneyed markets which even the greatest houses must feel a little, and in the bankruptcy of a great bookseller lately,[1] which always sets on foot similar reports of failures in the same line & Constable may have had some pinch for the moment. But men who refuse the loan of £2500 when offered and offer an advance of the same sum when it was not called for, cannot be in any real distress.

For the moment the bluff succeeded and Scott returned to Castle Street with a far lighter heart than when he left it. He settled down to continue his literary work and two days later commenced the inimitable record of his thoughts and actions which, had he written nothing else, would have ensured him the immortality that has now been accorded by a grateful posterity to Samuel Pepys. He decided to keep a journal[2] in which he daily recorded his memories, hopes and fears, and although he stated that he was prompted to do this by 'seeing lately some volumes of Byron's notes', a more likely explanation was that Pepys himself was the diarist he wished to emulate. The two-volume quarto containing the edited transcript of the shorthand notes made by the seventeenth-century Secretary to the Admiralty had appeared for the first time early that summer; Scott had read the entire work by December, and in the following January he sent Lockhart an article regarding it for inclusion in that month's *Quarterly*. Soon after reading Pepys's *Diary* he ordered from his binder two quarto volumes. These were to be bound in vellum and fitted with locks, and on the 20th November, 1825, he opened volume one, smoothed down the blank pages, and wrote the first words in the journal he was henceforth to keep, with only one or two short breaks, until the final months of

[1] George Byrom Whittaker, a wholesale bookseller of Ave Maria Lane, London, about whom Scott wrote (*Journal*, 18th December, 1826). 'Whitaker, the rascally bookseller, whose slip for £200,000 or thereabouts has brought ruin nearly on the trade, kept seven hunters and be damned to him. He must have ridden a fine weight to be sure with £200,000 of honest people's cash about him.'

[2] The journal was first published in two volumes in 1890 (second edition in one volume in 1891). Unfortunately, the editor, David Douglas, saw fit to correct 'obvious slips of the pen', as he called not only omissions and spelling mistakes, but any words or phrases he found difficult to decipher. In some cases this resulted in Scott's original meaning being completely obscured or even twisted to read the opposite to what he intended. Those wishing to refer to an accurate transcription of the work are advised to consult the three-volume definitive edition edited by J. G. Tait and published by Oliver and Boyd of Edinburgh in 1939–46. This text is taken from a photostat in the National Library of Scotland. The original journal is now in the Pierpont Morgan Library, New York, U.S.A.

his life. Its biographical worth is inestimable, both as a study of the man himself and of the age in which he lived. He revealed his innermost thoughts without reticence and with only the occasional posturing of a man who was well aware that his words would one day be read by the generations who were yet to come. Scott's journal is the most honest and sincere of all his productions, allowing us to glimpse the real personality behind the façade he was too often forced to erect to deceive an inquisitive world. Without it the annals of English literature would be much the poorer.

Meanwhile, a few streets away, Robert Cadell paced his room, unable to sleep as he wrestled with the problem of how they were to meet their December bills and discarding plan after plan as he sought to find a way to save Hurst, Robinson & Company from going under. On the 21st he wrote to Constable, telling him frankly that he now saw no alternative but to enlist Scott's aid to try and save the sinking ship. News of the financial panic in London was now common knowledge in Edinburgh, restrictions on credit were being imposed by the Scottish banks, and whichever way he looked at the situation things seemed to be going from bad to worse. On the receipt of his letter, Constable wrote him from Polton: 'I have just tried whether I could, *with any safety*, attempt walking or moving about so as to go to town and consult with you, but I find I must not attempt it. Tomorrow I hope I shall be stronger, and see you, which you cannot doubt I have deep anxiety to do. For this day deliberate, and let us be prepared to see Sir Walter Scott tomorrow. Perhaps you had as well enclose or give him Robinson's letter,[1] and just plump the question as to £10,000 through his influence. providing it can be without explanations to *banks*, which would ruin all. It must be in the way of two bonds, say £5000 each, Sir Walter getting Robinson's acceptances for the whole, their security and ours also to the bonds....If Robinson keep Glyn and Co. right,[2] and if all continues well with us and Dixon, there is not so much to dread; but either going wrong would be the first approach of ruin.'

'I have had no rest all night, my fears are so great,' Cadell

[1] J. O. Robinson had written to Constable requesting immediate aid to the extent of £10,000.
[2] Glyn & Company were the House used by Hurst, Robinson & Company for discounting their bills.

replied, heading his letter 'Half-past Five o'clock, Tuesday morning.' 'I am clear that we should, in candour to Sir W Scott, let him know how Robinson stands. If we don't, he might say, "*Why did you not tell me? I could have given you some aid.*"' Taking the bull by the horns Cadell walked round to Paul's Works and bluntly informed James Ballantyne that their London agents were having the greatest difficulty in meeting their obligations and at all costs funds must somehow be found to tide them over the next few weeks. Constable and Company had backed the bills of Hurst, Robinson & Company; James Ballantyne & Company had backed the bills of Constable & Company: all three concerns were roped together on a slippery slope of dissolving credit with none of them able to belay round one really solid security. Let any of them loose their grip—and Hurst, Robinson & Company were only holding by their finger-tips— and all the partners in all three of the companies would be dragged down into a common disgrace. Of these latter facts the agitated Ballantyne was already well aware, and before many hours had passed so was Sir Walter Scott.

13

'HERE IS MATTER for a May morning—but much fitter for a November one.' So wrote Scott in his journal as the realization of how deeply he was involved in the financial turmoil taking place in the City of London first dawned upon him. 'The general distress in the city has affected H. and R.,[1] Constable's great agents. Should they *go*, it is not likely that Constable can stand, and such an event would lead to great distress and perplexity on the part of J. B.[allantyne] and myself…I had a lesson in 1814 which should have done good upon me. But success and abundance erased it from my mind. But this is no time for journalizing or moralizing either. Necessity is like a sour-faced Cook-maid, and I a turn-spit whom she has flogged ere now till he mounted his wheel. If *Woodstock* can be out by 25th January it will do much, and it is possible…' Later: 'Could not write to purpose for thick-coming fancies; the wheel would not turn easily, and cannot be forced.'

The awakening had come. Before the month was out Scott signed a bond with Constable for £5,000 to help ease the pressure on their London agents. A few days later the Lockhart family left for London to enable the new editor of the *Quarterly* to take up his post. 'Left us early and without leave-taking; when I arose at eight o'clock they were *gone*. This was very right, I hate red eyes and blowing of noses. *Agere et pati Romanum est.* Of all schools commend me the Stoics…I have lost some of the comforts to which I chiefly looked for enjoyment. Well, I must make the more of such as remain—God bless them.' And, despite the weight of worry which now oppressed his spirit, Scott picked up his pen and drove himself to continue writing *Woodstock*.

For a few weeks Hurst, Robinson & Company managed to stave off the more pressing of their creditors by raising short term loans at whatever cost they had to pay, and the news reaching Edinburgh from London became a little better. But affairs

[1] Hurst, Robinson & Company.

in the City remained extremely precarious. The rickety foundations supporting so many of the businesses that had mushroomed
during the boom years meant that a large proportion of them
could collapse at the first sharp nudge of public doubt. These
speculative, under-capitalized concerns traded almost entirely
on credit of one sort or another, relying for their continued
existence on the goodwill of finance houses who were themselves
often egg-shell affairs. Banks, at that time, were able to grant
credit and issue notes without firmly backing these transactions
by gold and securities; so that the whole elaborate paper façade
of bills-of-exchange, accommodation notes, counter notes, and
I.O.U.s needed only a zephyr of doubt to collapse in a tangle of
ruin. The failure of several joint-stock companies was the first
indication that something was seriously wrong and in December
the whole elaborate commercial structure creaked and swayed
as company after company declared themselves unable to meet
their obligations. James Ballantyne was the first to hear that
things were again seriously amiss with Constable's London
agents, and after a sleepless night he hurried round to Castle
Street before breakfast to break the news to Scott. After hearing
the depressing tidings from the grim-faced printer, the author
retired with a sinking heart to his study and unlocked his vellum
bound journal.

December 18.
  Ballantyne called on me this morning. *Venit illa suprema dies.*
My extremity is come. Cadell has received letters from London
which all but positively announce the failure of Hurst and
Robinson so that Constable & Co. must follow and I must go with
poor James Ballantyne for company.
  I suppose it will involve my all. But if they leave me £500, I can
make it £1000 or £1200 a year. And if they take my salaries of
£1300 and £300, they cannot but give me something out of them.
I have been rash in anticipating funds to buy land, but then I made
from £5000 to £10,000 a year, and land was my temptation. I think
nobody can lose a penny—that is one comfort. Men will think pride
has had a fall. Let them indulge their own pride in thinking that
my fall makes them higher or seem so at least. I have the satisfaction to recollect that my prosperity has been of advantage to
many, and that some at least will forgive my transient wealth on
account of the innocence of my intentions and my real wish to do
good to the poor. This news will make sad hearts at Darnick and in
the cottages of Abbotsford which I do not nourish the least hope of

preserving. It has been my Delilah, and so I have often termed it; and now—the recollections of the extensive woods I have planted, and the walks I have formed, from which strangers must derive both the pleasure and the profit, will excite feelings likely to sober my gayest moments. I have half resolved never to see the place again. How could I tread my hall with such a diminished crest? How live a poor indebted man where I was once the wealthy—the honoured? My children are provided [for]—thank God for that. I was to have gone there on Saturday in joy and prosperity to receive my friends—my dogs will wait for me in vain. It is foolish—but the thoughts of parting from these dumb creatures have moved me more than any of the painful reflections I have put down. Poor things, I must get them kind masters. There may be yet those who, loving me, may love my dog because it has been mine. I must end this, or I shall lose the tone of mind with which men should meet distress.

The lands and buildings of Abbotsford were safely beyond the reach of his creditors; the settlement he had made in favour of his son and daughter-in-law had seen to that. But he knew that his life-rent of the property was vulnerable and that, if things came to the worst, he could be dispossessed. His furniture, antiques, books and personal belongings could be stripped from him and sold to pay his debts, the lands let out to farmers for the rent they would bring during his lifetime, and the property offered to whichever tenant would pay the most. This knowledge wrung his heart and dampened his thoughts with a forgivable measure of self-pity as he realized the full implications of what had happened.

I find my dogs' feet on my knees—I hear them whining and seeking me everywhere. This is nonsense, but it is what they would do could they know how things are. Poor Will Laidlaw! poor Tom Purdie! this will be news to wring your hearts, and many a poor fellow's besides to whom my prosperity was daily bread.

Ballantyne behaves like himself, and sinks his own ruin in contemplating mine. I tried to enrich him indeed, and now all—all is gone. He will have the journal[1] still, that is a comfort, for sure they cannot find a better Editor. *They*—alas—who will *they* be—the *unbekannten Obern* who are to dispose of my all as they will? Some hard-eyed banker; some of those men of millions whom I

[1] *Edinburgh Weekly Journal*, printed at Paul's Works, and of which James Ballantyne was editor in name, although his brother Sandy actually carried out the task.

described. Cadell showed more kind and personal feeling to me than I thought he possessed. He says there are some properties of works that will revert to me, the copy-money not being paid. But it cannot be any very great matter, I should think.

His wife and daughter, who were with him at Castle Street, had to be informed, and they naturally were shocked and angry at the news. Lady Scott was far from well; she had suffered from asthma for some years, but lately pains in her chest had become severe and she sometimes had the greatest difficulty in breathing. A weak heart was causing circulatory troubles and a tendency to dropsy. She took the news badly, her husband writing that she 'did not afford me all the sympathy I expected.... She thinks I have been imprudent, trusting men so far. Perhaps so—but whatsoever I do I must sell my books to some one, and these folks gave me the largest price.'

Scott seems to have remained most of the day in the seclusion of his study for his journal entry alone runs to nearly two thousand words. As his spirits rose or sank he penned his thoughts as the mood possessed him.

> ...to save Abbotsford I would attempt all that was possible. My heart clings to the place I have created. There is scarce a tree on it that does not owe its being to me, and the pain of leaving it is greater than I can tell. I have about £10,000 of Constable's,[1] for which I am bound to give literary value, but if I am obliged to pay other debts for him, I will take leave to retain this sum at his credit. We shall have some *kittle* questions of literary property amongst us. Once more, 'Patience, cousin, and shuffle the cards.'

At half-past eight that evening Robert Cadell suddenly burst in with the news that letters had arrived from London saying that Hurst, Robinson & Company had stood the storm that had brought other houses crashing down. They were clamouring for assistance from Constable & Company, but said that prices on the Stock Exchange had risen strongly indicating that confidence was being quickly restored. This last piece of news was quite untrue, as the quartette of Edinburgh business men discovered a few days later; but for the moment Scott's spirits rose and he thanked Cadell profusely for the tiding he had brought.

Knowing the vast amount of money he owed the creditors of James Ballantyne & Company, the relief Scott felt at the better

---

[1] This sum had been advanced by the publisher for novels as yet unwritten.

news can well be imagined. The fears he and James Ballantyne had entertained that their ruin was imminent evaporated somewhat and tension at Paul's Works and Castle Street relaxed in a way that the London and Edinburgh publishing houses had fervently hoped that it would. The breathing space which the falsely optimistic tidings from the City afforded was made use of by Constable and Cadell to raise money from their friends and business acquaintances by assertions of confidence in their own and that of their London agents' resources. These measures, hopeless in themselves, spread the range of disaster even further than it would normally have gone. Later, due to this charge being brought against him by men furious at the needless ruin he had helped to cause, Cadell found the banks unwilling to grant him his discharge from bankruptcy when he applied to them for relief.

During the whole of the latter half of December and the first two weeks of January, Cadell worked day and night to try and retrieve their financial position, at the same time taking certain measures which he hoped would stand him in good stead if the worst happened. For much of this period Constable was *hors de combat* but a continual stream of letters passed between him and his partner and J. O. Robinson in London. Pressure was put on James Ballantyne to raise every penny he could, but the financial affairs of the printing house were now as precarious as the publishers', for the credit squeeze had hit them just as hard. 'I missed you today by a few seconds,' Cadell wrote to his partner on the evening of the 13th December. 'You were driving round the corner of the Bridge when I emerged from Ballantyne's. I have there done what I considered a duty. I found Jas. B's matters covered to Saturday only, and at once got him to agree to represent along with me the *instant necessity* of Sir W borrowing £10,000 on Abbotsford. I wrote a letter on the spot which James B enclosed. George Hogarth came in at this moment and said he could get the money in twenty-four hours. The letter was despatched forthwith. I do not know how he may receive it, but I know this, if we do not all of us exert ourselves, our occupation will soon end...And now let me entreat of you to exert yourself; it is just now for all; I see it as clear as the sun; and if you have any means that you can make available, now is the time. I have done and am doing all that is practicable. I have from private friends £2500....Things are to me so gloomy that my countenance has obliged me to tell Mrs Cadell of the dangers that threaten us.'

On Christmas Eve Scott left with his family for Abbotsford 'with a light heart', having in the meantime taken advantage of the clause in the agreement that allowed him to raise a mortgage of £10,000 on the house and lands. He excused himself for doing this by stating that he intended to repay '£3000 due to old Moss's daughter, and £5000 to the Misses Ferguson, in whole or part', which were yet another series of debts he had allowed to accumulate during recent years. Regarding the debt of £3,000, this was itself a mortgage on the Kaeside part of the estate and had to be paid back and deducted from the total sum raised, as it ranked as part of the £10,000 he was authorized to borrow. He therefore received a cheque for only £7,000, and of this £4,000 went immediately to pay bills he had raised through James Ballantyne & Company and which they had no funds to meet; the rest went to Archibald Constable & Company to cover some of the bills which were being presented at their bankers and which otherwise would be dishonoured.

At this stage in the drama, Scott appears to have deluded himself that he and the company he owned were all but in the clear financially; although knowing the vast amount of bills bearing the firm's name that would shortly be clamouring for payment it is difficult to understand how he was able to deceive himself in such a fashion. 'I was damnable bilious till matters were safe,' he wrote to his son just before Christmas. 'All engagements I ever made with Constable and his friends have been most honourably acquitted and I have now less doubt of them than ever.' But the worry of the past few weeks had left its mark and on the 5th January he had what seems to have been a slight stroke. There was no paralysis or loss of speech; nevertheless the effects seriously alarmed him. He had been for a walk in the grounds with his friends James Skene and Colonel Russell before sitting down at his desk to start work. 'To my horror and surprise,' he wrote in his journal, 'I could neither write nor spell but put down one word for another, and wrote nonsense. I was much overpowered at the same time, and could not conceive the reason. I fell asleep, however, in my chair, and slept for two hours.' At first he comforted himself with the thought that the symptoms might have been caused by a sleeping draught he had taken the night before, but when he wrote to James Ballantyne a few days later, enclosing some sheets of manuscript, he added a note stating that he hoped they would not 'smack of the Apoplexy.' Later events show that his diagnosis was almost certainly correct.

He enjoyed a week or two's comparative peace at Abbotsford, working on *Woodstock* and making notes for his *Life of Napoleon*. But on the 14th January he was jerked into sudden awareness that the crisis was by no means over when he received a hurriedly scrawled note from Constable that renewed all his fears and brought back the sleepless nights he had experienced so frequently in mid-December. 'An odd mysterious letter from Constable, who is gone post to London to put something to rights which is wrong betwixt them, their banker, and another monied friend,' he wrote anxiously that evening. 'It strikes me to be that sort of letter which I have seen men write when they are desirous that their disagreeable intelligence should rather be apprehended than avowed. I thought he had been in London a fortnight ago, disposing of property to meet this exigence, and so I think he should. Well—I must have patience. But these tirrits and frights are truly annoying.'

Had he but known it, all was already lost. What the partners of all three concerns had dreaded for so long had finally come to pass. The first of the impending avalanche of dud cheques, worthless bills-of-exchange, and broken promises-to-pay had been returned marked 'Refer to Drawer'. The tender fabric masking their inadequacies had at last been rent: a bill for £1,000, made out by Robinson in favour of the Edinburgh publishing house (which had long since drawn the money and spent it) found no funds to meet it on the due date. The Bank of Scotland immediately informed all its branches and the head offices of other banks of what had occurred and the shutters came down with a bang.

Ill though he was, Archibald Constable braved the shaking discomfort of a dash to the south in a final effort to stave off disaster. The letters he had received from the London publishers just prior to payment being stopped had made it clear that disaster was imminent, and he posted day and night, heaving himself into one freshly horsed carriage after another and rising before dawn at coaching inns to catch the earliest stage, until he finally reached his destination at Osborne's Hotel in the City. The following day, in company with James Robinson and

Thomas Hurst, he made his painful way from one banker's or money-lender's office to another, cap in hand and beseeching aid at whatever price they liked to charge. Not one of these astute gentlemen would advance anything like the sum they required to meet their immediate obligations, and late on Sunday evening, 15th January, Robert Cadell wrote the letter that acquainted his exhausted father-in-law with the news that the struggle for survival was over.[1]

My Dear Sir,

I fear things are now coming to such a pass that A. C. & Co. will, before many days, cease to exist.

Robinson, as you will soon know, has returned one of his own bills; what bill that is I know not; but writing from this house I fear it is a bill for £1000 done at the Bank of Scotland, which, as you know, settles the business. Applegarth's bill is at Ramsay's tomorrow, Gale's will be at Sir Wm. Forbes & Co's on Tuesday also—in all, £5000.

We are dished at Ramsays; Bank of Scotland; British Linen Co., and Sir Wm. Forbes & Co. I leave you therefore to judge what my feelings are…now the tables are turned. Robinson's bills are back, which to us is death, and I can see it in no other light. Alas! alas! such is the end of all our hopes and expectations. I have struggled hard. I have fought as for my life. Last Thursday I did not expect this, but now I see no escape…Had you gone to London on the 2nd Jany. all this might have been different; but all is now, I fear, too late, and oh! there will be a sad din!

I am, my dear Sir, yours truly,

R. Cadell

The next day a reluctant Sir Walter Scott was forced to return to Edinburgh to resume his duties at the Court of Session.

Perhaps he guessed what was to come, but with his first glance at the ashen-faced James Ballantyne he must have known for certain that the game was lost. The elaborate fantasy he had woven with such care, the dream-like world he had inhabited for so long, were all soon to dissolve into a chill reality. Poor Scott!

[1] Once again Lockhart, in his Biography, took advantage of the fact that the person most concerned was already dead and therefore could not dispute the story, to dramatize his narrative with fictional embroidery. His tale has it that, on realizing that he was a ruined man, Archibald Constable lingered on in the town, 'until he hovered on the brink of insanity.' In fact, he left London for Edinburgh on the 19th January, and his letters to his partner on that day, and those immediately before, although showing him to be extremely depressed by the news (and who would not be) are perfectly coherent.

How can one feel anything but sympathy for a man so intensely proud, when one witnesses him confronted not only with the certainty of financial ruin, but with the knowledge that in a few days the whole world will know that for years he had been a secret speculator in commercial concerns and the hidden partner in a firm that his extravagance had helped to bankrupt. The secrets he had kept for so long from even his most intimate friends (and some were guilty ones in the sense that he advised people to have work printed at the Ballantyne Press without informing them that he owned the business and thus stood to benefit financially), these secrets were about to be divulged to any who liked to hear them. The world would soon know that it was the craving to supply funds to buy land and build his magnificent fairy castle on the banks of the Tweed that urged him to churn out novel after novel at such indecent speed; and not all the world applauded his motives. 'When I think of the wretched trash that the Lust for Gain induced him to publish for the last three or four years,' wrote S. T. Coleridge when he heard the news of his downfall, '...even my feelings assist in hardening me. I should indeed be sorry if any ultimate success had attended the attempt to unite the Poet and the Wordling.'

Long after the crestfallen Ballantyne had departed to break the news of his impending fate to his own wife and children, Scott sat silent and morose in the small back room at 39, Castle Street where he had written so many reams of costly manuscript. 'Came through cold roads to as cold news,' he penned despondently before he limped his way to bed. 'For myself the magic wand of the Unknown is shivered in his grasp. He must henceforth be termed the Too-well-known. The feast of fancy is over with the feeling of independence. I can no longer have the delight of waking in the morning with bright ideas in my mind, haste to commit them to paper, and count them monthly, as the means of planting such groves, and purchasing such wastes; replacing my dreams of fiction by other prospective visions of walks by

> *Fountain heads and pathless groves*
> *Places which pale passion loves.'*

Next day it had become public knowledge that Archibald Constable & Company had been forced to stop payment; dragged down, it was said, by the fall of their London agents. Then news

---

[1] *Unpublished Letters of S. T. Coleridge,* edited by E. L. Griggs, 1932, Vol. II.

leaked out that James Ballantyne & Company, whose printing workshops were known to have more orders in hand than they were able to execute, had also failed. But these scandalous tidings paled into insignificance when the rumour spread that Edinburgh's most revered and best loved figure, the legendary Sir Walter Scott, was in fact the secret owner of the Ballantyne Press and as such a totally ruined man. Many refused to believe that such a tale could possibly be true, or that a man whom they would have trusted above all others, could have set out to deliberately deceive them in this way. James Skene was the first to be told officially by the baronet of how matters now stood, a message having been sent round to his house early next morning asking him to come to Castle Street as soon as he was up. 'I went to see him by seven o'clock, and found him already by candle-light seated at his writing-table, surrounded by papers which he was examining. Holding out his hand to me as I entered, he said, "Skene, this is the hand of a beggar. Constable has failed, and I am ruined *du fond au comble*. It's a hard blow, but I must bear up; the only thing which wrings me is poor Charlotte and the bairns." '

There was no sidestepping the fact that his family had to be informed of all the impending consequences, and his journal reveals that Lady Scott, for one, was not disposed to meekly accept his excuses without telling him exactly what she thought of conduct that had resulted in such a humiliating downfall. 'A painful scene after dinner, and another after supper, endeavouring to convince these poor dear creatures that they must not look for miracles, but consider the misfortune as certain, and only to be lessened by labour,' he wrote after having thankfully escaped to his study. 'I hear of nothing but *money money*, and as speaking about it won't bring it back, I wish Papa would be quiet on the subject of pounds, shillings and pence,' his daughter Anne wrote to her brother Charles at Oxford. 'I look forward to a very lively life with Mamma for six months in the year, particularly as her Ladyship is very cross.' To her brother-in-law Lockhart, her father wrote a long letter explaining what had happened and detailing the events leading up to the failure and his own probable future course of action. 'I have been far from suffering by Ballantyne,' he stated. 'I owe it to him to say that his difficulties are owing to me—to be sure, so are his advantages, which will greatly predominate.'

What exactly Scott meant by the latter half of this assertion, it is difficult to comprehend. Left to himself, and with the Abbotsford wound staunched, James would almost certainly have established himself as a successful printer, as later events go a long way to prove. But for the moment he was a very frightened man, and with a wife and a growing family of children to support, who could blame him for exhibiting some signs of the agitation he must have felt. Surprisingly, however, and Scott's remarks confirm this, Ballantyne throughout the crisis seems to have conducted himself in a courageous and praiseworthy manner. 'James Ballantyne this morning—good honest fellow, with a visage as black as the crook. He hopes no salvation—has indeed taken measures to stop. It is hard, after having fought such a battle,' the senior partner wrote the day after his return to Edinburgh. The worry of recent months, and the knowledge, brought home to him by his brother Sandy and his brother-in-law George Hogarth, that the debts of the firm, instead of decreasing, were being swollen every month by the accommodation constantly demanded by Scott, had brought the little man to the verge of a nervous breakdown. The certainty that any failure of the business would mean that he, as a partner, might well have his house and furniture sold to pay the debts of the firm, and the wife and children on whom he doted, turned out into the street, kept him awake night after night. A more cruel symptom brought on by his worries, especially for a man who loved a well heaped platter and a table rich with food, was the nervous dyspepsia that had made itself increasingly evident during the last year. He was already suffering, as now appears obvious, from ulcers in the digestive tract, formed by the anxieties of attempting to run a hopelessly insolvent commercial concern.

Sir Walter's solicitor, John Gibson, was in the meantime hastily working out, as far as he could at that time, exactly how deeply Scott and the firm he owned were involved in the financial scandal, details of which were now the principal topic of conversation in the town. 'The opening of the year 1826 will ever be sad to those who remember the thunderbolt which then fell on Edinburgh in the utterly unexpected bankruptcy of Scott,' Henry Cockburn wrote in his memoirs.[1] 'If an earthquake had swallowed half the town, it would not have produced greater

[1] *Memorials of His Time*, Henry Cockburn.

astonishment, sorrow, and dismay. Ballantyne and Constable were merchants, and their fall, had it reached no further, might have been lamented merely as the casualty of commerce. But Sir Walter! The idea that his practical sense had so far left him as to have permitted him to dabble in trade, had never crossed our imagination. How humbled we felt when we saw him — the pride of us all, dashed from his lofty and honourable station, and all the fruits of his well-worked talents gone.'

Within a few days of the first news that Hurst, Robinson & Company had been forced to stop payment, it became obvious that the extent of the crash and the amount of money involved were far greater than even the most pessimistic forecasts had predicted. On the 21st, Gibson brought round to Castle Street a set of provisional figures he had prepared, and the full implication of what had happened was brought home to the numbed and incredulous author for the first time.

Susannah in *Tristram Shandy* thinks death is best met in bed, [he wrote that morning]. I am sure trouble and vexation is not. The watches of the night pass wearily when disturbed by fruitless regrets and disagreeable anticipations. But let it pass.

> *Well, Goodman Time, or blunt, or keen,*
> *Move thou quick, or take thy leisure,*
> *Longest day will have its e'en,*
> *Weariest life but treads a measure.*

Things are so much worse with Constable than I apprehended that I shall neither save Abbotsford nor anything else. Naked we entered the world, and naked we leave it. Blessed be the name of the Lord!

After another sleepless night, he opened his journal wearily next day:

I feel neither dishonoured nor broken down by the bad — miserably bad — news I have received. I have walked my last on the domains I have planted — sate the last time in the halls I have built. But death would have taken them from me if misfortune had spared them. My poor people whom I loved so well! There is just another die to turn up against me in this run of ill-luck — i.e. if I should break my magic wand in the fall from this elephant, and lose my popularity with my fortune. Then *Woodstock* and '*Boney*' may both go to the paper-maker, and I may take to smoking cigars and drinking grog, or turn devotee, and intoxicate the brain another way. In prospect of absolute ruin, I wonder if they would let me leave the Court of Session. I would like, methinks, to go abroad,

And lay my bones far from the Tweed.

But I find my eyes moistening, and that will not do. I will not yield without a fight for it.

James Ballantyne & Company, although its fall was precipitated by the failure of the publishing houses, in fact needed only the slightest push to topple, for the firm was hopelessly insolvent and had been for several years. It was a few weeks before the total damage could be accurately assessed, but when it was it revealed a prospect to instil gloom into the stoutest of hearts. A detailed list of the figures relating to the firm (or rather Sir Walter Scott, for the debts had almost all been contracted on his behalf) is given in the Sederunt Book of the trustees for the creditors, which is now in the National Library of Scotland. The amount Scott owed, when the ranking was finally adjusted, but not including the sum of £10,000 he had secured by a mortgage on Abbotsford, came to £116,838 11 3d.

This sum was made up as follows:

1.	Sir Walter Scott's private debts	£20,066	19	9d.
2.	Debts (apart from bills) due by J. B. & Co. or for which both partners were liable (in fact James Ballantyne owed only £45 17 8d of this sum; the rest was Scott's liability)	12,615	6	7d.
3.	Bonds for which Sir Walter was liable, but which had been contracted on behalf of Archibald Constable & Co.	9,129	9	0d.
4.	Bills discounted and in the hands of third parties	75,026	15	11d.
	Total	£116,838	11	3d.

Of this immense total, about £40,000 consisted of debts properly due by Constable & Company, but owing to the duplication and triplication of bills by the issue of accommodation notes and counter notes, Scott found himself saddled with the entire amount. Nevertheless, a glance at the figures given above reveals how far he must have been living above his income, for despite the amount of real value he had received during the last few years, there were still debts amounting to nearly eighty thousand pounds incurred on his behalf and now awaiting payment.

Archibald Constable & Company were made bankrupt, with a total deficiency, according to Lockhart, of £256,000, and their affairs were wound up under the Bankruptcy Act by a process of sequestration. They ultimately paid a dividend of only two shillings and ninepence in the pound, due partly to their most valuable assets being sold under the hammer at give-away prices to satisfy the demands of anxious creditors eager to retrieve at least part of their losses. Hurst, Robinson & Company were even deeper in debt and paid a final dividend of only one shilling and three-pence in the pound against debts amounting to some £300,000, thus spreading ruin through the ranks of scores of smaller firms. 'Who could have suspected Constable's timbers to have been rotten from the beginning?' Scott wrote bitterly in his journal on the 9th February, when at last he realized that the colossus who had advanced him such vast sums was in fact a man of straw. 'Constable paid well and promptly but, devil take him, it was all spectral together; moonshine and no merriment. He sowed my field with one hand and as liberally scattered the tares with the other.'

Taking advantage of his partner's absence in London, Robert Cadell had wasted no time in securing his own position as far as he was able. He had apparently made up his mind to break with Constable as soon as it became obvious that the company that bore his name would shortly cease to exist and he laid his plans accordingly. Constable, for his part, seems to have had more than enough of Cadell, and the two were at each other's throats from the moment they met. The younger man had done his best to sow doubts in Scott's mind regarding his partner's ability to manage the affairs of the publishing house in a manner likely to lead to its ultimate recovery, blaming Constable's extravagant mode of living for much of their present troubles and convincing the author that it was on Constable's insistence that the money raised by the Abbotsford mortgage had been tipped into the pit and lost. The squandering of this mortgage money rankled with Scott more than anything else that had occurred, and when he realized that the failure would have taken place with or without it he was loud in his condemnation of the man he blamed for its loss. It was an unjust accusation to level at Constable, and the letters Cadell wrote at the time prove that it was he, not his partner, who prodded James Ballantyne into asking for the loan.

On the 23rd January, the senior partner of what had been the leading publishing house in Scotland limped his gouty way into 39, Castle Street, having learned from Cadell that in future he would go his own way, but confident that the man to whom he had paid such immense sums for the right of publishing his manuscripts would stand by him in his hour of need and continue to favour him now that he needed his help and friendship as never before. Skene was present and has given his version of the meeting between the Author of *Waverley* and his publisher of long standing.[1] Constable hobbled into the back room where he and Scott were seated, 'puffing like a steam-boat'. He seemed to sense from the chilly way in which Scott greeted him that the decision on which of the two partners he should side with had already gone against him. What the author told him soon confirmed which way the wind was blowing, and also that Scott was determined to extract whatever benefit he could from the tangle of disappointed hopes with which he was now surrounded. It was a bitter blow to a man who was endeavouring to face misfortune at least as gallantly as the laird on whom he had showered gifts and wealth on a scale no other author had received before, and it came at a time when his health was broken and his pride had been brought low. Without Scott all hope of recovery was gone, but with the forced joviality of a desperately anxious man who had at all costs to please, he did his best to leave the door ajar for a future reconciliation. 'Come, come, Sir Walter,' he said as he turned to leave, 'matters may come round, and I trust that you and I may yet crack a cheerful bottle of port together at Abbotsford.' Scott was not in the mood for forgiveness. 'Mr Constable,' he replied coldly, 'whether we ever meet again in these conditions must depend upon circumstances which yet remain to be cleared up.'

The two never met again on anything like the old footing and it was with a feeling of relief that Scott turned to Cadell to fill the place the ailing Czar had now been forced to vacate. So it was that the man whose ideas should have made him the greatest publisher in the history of English literature passed out of the life of the man whom Lord David Cecil has called 'one of the

[1] *Memories of Sir Walter Scott*, James Skene, London, 1909.

greatest novelists that ever lived.'[1] Scott eased his conscience with resolutions to 'befriend him if I can, but Constable without Cadell is like getting the clock without the pendulum—the one having the ingenuity, the other the caution of the business. I will see my way before making any bargain,' he noted that night, 'and I will help them, I am sure, if I can without endangering my last cast for freedom.'

The words 'last cast for freedom' were to Scott no idle phrase, but referred to a carefully formulated plan he had prepared with the help of his solicitor and the benevolent cognizance of several of Edinburgh's leading bankers. 'If I am hard pressed, and measures used against me,' he wrote two days before the scheme was proposed to his creditors, 'I must use all means of legal defence and subscribe myself bankrupt in a petition for sequestration. It is the course I would have advised a client to take and would have the effect of saving my land, which is secured by my son's contract of marriage. I might save my library, etc., by assistance of friends, and bid my creditors defiance. But for this I would in a court of honour deserve to lose my spurs. No, if they permit me, I will be their vassal for life, and dig in the mine of my imagination to find diamonds (or what may sell for such) to make good my engagements, not to enrich myself. And this from no reluctance to allow myself to be called insolvent, which I probably am, but because I will not put out of the power of my creditors the resources, mental or literary, which yet remain to me.'

On the 26th January, John Gibson arrived at Castle Street 'with a joyful face' to announce that the creditors had unanimously agreed to the setting up of a private trust into which the author would contract to pay his entire revenue from literary sources and thus eventually clear his debts. 'This is handsome and confidential, and must warm my best efforts to get them out of the scrape,' Scott wrote with a lighter heart than he had had for weeks. There was at first some difficulty with one of his main creditors, the Bank of Scotland, which not only claimed that the works he had contracted to supply to Constable should be made part of the publisher's estate, but demanded that the trustees should instigate a lawsuit to demolish the marriage settlement. But the Bank finally withdrew their objections to the terms under

[1] 'Sir Walter Scott's Vision of Life', Lord David Cecil in *The Listener*, February 9th, 1950.

which the trust had been set up; being swayed by the thought that, with *Woodstock* nearly completed and the *Life of Napoleon* considerably advanced, they would not have long to wait before substantial sums were paid in and a first dividend declared. These gentlemen had been reassured by John Gibson and Sir William Forbes, himself now a leading Edinburgh banker and a close friend of Scott's since the days of his youth.

Only one creditor refused to be swayed by the blandishments of Gibson and Forbes. A firm of London bill-brokers by the name of Abud insisted that Scott should either be made bankrupt and his assets disposed of, or that they should immediately be paid in full. To back up their demands they threatened court proceedings to recover their money. 'They are Jews, I suppose,' Scott wrote when he was told the news. 'The devil baste them for fools with a pork griskin.' Gibson did all he could to make the firm see reason; appealing to them to wait with patience like the other creditors, and assuring them of his belief that everyone would eventually be paid in full. But the financiers who owned Abud & Company were adamant and his appeal fell on deaf ears. Eventually, with court proceedings pending, Sir William Forbes secretly paid them the whole sum demanded, amounting to nearly £2,000; at the same time taking care that his friend's pride was not bruised by misinforming him that the bill-brokers had decided to drop their case against him and had agreed to abide by the recommendations of the trustees. Forbes allowed the sum he had advanced on Scott's behalf to rank as a debt with those of the ordinary creditors, taking his chance with the rest as to the amount he would eventually be repaid. It was not until after the banker's death the following year that a grateful Sir Walter learned for the first time how generous his friend had been.

A wave of sympathy had swept the country when news of Scott's plight became known, and the esteem in which he was held at that time has probably never been accorded to any other writer before or since. Offers of help poured in from all quarters, while letters appeared in the newspapers calling on men of goodwill to rally to the assistance of a 'popular author fallen on evil times'. When an incredulous Earl of Dudley, seated at his breakfast table in distant Brighton, read of his downfall, he crumpled his newspaper with an oath that startled the entire room. 'Scott ruined!' he thundered. 'The Author of *Waverley* ruined! Good God, let every man to whom he has given months of delight give him sixpence, and he will rise tomorrow morning richer than Rothschild!'

It is doubtful if any other debtor in Britain would have been let off the hook in quite so generous a fashion as Scott was by the bankers and money-lenders of London and Edinburgh in the spring of 1826. Unlike the other unfortunates struggling in their net, he was allowed to escape at least some of the worst consequences of his folly. His bankruptcy would have been considered little short of a national disaster and this alone caused many of his creditors to stay their hands; while for those who knew him personally, like Sir William Forbes, there was the added inducement of a genuine affection and a wish to help a man they both liked and admired. But bankers are not renowned for letting sentimental considerations soften their flinty hearts. These hard-headed and commercially minded gentlemen had the added consolation, not only of the warm euphoria engendered by an act which brought them the grateful thanks of many of Edinburgh's leading citizens and a good deal of not unwelcome publicity, but also of the knowledge that the gamble they were taking on Scott's ability to continue writing best-sellers might very well come off. Just in case of accidents, they hedged their bet to some extent by insisting that he take out an immediate policy of insurance on his life, by which a capital sum of £20,000 would be payable to the Trust in the event of his death. With everything nicely buttoned up they departed, to wait expectantly what the first year's writing would bring.

From the author's point of view the setting up of the trust fund was by far the most satisfactory arrangement that his creditors could have made. They had agreed, amongst other things, that he should continue to receive the benefits of his official salaries, now amounting to £1,600 per annum, which defaulters in similar circumstances were usually forced to mortgage to help reduce their indebtedness. Number 39, Castle Street, which had been his town house almost from the first days of his marriage, he voluntarily sold, together with most of its contents, in order to cut down his expenses and to bring in some cash to meet personal debts of a pressing nature. But the Abbotsford he loved so well, with all its rolling acres of land, was his to do with as he pleased, and his life-rent of the property was as secure as it had ever been. Its furnishings and antiques, its fine library and valuable pictures—these he and his family could continue to enjoy indefinitely, providing no decision was made by the trustees to the contrary. Much of their anxious uncertainty about these personal possessions (conservatively valued as being worth not less than £12,000) was allayed when Alexander Cowan,[1] who had been elected chairman of the trust, hinted that the members could confidently be expected to take an extremely benevolent attitude regarding their disposal if his literary profits came anywhere near as high as their hopes.

And so it was that a chastened Sir Walter Scott made arrangements to settle down at his Tweedside home full of heroic resolutions to work hard and practise economy; although it quickly became obvious that he found the first of these laudable sentiments easier to comply with than the second.

[1] The head of the Edinburgh paper-making firm of the same name.

14

BUT THE BANKERS, smarting under losses now known to amount to hundreds of thousands of pounds, made certain that the lesser fry involved in the sorry affair did not escape with a penny more than the law allowed. The screws were immediately put on Constable, Cadell, and the two Ballantyne brothers, and put on hard.

Archibald Constable was stripped of every asset his creditors thought saleable: his house, furniture, pictures, library, horses, and personal possessions of every kind—all were sold under the hammer to the highest bidders. Within a few weeks he and his wife and eight children retired to a few rooms in Park Place, a sparsely furnished apartment in complete contrast to the luxury of Polton and the confidence-inspiring solidity of the Princes Street offices. He did his best to save the collection of first editions he had painstakingly built up during his years as a bookseller, but they were taken from him and disposed of, as were the thirteen original manuscripts of Scott's works, presented to him in 1823 by the author. These were auctioned in London and fetched a total of £317, their late owner being reduced to tears when the news of their forced sale appeared in the Edinburgh papers. 'The most eminent publisher that Scotland ever produced,' as the *Caledonian Mercury* called him,[1] was now a broken and enfeebled man, deserted by most of his friends, doublecrossed by his partner, and an increasing burden on his wife and family. His eldest son, David, suffered a nervous breakdown and for a time became insane, due, it was said, to the shame and worry brought on by his father's fall from power.[2] But thoughts of the fortune to be made if only his Miscellany could be launched on a large enough scale kept the ex-publisher busy dictating appealing letters to possible backers of the enterprise, and by January 1827, he had managed to scrape together suffi-

[1] In the issue for 23rd July, 1827.
[2] *Archibald Constable and his Literary Correspondents*, Vol. III.

cient funds to allow the first three volumes, comprising the voyages of Captain Basil Hall, to appear. These were excellent value at three shillings and sixpence apiece, and were well received by the critics, but their proprietor knew that success could only come if capital was available to launch the project on an immense scale, and with the stigma of bankruptcy upon him this could never be. Gradually he lost heart and then started to go downhill, his appetite for food seeming to decrease in direct proportion as his appetite for life itself slowly waned. To those who remembered his portly figure of a few months before, his wasted features were almost unrecognizable. By midsummer his family had given up hope of his recovery, and on the morning of the 21st July, while his wife and the younger children were away at Portobello, he called his son Thomas to the sickroom where he had been confined for many weeks. He whispered to the young man who was one day to re-establish his publishing business, and, in 1839, be created the Queen's Printer for Scotland: 'Dear Tom. I leave you very poor; had it pleased God to spare my life for a few years, it might have been otherwise; but I trust that at least you will find the name you bear no disadvantage to you.' A few hours later he had a heart attack and died. 'Poor fellow,' was Scott's only recorded comment when he heard the news. 'If he deceived others he was deceived himself.'

Archibald Constable's ex-partner had no regrets at the passing of the man who had once been his father-in-law. To the proprietor of the *Foreign Quarterly Review*, R. P. Gillies, who had applied to him about the possibility of persuading Scott to contribute an article to his magazine, Cadell was bitter in his condemnation of the man who first started him on his career as a publisher. 'Constable is now in a small space—poor man he died very easily,' he wrote when he broke the news. But having unburdened himself of these few kindly words, he trenchantly asserted, 'Thus has gone one of the vainest and most absurd men you have ever known....Originally ill-educated, he picked up from his intercourse with others a smattering of passable letter-writing, which, with some knowledge of books, made a great show to ordinary persons. He had besides an ingenious mind, but I have not the slightest doubt that many of his projects were suggested by others and fathered by him. He was *not* a liberal minded man—he was the very reverse. A liberal minded person is liberal in all things. Mr C made liberal offers of money, which were the offspring of sagacious calculation, but he almost always grudged his liberality so soon as it was emitted—and used to curse his folly. His liberality was vanity. Do you call it liberal to allow merit to no one else, to be jealous of others in the same trade, and to do petty things to annoy and vex them? Mr C took the absurdest likings to persons—and before long equally absurd hatings—and when he did hate it was the most malignant hatred. In a word, in Mr C there was nothing really amiable; he quarrelled first and last with every friend he had—wife—son—and daughter. He was at one time a successful projector—and died a Bankrupt from want of knowledge of business and calculation.'[1] Thus wrote Robert Cadell a few days after Archibald Constable's death. It was an epitaph that reveals as much about its writer as about the man at whose grave the stone was flung.

Due mainly to the good offices of Alexander Cowan, chairman of the trustees, and from whose paper-making firm the printer had bought his supplies since his earliest days in Edinburgh, James Ballantyne was treated by the creditors somewhat better than the unfortunate publisher. His house at 3 Heriot Row, into which he was just about to move with his wife and growing family of children, was sold to help pay some of the debts of the Ballantyne Press, for which, as a partner, he now found himself liable.[2] The few *objets d'art*, pictures and antiques at St John Street which were thought to be of value were also sold, but he was permitted to continue living there, and his furniture and personal possessions other than these were left intact. He was once again demoted to the post of manager of the printing business, this time under the strict surveillance of John Gibson, W.S.'s agent for the trust, and allowed a salary of £400 a year but with no other benefits whatsoever. This was barely enough to live on, his standard of living declined abruptly, and it soon became a struggle for him and his wife to make ends meet.

His brother Sandy was also hard hit. Most of the money he had received from the sale of the *Kelso Mail*, amounting to about £1,600, had been invested to buy a share in the *Edinburgh Weekly Journal* or loaned to his brother to help Constable & Company before the crash. He was innocent of the type of

[1] Cadell MSS., National Library of Scotland.
[2] The house fetched £2,700, but one thousand pounds of this sum was needed to pay off the mortgage which James had taken out in order to finance its building.

pecuniary guile practised by Scott and James during the financial intrigues necessary to keep the printing business afloat long after it had become insolvent; but he now found himself sucked into the vòrtex created by the crash and whirled into a cloud of worry and anxiety on a scale he had never imagined possible. With little or no chance of retrieving his losses, and with a wife and eight young children to provide for, he at first thought of taking the little capital he had left and hastily moving to the continent, where he could live cheaply until he could find work as a printer. But before any plan for flight could be formulated, the pressing attentions of his creditors (for he found himself liable for certain accommodation notes and counter bills put into circulation by the publishing houses) caused him and his family to leave Ann Street, and move in with their friends, David Cowan and his wife, who had offered them rooms in the Regent Moray's House, in the Canongate. The months passed slowly, as he and his brother strove to keep their heads above water, and only the news that his creditors had decided to allow him to resume the management of the *Edinburgh Weekly Journal* at a salary of two hundred pounds per annum persuaded Sandy to renounce, at least for the present, the plans he had made for making a home abroad.[1] The few hundreds he had left out of the several thousand pounds he was worth at the time of the death of his brother John, he had generously offered to make available to help his hard-pressed brother James. He refused it, knowing that Sandy and his family were equally in need. In the meantime, Scott, with only his salaries to live on pending the payment of certain monies for articles written for magazines (which he hoped to pocket without his creditors discovering what he had done) had been forced on several occasions to borrow sums from his solicitor. In addition, he had been embarrassed to learn of the size of the bills Lady Scott had run up at the houses of Edinburgh tradesmen during the previous twelve months. With the example her husband had set her it is hardly surprising that she had seen fit to disregard measures of household economy, but some of the accounts that poured in when Sir Walter's financial difficulties became known were a good deal higher than the laird had ever imagined possible. William Child, a glass and china merchant of Catherine

---

[1] Details of the struggle made by the Ballantynes to retrieve their fortunes and their subsequent family histories can be read in *Ballantyne the Brave*, a biography of R. M. Ballantyne, Rupert Hart-Davis, 1967.

Street, presented a bill for £390 19 5d., and a shoal of smaller fry were soon clamouring to be paid by return. All these invoices Scott was forced to send to John Gibson to be cleared, promising that the amount involved would be refunded as soon as cash became available. Daniel Terry was also asking for help. In April the previous year, Scott had provisionally promised to stand guarantor to the amount of £1,250, in order that the actor-manager and his friend Frederick Yates could become joint lessees and managers of the Adelphi Theatre, London, which the proprietors had advertised for sale at £30,000. Terry was now asking that £170 should be forwarded immediately, and, in spite of his own embarrassments, Sir Walter had no alternative but to comply.[1] Number 39, Castle Street had not yet been sold,[2] and Gibson had made it clear that this was not the sort of obligation that he, as agent for the trust, could be expected to take care of, even as a temporary measure. The money had to be found, however, and Scott was determined not to let down the man who had been his friend for very many years, and who had not only given invaluable assistance in the furnishing of Abbotsford, but had dramatized and produced many of the *Waverley* novels on the English and Scottish stage. Scott had learned from James that his brother had a hidden reserve of cash and he decided to approach Sandy with a view to a loan. 'I hope to settle your friendly accommodation in the course of a day or two,' he wrote to his solicitor on the 12th May, 'and believe I can also arrange Terry's matter without troubling you. But I am not quite certain yet.'

It says much for the youngest Ballantyne brother's loyalty and deep respect for the man whose extravagance had been largely responsible for plunging the entire Ballantyne family into debt, that without hesitation he handed over a total of £500 in bank-notes as soon as Sir Walter made his appeal. This was all he had left, and he had preserved this sum as a means of settling abroad if the scandal of their downfall became too much for his wife Randall to bear, or as a final resort in the event of their staying

[1] The guarantors, luckily for Scott, were never called upon to pay up; but on Daniel Terry's failure the author received a dividend of only 10/- in the pound on the total of £500 he had actually lent. The other £250 was not recovered.

[2] The house was sold in July, 1826, and fetched £2,300. 'It is worth £300 more,' wrote Scott, 'but I will not oppose my own opinion, or convenience, to good and well-meant council. So farewell, poor No. 39.' (*Journal*, 28th June.)

in Scotland and of his being unable to find employment there. One immediate consequence of his loaning Scott the money was the sale of his beloved Stradivarius violin and the purchase of a much cheaper instrument with part of the proceeds.[1] One can sympathize with the author in his predicament over the money needed for Daniel Terry, but to ascertain from James the amount his brother Sandy had concealed and then to borrow the entire sum betrays a selfishness that is difficult to forgive. Scott himself appears to have suffered some qualms of conscience about the loan, for he wrote in his journal that night:

> As I must pay back to Terry some cash in London, £170, together with other matters here, I have borrowed from Mr Alexander Ballantyne the sum of £500, upon a promissory note for £512.10s. payable 15/18 November, to him or his order. If God should call me before this time, I request my son Walter will, in reverence to my memory, see that Mr Alex' Ballantyne does not suffer for having obliged me in a sort of exigency—he cannot afford it, and God has given my son the means to repay him.

Out of all those who suffered financially to greater or lesser degree by the failure of the three principal companies involved, only the shrewd and commercially astute Robert Cadell derived ultimate benefit. The events that toppled the ailing Czar and split the partnership set his feet on the road to fortune and the respect purchased by a wealthy old age. By a series of calculated manœuvres Cadell not only succeeded in securing the literary services of the Author of *Waverley* for his own exclusive use, but squirmed out of his obligations to his creditors for a payment (according to letters he wrote at the time) of only one shilling and fivepence in the pound. Within a few months of this settlement being agreed the re-established publisher was bobbing like a cork on the surface of the commercial affairs of the city that had recently witnessed the downfall of his erstwhile partner and himself; his pockets jingling with sovereigns and with a balance of nearly four thousand pounds in the bank. How he so quickly managed this somersault from bankruptcy to affluence is something that has never satisfactorily been explained. It leads one to suspect that he might well have had assets that his creditors knew nothing about. His conduct immediately prior to the crash

[1] According to a letter found in Sandy's papers, his Stradivarius violin was offered to a London dealer for £25. As far as the present members of the Ballantyne family are aware, this was the sum finally obtained.

strengthens the theory that, knowing full well that all was lost, he nevertheless set about laying his hands on all the cash he could before the news that Archibald Constable & Company had stopped payment became public.

The day before the company of which he was a partner defaulted (or rather Hurst, Robinson & Company, which amounted to exactly the same thing, for the Edinburgh publishing house were entirely dependent on them for their continuing existence), Cadell persuaded the cashier at the Bank of Scotland to allow him to draw nearly two thousand pounds out of his firm's cash account. The bills he presented to cover this amount were next day proved to be practically worthless, as Cadell, having heard from London, had every expectation they would be. On top of this he had raised over three thousand pounds during the previous six weeks from personal friends and Edinburgh businessmen by promising high rates of interest and security he insisted was perfectly sound. When his promises proved as worthless as the bills-of-exchange and post-dated cheques he had handed over, these gentlemen were quite naturally incensed at their losses and determined to make Cadell's life as unpleasant as possible for some time to come. The Bank of Scotland took legal advice with a view to proceeding against him for fraud, believing that he was fully aware that the bills of Hurst, Robinson & Company which he paid in to enable him to draw the money were worthless or would be in a matter of days. Learning that the bank was seeking a warrant for his arrest, the publisher fled from Edinburgh and went into hiding. Scott discovered this on the 4th February, when he called into the Princes Street offices to inquire his whereabouts. 'Returned from Court by Constable['s office], and found Cadell has fled to the sanctuary,[1] being threatened with ultimate diligence, by the B[ank] of S[cotland] — about some £1900 drawn out of their cash accot. the day before the stop. If this be a vindictive measure, it is harsh, useless, and bad of them, and flight, on the contrary, seems no good sign on his part. I hope he won't prove his father or grandfather at Prestonpans:

[1] The sanctuary to which Scott refers was in the precincts of the Palace of Holyroodhouse. The western boundary was marked by the Girth Cross at the foot of the Canongate. Debtors were able to hide here, safe from duns, until the privilege was abolished sometime in the 1830's. The Isle of Man offered similar refuge.

And Cadell dressed amang the rest,
  Wi' gun and good claymore, man,
On gelding grey he rode that day,
  Wi' pistols set before, man.
The cause was gude, he'd spend his blude
  Before that he would yield, man
But the night before he left the corps,
  And never faced the field, man.'

Scott had little patience with those who refused to stand their ground in the face of adversity and had no sympathy, as he put it, with the virtues 'that escaped in salt rheum, sal-volatile, and a white pocket handkerchief.' Walking into the Court of Session for the first time after his downfall must have been a considerable ordeal, and he 'like a man with the large nose, thought everybody was thinking of me and my mishaps'. But to those who offered help he returned a polite refusal, saying as he walked away to take his place at the table under the judges' dias, 'My own right hand shall pay my debt.' He was grateful to the scourge of economic necessity that drove his pen from that time onwards; he had gambled thinking the odds were in his favour and he had lost his bet. So, at the age of fifty-five, suffering from the occasional warning symptoms displayed by one whose blood-pressure was creeping higher than his years warranted, yet outwardly physically fit, he took a grim pleasure in the penance imposed by fate and set about clearing up the mess into which he had involved himself. He entertained no guests and refused to be entertained himself; spending every spare minute he could snatch from his duties seated at his desk, quill pen in hand, while the written sheets piled higher in his tray ready to be folded and despatched to the printing office by the morning's post.

By the end of March *Woodstock* was finished. John Gibson had been delegated to handle its publication rights and he offered it to several of the largest London houses. He stipulated that either banknotes or unshakeable security for the entire amount agreed must be laid down on the table before the contract was signed and Murray and Longman accepted this condition and both made bids. The latter ultimately became the publisher, the trust benefitting by a clear profit of over £6,000. Scott's creditors were extremely impressed that such a large sum should have been raised from the sale of a work he had begun only the previous November and they waited with hopeful expectancy to see the outcome of his next literary effort. His sincerity of purpose was now accepted by them all and the flintiest-hearted amongst them applauded their own good sense in allowing the trust to be formed.

The fact that he felt himself under an obligation to the gentlemen of the banking world was a source of irritation to Scott, who never liked to be beholden to anyone if it was possible to prevent it. He believed that, on the whole, they had behaved handsomely towards him, and he was on the lookout for some way of repaying what he thought to be their kindness by not insisting that he should be pursued with the full rigour the law allowed. Quite unexpectedly, an opportunity occurred that gave him an outlet for these repressed feelings of obligation and he waded in with a gusto that surprised even his closest friends. He had long resented what he called the purposeless changing of the ancient Scottish legal customs by the entrenched bureaucracy in London, and their latest efforts to modernize and bring into uniformity the currency of the whole of the British Isles by abolishing the rights of the Scottish banks to issue their own paper-money roused his nationalistic instincts to a fury. He composed a series of 'Letters of Malachi Malagrowther' which the Ballantynes published in the *Edinburgh Weekly Journal*, and in these he launched a passionate appeal to the spirit of the Scottish people and to that 'feckless' group, the Scottish members of Parliament, the 'time-serving *faineants* who call themselves the Representatives of Scotland.' The letters gave a great deal of offence to many of his own political friends—Canning, Melville, and Croker amongst others. To the latter he said: 'If you unscotch us, you will find us damned mischievous Englishmen.' The letters were reprinted by Blackwood and issued as a pamphlet, and, like Swift's *Drapier's Letters*, on which to some extent they were modelled, caused a tremendous stir, sufficient as it turned out, to lead to the withdrawal of the scheme as far as the Scottish banks were concerned. Thanks to Scott's efforts in 1826, they still issue their own notes to this day.

With *Woodstock* finished, he turned his attention once again to *Napoleon*, the 'tautologies and inaccuracies of which' James Ballantyne complained, 'cost me 5 hours labour on every one sheet, if it costs me five minutes.' The task was a long and arduous one for an author who disliked having to verify every incident he portrayed and who found the discipline of biography irksome after the free reign he was able to give his imagination when writing his novels.

But tragedy was looming. Lady Scott was now seriously ill. Her weak heart was causing circulatory troubles and affecting the efficient working of her kidneys, giving rise to dropsy with all its attendant pain and disfigurement. With her daughter Anne in attendance, she joined her husband at Abbotsford on the 23rd March, having stayed on in town to try the effects of a new medicine recommended by her physician, Dr Abercromby. This was the last journey she made in life and shortly afterwards she took to her bed, dosed heavily with digitalis, and her appearances downstairs became more and more infrequent. In an unpublished letter[1] to James Ballantyne, her husband shows the increasing anxiety he felt on her behalf:

[4th May, 1826]

Dear James,

I thank you for your news. Lady Scott's health continues extremely precarious — She makes no advance & that in such a case is to retreat. When she came here she walked a little abroad — till a month ago she came downstairs & this last week she has taken her bed intirely — a sad prospect.

Sir Robert Dundas,[2] too, is unwell, which makes my coming to town on the 11th a matter of peremptory necessity. One good thing is that my niece Anne Scott has arrived here which gives us some assistance in our sorrows.

You will not be surprised if these domestic scenes check my fluency of composition, but there is no use in suffering oneself to be overcome & what must be done shall be done. I agree with you, the sooner & faster we can get out the new editions the better. We have in Cadell a purchaser under the lee, and I think you would not offer without such views of profit as will occur to others. I should wish to glance my eye over the copy to be used at press.

Yours truly
W.S.

friday
morning
Are you able to follow the battles with a tolerable degree of distinctness? Maps are really necessary to read such details with but I endeavour to make them as concise as possible.

[1] This letter is in my own collection.
[2] Sir Robert Dundas was one of Scott's colleagues at the Clerks' Table in the Court of Session.

On Thursday the 11th May, although it was now obvious that his wife was dying, he left her in the care of the two Anne Scotts, niece and daughter, and departed for Edinburgh to resume his legal duties. 'I have foreseen for two years and more that this menaced event could not be far distant,' he wrote as his carriage rolled towards the town. 'I have seen plainly within the last two months that recovery was hopeless—and yet, to part with the companion of twenty-nine years when so very ill—that I did not, could not foresee. It withers my heart to think of it, and to recollect that I can hardly hope again to seek confidence and counsel from that ear to which all might be safely confided. But in her present lethargic state, what would my attentions have availed? and Anne has promised close and constant intelligence. I must dine with James Ballantyne to-day *en famille*. I cannot help it but would rather be at home and alone. However, I can go out too.' Later that night he wrote: 'I passed a pleasant day with honest J.B. which was a great relief from the black dog which would have worried me at home.'

It seems strange that he did not apply for a substitute to undertake his duties at the Court of Session, for despite his colleague's illness the routine task of noting the court's findings and preparing the legal papers could have been delegated, as it had been on other occasions, with very little trouble. He knew when he left his house that it was hardly possible for him ever again to see his wife alive; she had been only semi-conscious for several days and to even a layman's eyes she was sinking. The court did not resume until the following Monday, and to stay at Abbotsford over the week-end, although inconvenient (as he had to move into his new lodgings in the city and there was the £500 loan from Sandy Ballantyne to be arranged), could nevertheless have been undertaken with only slight disarrangement of his plans. But he hated gloom and had succeeded in convincing himself that it was illogical for him to remain where he could do little to help.

Late on Monday night he was back in his Tweedside home, having received that morning, at Mrs Brown's lodgings in North St David Street, 'the melancholy intelligence that all is over at Abbotsford.'

'I have seen her,' he wrote the following day. 'The figure I beheld is, and is not, my Charlotte—my thirty years' companion. There is the same symmetry of form, though those limbs are

226

rigid which were once so gracefully elastic—but that yellow masque, with pinched features, which seems to mock life rather than emulate it, can it be the face that was once so full of lively expression? I will not look on it again....If I write long in this way, I shall write down my resolution, which I should rather write up, if I could....But I will not blaze cambrick and crape in the publick eye like a disconsolate widower, that most affected of all characters.'

After the funeral his butler, Dalgleish, insisted on sharing his solitude in the Edinburgh lodging house, caring for his clothes, preparing an evening meal, and doing whatever domestic chores were necessary for his master's comfort. With *Woodstock* out of the way, Scott settled down to labour steadily at *Napoleon*, for which Longman, in October, agreed to pay him the staggering total of 10,500 guineas. By the autumn he had run out of facts, and in October he left Scotland to visit London and Paris in search of information. He visited Morritt at Rokeby on the way, dined with bevies of the famous in London, and was received by the King at Windsor.

In Paris, Scott was feted in much the same style as he had been in Dublin. *Ivanhoe* was performed as an opera, with, as he put it, 'the story greatly mangled, and the dialogue in a great part nonsense'. 'I believe I must give up my Journal till I leave Paris,' he wrote on the 5th November. 'The French are literally outrageous in their civilities—bounce in at all hours, and drive one half mad with compliments.'

For weeks after his return to Scotland he was plagued with a complaint akin to dysentery and at times even a drink of lime water meant a hasty retreat to the nearest closet within minutes of setting down the glass. He lost several stones in weight, and was hardly on the road to recovery before his one good knee locked solid with rheumatism and he had to be lifted bodily from the coach that brought him back to Abbotsford from the city. Most of Christmas he was forced to spend in bed, but by the 30th he was feeling better and Anne tried to arrange a small party to cheer him up a little.

It is *not* the last day of the year, but tomorrow being Sunday we hold our festival of neighbours today instead. The Fergusons came *en masse*, and we had all the usual appliances of mirth and good cheer. Yet our party, like the chariot-wheels of Pharaoh when involved in the Red Sea, dragged heavily. Some of the party grow old and infirm; others thought of the absence of the hostess, whose reception of her guests was always kind. We did as well as we could, however.

> *It's useless to murmur and pout—*
> *There's no good in making ado;*
> *'Tis well the old year is out,*
> *And time to begin a new.*

...Why should we give up the comfort of seeing our friends, because they can no longer be to us, or we to them, what we once were to each other?

15

CADELL, IN THE meantime, had been chased from one refuge to another by creditors eager for his blood. But during 1827 the pressure upon him eased considerably, due partly to the influence Scott brought to bear on his behalf by letting it be known that, with Cadell's help, literary adventures might be undertaken that would result in a payment all round of twenty shillings in the pound. From the very first, James Ballantyne had been a firm supporter of the Cadell camp against that of Constable. 'Rely on it that months hence, when this business is settled, as settled it must be one way or another, you, if you choose it, will be the publisher of Sir Walter Scott,' he had written the younger man as early as the fatal 16th January, 1826; but he had reason in later years to regret that he had advised Scott to throw in his lot with a man who used friends and acquaintances for his own ends and cold-shouldered them as soon as their usefulness was over.

Cadell's objective was to gain control of what remained of the firm of Archibald Constable & Company by persuading the trustees to sell him a sufficiently large block of shares in the concern. This he hoped to do with funds subscribed by a brother and other friends; but the suspicion remains that it was Cadell himself who supplied the money that his brother was to advance, and that these funds came from assets he had managed to conceal at the time of the bankruptcy. A discharge from further obligations to his creditors, to whom he offered a total of one shilling and fivepence in the pound, was not to be obtained as easily as he imagined, the banks objecting that he had 'gone about to the last moment declaring that no insolvency was to occur and thereby obtaining sums from individuals down to the very day when payment was stopped.'[1] It was as late as 1829, after a stormy meeting, that a discharge was finally obtained, and it was only through Scott's insistence that Cadell was the man he

[1] Letter written by William Bell to Sir Walter Scott, 31st December, 1828.

wished to publish the collected and annotated edition of his works, a sure-fire best-seller they had privately christened the *Opus Magnum*, that the banks, scenting profit from afar, relented and gave the settlement their blessing.

With the formation of Cadell & Company in 1827 the publisher's fortunes improved so dramatically that the impediment of still being an undischarged bankrupt could have had little if any effect. From behind the back of his brother and his other nominees he played his cards carefully; his first and over-riding objective being to secure the services of Sir Walter Scott for himself alone. His initial manœuvre in this direction was to offer the baronet help in the payment of the doctors' bills and funeral expenses occasioned by the illness and death of Lady Scott. Despite his resolutions regarding economy, it was already becoming apparent that there was not the slightest chance of the author being able to live on the £1,600 a year his official salaries brought him in. If he was to toil like Sampson 'eyeless in Gaza, at the mill, with slaves' on his creditors' behalf, then he insisted on having elbow-room in which to work; and elbow-room to Scott meant sufficient of the good things in life to make writing a pleasure not a pain. Before *Napoleon* was completed, Scott had made arrangements with Cadell for a new series of stories, to be called *Chronicles of the Canongate*, or *The Traditions of the Sanctuary*, by the Author of *Waverley*. For this work the publisher agreed to give the author £500 for a sufficient number of copies to allow him to show a small profit; thereafter the trustees were paid £2,228 for the remainder of the issue, Cadell contracting to pay the overhead expenses and all other costs. This £500 went into Scott's own pocket, and for many years secret arrangements were made between the two men for a thin skimming of cream to find its way to Abbotsford at the expense of the Trust. Thanks to Ballantyne's influence, Cadell also acquired an interest in the nine volume *Napoleon*, which appeared at the end of June 1827, bearing the inscription: 'Printed by Ballantyne & Co. for Longman, Rees, Orme, Brown and Green, London, and Cadell and Co. Edinburgh.' The first series of the *Chronicles of the Canongate* followed in November, and by this time Sir Walter Scott was firmly in Cadell's hands, with financial obligations once again creeping slowly upwards and cementing their business relationship with a firmness time only helped to harden. 'I find myself short £85 till the 21st of next month,' the author wrote his publisher from his recently acquired furnished house in Walker Street, in May, 1827. 'I do not wish on any account to commence a new system of advances, but perhaps you may be able to lend me the said balance for said term.' Cadell saw to it that the money was despatched immediately, as he was only too pleased to do on several other occasions.

Three days later Scott wrote in his journal: 'A good thought came into my head: to write stories for little Johnnie Lockhart from the History of Scotland, like those taken from the History of England.' He informed Cadell of what he intended and the publisher replied with a sly hint that a little cash might well be made on the side by one who had laboured so hard for the benefit of his creditors. 'I hope you do not intend the proceeds of this little book for Mr Gibson's money-bags—it would be both a sin and a shame, permit me to say, to let the amount travel such a road after having done such wonders this year already.' On the 30th the publisher made a firm offer which included £500 to be paid to Gibson as a sweetener. But after taking over the publication, Cadell paid Scott 750 guineas for ten thousand copies, with provision that a similar sum was to be paid if a like number of copies were printed for a second edition. The trust received nothing—but they somehow found out what had occurred. In 1831 they recorded the note: '*Tales of a Grandfather, History of Scotland* for Lardner's *Cyclopaedia*, and *Letters on Demonology*, were kept by Scott for current expenses and this the trustees have passed over.'

The financial success of *Napoleon* and *Woodstock*, and the warm welcome the public had extended to *Tales of a Grandfather*, coupled with the start of Cadell's great scheme for the Collected Edition of the Works of the Author of *Waverley* did much to raise his spirits and set him once more in harmony with the world. The trustees were quick to express their gratitude of the immense efforts he had made on their behalf, and let it be known that they would eventually make him a present of his library, antiques and furniture, which was then estimated as being worth a payment of two shillings in the pound, had they been sold for the benefit of the Trust. With the money received from his books, a first payment was made to his creditors, amounting to six shillings in the pound towards the extinction of his debts. It is perhaps forgiveable, therefore, that Scott should have thought himself entitled to keep sums earned by the writing of minor works. By their help, and occasional loans from friends, he maintained both Abbotsford and the house he had rented in Walker Street, managing at the same time to live in stylish comfort while affording the two youngest members of his family considerable support.

In the middle of writing *Tales of a Grandfather* he was asked by Cadell: 'what is to follow *Chronicles* and *Tales*: I have no hesitation in stating that a three-volume novel would be well received after this.' And in August the publisher baited the hook by offering to purchase three novels in advance. 'Had a packet from James,' Scott wrote, 'low about the novel, but I had another from Cadell, equally uppish. He proposes for three novels in 18 months, which would be £12,600. Well, I like the Bookseller's predictions better than the printer's. Neither are bad judges, but James, who is the best, is not sensible of historical descriptions and likes your novel style out and out.'[1] The ghost of Archibald Constable must have smiled at the sight of his protégé emulating his old master in such a fashion; but Cadell was hard-headed enough not to risk deeper water than he could comfortably negotiate. In April, 1828, the publisher reported to his London agent that 'the *Chronicles* Second Series, entitled *The Fair Maid of Perth*, will be out immediately'. In March, the same year, he urged Scott to squeeze out of his capacious mind 'a steady flow of novels...the enthusiasm in the public mind in favour of your writing, I do maintain, is unabated—no sooner is one book done than we receive orders for the next although not yet named—and then a universal cry—"if this is not so good as its predecessors it is far, far beyond any thing else." I have a dread that a pause might coincide with the abatement of the public interest.' With such inducements and the overwhelming desire to be freed forever of the millstone of debt, the aging baronet worked at his desk far into the night, writing doggedly hour after hour; the pages piling and the candles burning low as he covered reams of Cowan's best laid paper with the crabbed hieroglyphics that the Ballantynes deciphered with almost reverent care next day. He suffered frequent headaches and from an occasional light-headedness, the blood pounding in his ears like tautened silk as he bent low to retrieve his pen; but his rheumatism had gone into hiding even if his stiff right leg was

[1] *Journal*—22nd March, 1828.

an increasing disability as the years rolled on. Court work he found such an unmitigated bore that he sometimes had the greatest difficulty in staying awake. His appearance there attracted far more attention from his admirers than did the weighty legal arguments that droned on around him. Many of his devotees travelled miles for the pleasure of sitting in the oak-panelled room to watch their idol fulfilling the monotonies of his task as a Clerk; their gaping hero-worship irritating him extremely.

The moment I entered the Court of Session I recognized him at once, [one such admirer wrote in later years].[1] Portrait and bust had made his face familiar. He sat as one of the clerks of court in front of the Judges' bench. Above him were divers senators, in the dignity of their official robes, and eminent, no doubt, in law; but my gaze was fixed on the sagacious features, ruddy complexion, and high silvery head of the one man who, while occupying a lower professional level, towered above them all. A homely and unpretentious man Sir Walter looked, though crowned of Apollo and the gods. With what awe did I contemplate the hand that had taken the 'harp of the North' from its witch-elm and struck immortal music from its cords! Yet that hand was now engaged putting past vulgar papers. I even declare that I beheld Scotland's greatest living son repeatedly yawn like an ordinary mortal, as if weary of his drudging occupation!
In a little while he rose, found his hat, and made for the door, passing close to where I sat. For a moment he paused within inches of me, on meeting a professional friend in gown and wig. With this gentleman he exchanged a few words whisperingly, but loud enough to enable me to hear his voice, with its soft, south-country burr. Then out the great man went into the open street. In person he was tall and stoutly built. Attired in a black dress-suit, and wearing a white cravat of sundry folds, he had much the appearance of an old country clergyman. His lameness was conspicuous. In his right hand he carried a strong staff, pressed it to his side, bending over it at every step, and proceeded down the High Street at a leisurely pace, with a lofty swaying motion.

Novels, biographies, critical articles and reviews for magazines, and even a couple of sermons to aid his secretary, George Huntly Gordon, (who promptly sold them for £250) came from his pen in a never ending stream during the years following the setting up of the Trust. His miscellaneous prose works were reprinted

[1] *Backward Glances*, or *Some Personal Recollections*, James Hedderwick, 1891.

233

for sale as a six-volume set and published in 1827; but the judge who was called upon to decide where the profits from this issue should go, assigned them to Constable's trust on the grounds that the publisher had bought and paid for them (in bills subsequently dishonoured) before the bankruptcy took place. Cadell was thus thwarted in his design to keep control of the copyrights vested in this work. But the copyrights in Scott's earlier novels, which Constable's trustees also owned, were now advertised for sale on behalf of his estate, their value being set at £4,000 as a guide to those who might be induced to bid at the forthcoming auction. This was the opportunity which Robert Cadell had long been seeking; the chance to gain control of the copyrights of Scott's fictional prose works, thus opening the way for an issue of the entire collection of novels at a price that would tempt thousands to invest in a set. With Scott's backing he persuaded John Gibson and his fellow trustees to allow him to borrow the sum he had undertaken to pay for the second series of the *Chronicles*, amounting in all to some £4,000, and with this to purchase the copyrights when they were auctioned. To his dismay however, they went for over £8,000, and had the Trust not stepped in and bought half of them, the publisher buying the remainder, Cadell's grand scheme for a complete reissue would have been doomed to failure. In this manner the decks were at last cleared for what had originally been Archibald Constable's dream and was now to be his ex-partner's fortune-spinning publication — the *Opus Magnum*, as the coterie of author, publisher, and printer came to call it, or the Collected Works of Sir Walter Scott, Bart.

The author was jubilant at the way his indebtedness to his creditors was diminishing with each passing month, and by the end of 1828, thanks largely to the sales of *Woodstock* and *Napoleon*, the Trust had benefited by no less than £35,000. Scott now looked forward with confidence to the day when the final payment would be made that would extinguish his obligations towards them forever. The two Ballantyne brothers were also faring better and the pressure of their creditors' demands had eased considerably during the previous twelve months. There were many leading businessmen in Edinburgh who were fully aware of the reasons for the insolvency of the Ballantyne Press: the laird of Abbotsford had ruined a thriving firm by his constant demands for funds, and they attached no blame to Ballantyne who they knew had been powerless to interfere. Proof of their confidence in the printer's ability to manage his own affairs, now he was at last free to do so, is given in their attitude towards him and his brother when Scott's connection with the firm was severed. Alexander Cowan decided that his confidence in the commercial integrity of the two brothers was sufficient for him to reinstate the eldest at the head of the printing company's affairs. With James's knowledge and approval, he offered the trustees £10,000 for the printing house as a going concern, and this the creditors accepted. An agreement was signed, whereby Ballantyne contracted to repay him this capital sum, with interest, during the course of the following years, the business in the meantime becoming once again his own property to manage as he wished. There were one or two strings attached to the deal; James was to obtain the paper used at the Press only from Cowan & Company, and assurances regarding the continuing goodwill of Sir Walter Scott towards the firm in respect of the printing of his works, were sought and obtained. James grasped with both hands this heaven-sent chance of eventually becoming independent and expressed his eager gratitude to Cowan for advancing the loan. Shortly afterwards he admitted his brother Sandy into partnership. Their financial affairs gradually improved; the firm of James Ballantyne & Company increased its turnover and was soon managing to show a profit at the end of each financial year; repayments of the Cowan loan were made each quarter day, and by the end of 1832 the entire debt had been paid off and the company was once again in a fully solvent state. The *Edinburgh Weekly Journal* continued to appear each week-end and was steadily increasing its circulation, and the new year of 1829 dawned for the Ballantynes after a Hogmanay warmed with the spirit of optimism and the hand-clasping cheer of brothers who believed that the worst of their penance might already have been performed.

Much of Scott's time was now occupied in writing fresh notes and prefaces to add to the forthcoming issue of his Collected Works, the first volumes of which, comprising the novel *Waverley*, were soon to be advertised in the trade press. Cadell was insisting that there were still large profits to be made out of yet another work of romantic fiction, and the thought of the thousands he could acquire for a few month's hard work, the plot for which he had already roughly sketched out, set Sir

Walter once more labouring at his desk, this time on the opening chapters of *Anne of Geierstein*. It was to prove difficult going almost from the commencing lines. 'The materials are excellent, but the power of using them is failing,' he wrote in his journal on the 26th January. Not only was he finding it increasingly difficult to maintain his output, but he realized, scanning the proof-sheets as they came from the press, that the quality of his literary composition was beginning to deteriorate. The high blood pressure from which he suffered, with its attendant symptoms of head-pains and giddiness, had resulted in a tetchiness of mood that made him resent criticism, something that he had always maintained caused him not the slightest unease. The time was not far distant when his unaccustomed sensitivity to comment on what he had written helped sour his friendship with James Ballantyne that had existed since his schooldays in Kelso. A slight coolness towards the little printer first became apparent when James reviewed the opening chapters of Scott's latest novel in a far from favourable fashion. But in the middle of seeing this book through the press, Ballantyne suffered the prostrating shock of losing his wife, a partner he had been devoted to ever since their marriage. Despite the best efforts of her doctors, she died within a few days of contracting a fever,[1] leaving her St John Street home desolate with the weeping of her husband and children. To his friends and wellwishers Ballantyne appeared to be plunged into such black despair that many of them had serious forebodings that he might lose his reason or even take his own life.

Scott could never sympathize for long with anyone who paraded his grief in so ostentatious a fashion, and it was not many days before he began to show signs of irritation at Ballantyne's prolonged absence from business. It was James that he relied upon to smooth his narrative style and detect the many errors of grammar and syntax which inevitably crept into the work of one who composed so hastily, then despatched the written sheets to the printer without any attempt at revision. With Ballantyne away in mourning, Sir Walter's manuscript piled up at the printing office, the proofs, which usually arrived for his approval by every other post, failing to appear.

The author had revealed that he now had doubts about his

---

[1] It seems probable from the symptoms that Mrs Ballantyne died from pneumonia.

ability to continue writing works of a quality that the public would be eager to accept, and he was well aware that one poorly written novel, published at this stage, might have a serious effect on the sales of his Collected Works on which all his hopes were based. Apart from the vivid portrait of Charles the Bold, and the colourful picture of the court of René, the king of the Troubadours, *Anne of Geierstein* flags into leaden-footed verbosity almost from the start. It points to the detrition of mind which Scott's tremendous output of the previous years had caused, and this intellectual tiredness, coupled with the bodily fatigue brought about by advancing age, was dulling the edge of his once incisive imagination. This fact became even more obvious to his readers in the years that followed, and finally led his publisher to issue an appeal that he should rest on his laurels and lay aside his pen for good. But for the moment, Cadell contented himself with proposing that the publication of *Anne of Geierstein* should be delayed 'at any rate, during the full rage of the Catholic question'. To this suggestion the author at first agreed, only to change his mind after a further reading of the printed sheets. The work appeared early in 1829, and, as Ballantyne had predicted, met with less than moderate success.

Even at this stage, although an open breach between the two did not occur until some time later, Cadell was already preparing the ground for a break with the printer. He resented having to comply with Scott's wishes that the printing of his own works should be carried out only by the Ballantyne Press. This Sir Walter had made clear to the publisher as early as January 1828, when he wrote him regarding the reprinting of the *Tales* which Cadell was proposing to place elsewhere. 'I need not remind you,' he wrote on the 3rd, 'that we three are like the shipwrecked crew of a vessel cast upon a desolate island and fitting up out of the remains of a gallant vessel such a cock-boat as will transport us to some more hospitable shore. Therefore, we are bound by the strong tie of common misfortune to help each other in so far as the claim of self-preservation will permit & I am happy to think the plank is large enough to float us all.' And again on the 8th: 'Besides my feelings for my own old friend & school fellow with whom I have shared good and bad weather for so many years, I must also remember that, as in your own case, his friends have made great exertions to support him in the P[rinting] O[ffice] under an implied hope & trust that these publications will take in ordinary cases their usual direction. It is true no engagement was, or could be, proposed to this effect, but it was a reasonable expectation which influenced kind & generous men & I incline to pay every respect to it in my power.'

In other words, a clear indication to the publisher that he would be displeased if the little printer was left to his fate now that Cadell was able to dispense with his services. His wishes were complied with in this instance, but Constable's ex-partner was only biding his time, waiting for a more favourable opportunity to occur. Scott's connection with the Ballantyne Press was now severed. He derived no benefit from any profits made by the establishment; but the loyalty bred by years of friendship and business association made him insist on helping James in any way he could. Whether he ever mused on the fact that the entire Ballantyne family was now ruined as a direct consequence of their association with the man they still revered, and that fate might well have dealt more kindly with them had they been left as small-town businessmen in Kelso, is open to conjecture. In a fit of depression he once wrote in his journal: 'It is written that nothing shall flourish under my shadow—the Ballantynes, Terry, Nelson, Weber, all came to distress. Nature has written on my brow, "Your shade shall be broad, but there shall be no protection derived from it to aught you favour."'[1] If his conscience pricked him occasionally he consoled himself by the thoughts of the benefits he imagined he had brought them.

By an insidious process of hints and innuendoes Cadell now set about driving a wedge between Scott and the printer, hoping by so doing to free himself from any obligation to channel his orders to Paul's Works. With the ruthless commercialism for which he later became notorious, the publisher started to pit the estimate of one printing house against the next, running a Dutch auction in price-cutting to obtain rock-bottom quotations. He was determined that James Ballantyne & Company should receive no preference, despite the high quality of the work they turned out, but he had to be careful not to offend the man whose favours he knew could lead him to fortune.

Proof-sheets and corrected printings from the *Opus Magnum* continued to arrive in fits and starts but, much to the author's annoyance, little or nothing of the nearly completed *Anne of Geierstein*. 'I hear bad news of James Ballantyne,' Scott wrote

[1] *Journal* — 15th April, 1828.

238

on the 9th April. 'Hypochondriac I am afraid, and religiously distressed in mind.' The seeds of future discord between the two were being sown with subtle skill by Cadell, who knew of the laird's scarcely concealed aversion to formalized religion in general and tub-thumping evangelicism in particular. In letters to Abbotsford he was emphasizing James's new-found piety and preoccupation with spiritual matters, at the same time pointing out the difficulties his absence was causing at the Ballantyne Press. A harshly worded and, as the author put it, 'painful letter to Ballantyne' was despatched informing James that he must 'awake, arise, or be for ever fallen'. But still the grief-stricken printer stayed in hermit-like seclusion, and not only the new novel (which the author was now determined should be published as soon as printed) but also his money-spinning Collected Works were in serious danger of being delayed. 'I find J.B. has not returned to business, though I wrote him how necessary it was,' an exasperated Scott noted sourly on the 18th. 'My pity begins to give way to anger. Must he sit there and squander his thoughts and senses upon cloudy metaphysics and abstruse theology till he addles his brains entirely, and ruins his business? I have written him letter third, and, I am determined, last.' If 'letter third' did not do the trick, an advice from Cadell that he wished for part of the Collected Works to be printed elsewhere in order to speed production, achieved the desired effect and sent the printer scuttling back to his Canongate office.

The demand of the booksellers for the first volume of the *Opus Magnum*, which appeared with the prospectus in May 1829, was so enormous that Scott and his excited publisher felt like dancing in the streets with delight. On the 2nd June, he wrote to his son Walter, 'I write to send you a copy of the *Waverley* novels which I will put under Croker's frank. The sale is pro-di-gi-ous! If I live a few years it will completely clear my feet of former encumbrances and may perhaps enable me to talk a word to our friend Nicol Milne.'[1]

With Ballantyne's presses working night and day to turn out the printed sheets of the *Opus Magnum* for the binders, and with practically the whole production of Paul's Works geared to complete this one huge order in the stipulated time, Cadell picked

---

[1] Even at this stage in his career Scott was still dreaming of one day buying Nicol Milne's land adjoining Abbotsford, the estate of Faldonside, for which his neighbour was asking £30,000.

this moment to apply pressure on James and his brother, just when he imagined they could least afford to resist it. Ballantyne had quoted the publisher a figure of fourteen shillings a ream for printing this work, and this had been accepted by Cadell several months before the first volumes appeared in the bookshops. Upon the acceptance of his estimate, Ballantyne had been forced to borrow a considerable sum to finance the project, for the printing of several hundred thousand octavo volumes called for a considerable outlay in paper, inks, type-faces, and materials of all kinds. Two new presses were purchased and extra labour taken on, orders from other sources having to be refused until the bulk of the Collected Works of the Author of *Waverley*[1] had been completed. Soon after the first sets of sheets had been cased up and despatched to the booksellers, James received a complaint from Cadell that he thought the work had been printed with less than his usual skill and therefore the price charged per ream ought to be reduced accordingly. His communication contained the threat that he would find another printer to finish the order if his demand was not acceded to. The methods he employed to try and blackmail James into submission can best be perceived by reading the letter of bitter complaint which the printer sent to Scott in the hope of inducing him to demand that Cadell should withdraw his threat.

> *Printing Office.*
> *Edinbr. Septr. 4, 1829*
>
> Dear Sir Walter,
>   Several months since, I informed you of my belief that I had nothing to depend upon from Mr Cadell, as manager of the Magnum, in the way of being employed in that work any farther or longer than he felt compelled to employ me. I said that I wished nothing to be done in the way of interference then; but that when the time came, as I knew it would come, that my apprehensions were realized, I should then solicit your aid and support. Your answer came to assure me of your support, should that time come. 'Do not doubt,' you were kind enough to say, 'that I will attend to you. I have told Mr Cadell that we are like three mariners, escaping from common shipwreck; and as the plank is broad enough for all, I cannot think it right to push any off from it.' Emboldened by this kindness, and respectfully reminding you that this is the very first

---

[1] On the 23rd February, 1827, at a dinner at which he presided in Edinburgh, Scott publicly acknowledged the authorship of the *Waverley* novels for the first time.

time since the unfortunate month of January 1826 that I have ever intruded upon you a syllable respecting myself, I solicit your careful attention to the following brief statement.

1. Previously to the commencement of the Magnum, we gave in Estimates for printing it. No. 1 was at 14/– per ream; No. 2 at 12/–. No. 1, the highest, was adopted. Hot-pressing 1/6 per ream.

2. The work was published; the whole periodical press was loud in praise of the printing; and the success has been unequalled. But Mr. Cadell was *not* satisfied; and I submitted to charge only 12/– in place of 14/–.

3. Upon this principle, the 2 volumes of *Waverley* were settled *and paid* 12/– for *printing* per ream; and 1/6 for *Hot-pressing*. Be pleased to mark this.

4. Now, however, Mr. Cadell refuses to pay for the hot-pressing, thrown into the bargain by others; and therefore is determined to extort it from us under the penalty of withdrawing the work from our press.

5. We answer, we cannot submit to this; and that it would be unjust and unfair to remove the work on any such grounds. No doubt, in the present distressed state of trade, he could get even greater concessions. But that was nothing to us. On the faith of an adopted estimate, we had laid out all our own, and much of our friends' money, to the extent of upwards of £4000, with a view to the Magnum alone; and that, *all this being done*, his now insisting that we should agree to a measure which would be greatly *injurious* to us, under the threat of another which would be *ruinous*, is unkind, unreasonable, and unjustifiable.

This, dear Sir Walter, is a brief statement of the point at issue; but I inclose a copy of the letter sent by us to the Trustees, and the correspondence between Mr Cadell and us. I know your dislike of such details; but this is a truly serious matter to me and my family, and to those friends who have come forward to help me in my misfortunes. I only beg you to examine these documents, and then to do as you think fair, whatever may be the effect upon me.

The truth is, and I say it without hesitation, that Mr Cadell is as yet only feeling his way. He will, if he can, beat us down till we shall have the mere shadow of profit. Should his present unreasonable demand be acceded to, it would only make way for some new encroachment. He always has it in his power to say 'Gentlemen, I can get the work done still cheaper. You must come down 20 per cent. more or my duty to the concern will make me remove the work.' And it is true he *could* get the work done much lower, by persons who, having no work, are willing to make any sort of concessions for employment. But he talks in this way too late. It would have been all quite right before we had laid out £4000, depending both on the stability of the price, and the permanency of the job. Then he would have been perfectly justifiable in going wherever he could get the thing done cheapest. But, surely, what was right then is not right now. We have embarked more than our all to meet this employment, *and will be ruined* if it is taken away, or only retained by working for nothing.

From 14/- per ream, he has got us down to 12/-, and now meditates, by compelling us to hot-press for nothing, to lower that last charge to 10/6d; or 20 per cent. below the original estimate. This is hard, surely. I have printed *Blackwood's Magazine* twelve years, and have never heard one word of deduction simply because he thinks our charges fair, and does not attempt to beat us down because he knows he could. This last sentence is not quite germain to the matter; but it has slipt out, and I entreat you to forgive it.

I am, dear Sir Walter, most respectfully yours,
James Ballantyne[1]

On this occasion Scott intervened on Ballantyne's behalf, causing Cadell to modify his demands so that a compromise solution could be reached.[2] But he was none too pleased at being dragged into a commercial squabble to act as referee. The publisher was proving a most useful friend whenever he was in need. On numerous occasions during the past few years he had lent, without demur, comparatively large sums of money to the author, besides plying him with gifts of considerable value in the form of wines and spirits. The result was, as Cadell had no doubt hoped, that Scott found himself in a position of some embarrass-ment when he came to take Ballantyne's part, even though right was manifestly on the printer's side. He therefore let James know that the affairs of the Ballantyne Press were solely his own

[1] *The Private Letter-Books of Sir Walter Scott*, edited by Wilfred Partington, London, 1930.

[2] 'I have had a long letter from Ballantyne about his charges, which I find he has very foolishly sent to the trustees. The matter might have been much better settled, without troubling them, amongst our three selves. I have endeavoured to make him sensible that he ought not, on so long a job, to expect more profit than other folks of his trade, and that a preference at the same rates is a very considerable favour. On the other hand, I think it may be remembered in his favour that he has put himself into a condition to execute the work with speed and exactness and that, if he should take the pet (which he is quite capable of) we should hardly be able to get on the work elsewhere; at any rate a great delay must needs take place. It is the interest of both parties to settle the *prix juste* without loss of time and some sacrifice must be made by each.' Letter to Robert Cadell, sent from Abbotsford, 7th September, 1829.

responsibility, and that henceforth he must be prepared to stand on his own feet when it came to fighting battles in the commercial jungle.

All pretence of a personal friendship between printer and publisher was now abandoned, and in course of time Cadell's ruthlessness in business affairs lost him the majority of friends in the trade who had taken pleasure in visiting the offices of his company in Constable's day. He had by this time so far insinuated himself into Scott's financial affairs that the author turned to him automatically whenever funds ran low; something that happened with frequent regularity, for his salaries and occasional literary windfalls were never enough to cover his living expenses. He still lived well above his income and debts of a personal nature had increased by over three thousand pounds by the autumn of 1832. Scott appears to have admired Cadell, both as a businessman and as an individual, despite the fact that the publisher made no bones about viewing any literary work purely from the standpoint of its saleability as an article of commerce. Had he been originally apprenticed to a draper or a horse vendor, he would have been just as calculating in his assessment of the relative profitability of the goods he was offering for sale. He would no doubt have pushed those articles that gave him the greatest return on his original outlay, and have been as efficient in purveying holland sheets or a high spirited hunter as he was in disposing of the latest novel from the Author of *Waverley*. Within a few years he had made Cadell & Company into one of the leading Scottish publishing houses, while at the same time amassing a personal fortune that at his death amounted to more than one hundred thousand pounds.

Ballantyne he found useful as a literary critic, recognizing that he had a flair for detecting what the public would, or would not, buy. He frequently used him as a buffer between himself and Scott, a device that came in useful when it was necessary to advise the author that a novel on which he had laboured for months needed modification before it could be published with any hope of success. Scott was well aware that any criticism Ballantyne offered was usually well merited, but even so, especially in his last few years, he came to identify the printer as one whom it was well nigh impossible to please and the little man became an increasing source of irritation to him. If Cadell had any unpleasant news to impart, he always did it through

Ballantyne, excusing himself from approaching the author direct by flattering the printer, addressing him as Sir Walter's agent. The first jolt of this kind, administered by his new publisher, had been felt by Scott in December 1827, when he noted that the Second Series of *Chronicles of the Canongate* had not been well received: 'Had a formal communication from Ballantyne, enclosing a letter from Cadell of an unpleasant tenor. It seems Mr Cadell is dissatisfied with the moderate success of the 1st Series of *Chronicles* and disapproves of about half the volume already written of the Second Series, obviously rueing his engagement.' In this instance, like those tactful remonstrances that came about later works, it was Ballantyne, not Cadell, who showed signs of disquiet after perusing Scott's manuscript. But the publisher was quick to take alarm as soon as he noted James's hesitation, for he had little confidence in his own judgement in literary affairs and relied almost entirely upon Ballantyne's critical opinion. On this occasion Scott accepted James's strictures with a good grace, and two of the stories in the series, comprising *My Aunt Margaret's Mirror* and *The Laird's Jock*, were cancelled. But he continued writing *The Fair Maid of Perth*, despite its manifest imperfections. The short story *My Aunt Margaret's Mirror* was later partly rewritten and sold to Frederic Mansel Reynolds for inclusion in his newly founded Christmas annual *The Keepsake*. It appeared in the second issue of this expensive and highly ornamental publication in 1829, along with contributions from an impressive list of writers, who included Wordsworth, Southey, S. T. Coleridge, Shelley, Thomas Moore, Henry Luttrell, and Scott's son-in-law, Lockhart. The £500 he received from this little effort he placed in his own private account, saying nothing to either Cadell or the Trustees about this most acceptable piece of good fortune.

By now Scott was far from well and the head pains and spells of giddiness from which he suffered were becoming increasingly frequent. During January, 1830, chilblains prevented him from taking up his pen for several days, while his rheumatism lurked ready to stiffen his one good knee at the most awkward and inconvenient of times. But these were chronic complaints of long standing and he had learned to accept them as one of the penances extracted by Anno Domini. There now came a far more serious manifestation of advancing age and the indulgences he had permitted himself since the days of his youth. After returning to the

Parliament House on the 15th February, he was suddenly felled by a cerebral haemorrhage that left him speechless at the feet of his daughter Anne and Violet Lockhart, his son-in-law's sister. A few minutes before he had been sitting conversing with the elderly Miss Young of Stockbridge, whose father, the late Dr Young of Hawick, had once rendered him some service of a political nature. This good lady was appealing to Sir Walter to present a petition, on behalf of herself and her ailing sister, to the Duchess of Buccleuch, in order that they might obtain a pension. Scott had been discussing the project with her for some time, but when he rose to take his leave he staggered and fell heavily to the floor. He was unable to speak and it was soon obvious to those who crowded round that he had suffered some sort of a stroke. The surgeon who was hurriedly sent for bled him there and then, and after showing some signs of recovery he was helped to a carriage and taken home to his bed. He was cupped again the same evening, and a day or two later most of the symptoms that had so distressed his daughter and the rest of the family had almost disappeared. He still slurred his words a little and there was a downward droop to the right-hand side of his mouth, but otherwise he appeared to be back to normal. What paralysis there was had left him completely in the course of the next few weeks, and the fact that it was his right side that had been affected was disguised by his lifelong limp. He was now forced to accept a strict diet, scarcely touched wine or spirits, and regretfully laid aside the comfort of the cigar he had permitted himself in the evenings. His doctors thought it best to inform him that the attack had come 'from the stomach'; but one who had already lost his father and elder brother from the same complaint was well aware of what it was that had struck him. 'It looks woundy like palsy or apoplexy,' he wrote. 'Well, be it what it will, I can stand it.'

He was resolute in his determination to continue his writing in spite of his doctor's orders to the contrary, and during 1830 his output did not fall far short of that of the previous few years. Lockhart and his wife had become seriously alarmed at the state of his health and tried to wean him from what his son-in-law called 'the exciting and feverish composition of novels'. This was the class of writing that Scott found absorbed his attention and satisfied his desire to create to a greater degree than any other type of literary composition, but he nevertheless agreed to sandwich a non-fictional work between his last novel and the next. He commenced writing a series of letters devoted to explaining the darker side of demonology and witchcraft for Murray's Family Library, and in a few months had netted, unknown to his trustees, a total of £700 in fees. Part of each week was spent in writing notes and introductions for his eagerly awaited Collected Works, one volume of which issued from the press every month before being snapped up in their thousands by booksellers from John O'Groats to Penzance. Any spare time he had left was taken in replying to the numerous letters that arrived at Abbotsford every week; in composing a series of *Essays on Ballad Poetry*; and in completing a review of Southey's *Life of John Bunyan* which Lockhart had commissioned for the *Quarterly*. In the midst of all this he managed to complete a Fourth Series of *Tales of a Grandfather*.

This year was his last as Clerk to the Court of Session. It had become obvious to their Lordships that their faithful servant of a millennium of torts and retorts, arguments and counter-arguments, was now visibly infirm and finding the effort needed to sit patiently through long hours of legal discourse an increasing burden and an irritation from which he would be glad to escape into peaceful retirement. By the late autumn he was free at last to live all the year round at his Tweedside home, and was in receipt of a pension of £800 a year to sweeten his leisure hours. But although he was now his own master of the means by which he passed his days, his time was totally absorbed by his social activities and literary work. During the summer the Lockharts arrived to spend a holiday and it did not take them long to realize that he had already allowed himself to drift back into his old style of lavish entertaining, coupled with the attendant expense this always entailed. Minor vexations put him out of temper more easily than in the past and he was exhibiting political attitudes that were reactionary to a degree that nonplussed even his right-wing son-in-law.

By the autumn so much money had been contributed to the Trust by the continuing heavy sales of the Collected Works that a second dividend, this time of three shillings in the pound, was distributed to the creditors. These most obliged and grateful gentlemen thereupon passed a resolution according Sir Walter Scott their heartfelt thanks 'for the unparalleled and most successful exertions he has made, and continues to make for them.' They also set their official seal upon the gift they had made him of his library and other personal possessions, amounting, as they noted, to the equivalent of a further two shillings in the pound. This was the last dividend to be paid them in the author's lifetime, but already nearly half of the debts he had been forced to shoulder in January 1826 had been cleared and he expressed his confidence that two more years would sweep away the last of his financial obligations towards them.

By the 22nd July, 1830, he was writing to John Murray, the London publisher, that he had 'corrected the last sheets of the ghosts' (as he termed his *Letters on Demonology and Witchcraft*)[1] and asking him to kindly send on the £700 copy money. He was already working on the two stories that together were to form what proved to be his last published novel, *Count Robert of Paris* and *Castle Dangerous*. For both tales he had been offered large amounts by Cadell, *Castle Dangerous* alone bringing a promise from the publisher that he would 'carry to Sir Walter's cash account the sum of £1,200'. He was working on these stories throughout the autumn, dictating to his amanuensis William Laidlaw, for since his stroke he had experienced difficulty in gripping his pen firmly and his eyes were now no longer able to read back the scrawled pages of manuscript.

In December Ballantyne dampened his spirits by an adverse criticism of the opening chapters of *Count Robert*, but admitted 'It is far too early to pretend to give an opinion, far less to decide, about *Robert of Paris*. I confess I think 24 pages an enormous length for a single conversation, of no great interest perhaps, between Achilles & Hereward; but it would be grievous to stop before the experiment is fairly made. *You* are of the opinion the subject is an excellent one; whereas *I* do not even know what the subject is.'[2]

Meanwhile Scott reported in his journal: 'I wrote with Laidlaw. It does not work clear; I do not know why. The plot is, nevertheless, a good plot, and full of expectation. But there is a cloud over me, I think, and interruptions are frequent. I creep on, however.'

In February he gave a *résumé* of his working day. 'Rose at

[1] Published in 1830 as a collected series of ten letters. It appeared as an octavo, with a frontispiece by James Skene, and with twelve spirited copper-plates (hand-coloured in some copies) by George Cruikshank.
[2] MS. 869, National Library of Scotland.

seven; dressed before eight, wrote letters, or did any little business till a quarter past nine. Then breakfast. Mr Laidlaw comes from ten till one. Then take the poney, and ride *quantum mutatus* two or three miles, John Swanston walking by my bridle-rein lest I fall off. Come home about three or four. Then to dinner on a single plain dish and half a tumbler, or by'r lady, three-fourths of a tumbler, of whisky and water. Then sit till six o'clock, when enter Mr Laidlaw again, and work commonly till eight. After this, work usually alone till half-past nine, then sup on porridge and milk, and so to bed. The work is half done. If any asks what time I take to think on the composition, I might say, in one point of view, it was seldom five minutes out of my head the whole day. In another light, it was never the serious subject of consideration at all, for it never occupied my thoughts entirely for five minutes together, except when I was dictating to Mr Laidlaw.'

His butler, Dalgleish, had been forced to retire by ill-health; a young man of the name of John Nicolson, who had worked on the Abbotsford estate from boyhood, taking his place as a personal valet. Scott's doctor gave the lad exact instructions on how to use the lancet should an emergency call for the immediate bleeding of his master, for it seemed obvious that another stroke might not be long delayed. He had suffered a slight one in November, collapsing with a thud on his bedroom floor, but recovering sufficiently to drag himself into bed without disturbing the rest of the family. Yet a month later he presided at a Selkirk court called with the express intention of meting out summary punishment to salmon poachers, which many of the surrounding land-owners would have cheerfully seen hanged. The jury found four of the 'black-fishers' guilty and Scott sentenced them to imprisonment under the terms of a new Act proscribing heavy penalties for the offence. One of the unfortunate poachers tried to escape, giving Sir Walter a chance to display his valour by barring his path to the door. 'One of the criminals tried to break out. I stopped him with my own hand,' he wrote that night. An eye-witness to the drama was the Procurator-Fiscal: 'The prisoner, thinking it a good chance of escaping, made a movement in the direction of the door. This Sir Walter detected in time to descend from the Bench and place himself in the desperate man's path. "Never!" said he; "if you do, it will be over the body of an old man." Whereupon the

248

other officials of the Court came to the Sheriff's assistance and the prisoner was secured.'[1]

Scott had more than once confided to his journal his belief that the novel on which he was then engaged would be the last he would have the strength to complete. On the 16th April, 1831, he made the entry: 'About one hundred leaves will now complete *Robert of Paris. Quaere*, if the last. Answer—not knowing, can't say. I think it will.' He was feeling unwell when he made the entry with what he described as a 'muddiness of brain' that clogged his reasoning and often caused him to set down one word in place of another. For much of that week he had relaxed his guard against rich food and wines, and had partaken of both in a manner extremely unwise for one with his past medical history. Lord Meadowbank, his old friend from the judges' bench, was staying at Abbotsford, as he nearly always did when on the Jedburgh circuit, and his host had done his best to enliven his visit by inviting a number of friends and neighbours to dine there. Several others were house guests, including James Skene and his son William, to whom we are indebted for a first-hand account of what transpired. On the 14th and 15th there had been lengthy dinner-parties, at both of which Scott had consumed a quantity of champagne after finishing his mealtime allowance of whisky and water, but refusing the port and claret with which the rest of his guests were regaled. Next day was a Saturday and he was obviously far from well, keeping to his room for most of the day, although he walked a little with Skene and his son in the morning. This young man kept a diary in which he made the following notes:

On Sunday Sir Walter did not come down to breakfast, but sent a message to say that he had caught cold and had taken some medicine for it the night before, which had made him ill, and he would, therefore, remain in bed. When we sat at either lunch or dinner, I do not recollect which, Sir Walter walked into the room and sat down near the table, but ate nothing. He seemed in a dazed state, and took no notice of any one, but after a few minutes silence during which his daughter Anne, who was at table, and was watching him with some anxiety, motioned to us to take no notice, he began in a quiet voice to tell us a story of a pauper lunatic, who, fancying he was a rich man and was entertaining all sorts of high persons to the most splendid banquets, communicated to his doctor in confidence that there was one thing that troubled him much, and

[1] *Selkirkshire*, Craig-Brown, Vol. II.

which he could not account for. This was that all these exquisite dishes seemed to him to taste of oatmeal porridge. Sir Walter told this story with much humour, But after a few minutes' silence, began again, and told the same story a second time, and then again a third time. His daughter, who was watching him with increasing anxiety, then motioned to us to rise from table, and persuaded her father to return to his bedroom.

With the help of his valet, he managed to negotiate the stairs, but on reaching his dressing room he collapsed and almost immediately lost consciousness. One of the servants was sent post haste to Selkirk to fetch Dr James Clarkson, and on the surgeon's arrival at Abbotsford he immediately instituted all the usual remedies then in favour in cases of apoplexy. Scott had in the meantime regained his senses but was paralysed down the right side and had completely lost the power of speech. Clarkson bled him; shaved his head in order that he might blister it 'to relieve the pressure on the brain'; and issued strict instructions to Anne that henceforth her father was to be kept on the most spartan of diets. When his faculties returned sufficiently for him to be able once more to think coherently, poor Scott found himself in the most dismal of conditions. The copious bleeding he had undergone had left him weak as a kitten; the muscles of one side of his face had sagged in a grotesque fashion; while the whole of that side of his body was numbed and almost without feeling. These symptoms became less severe during the course of the next few days and he was soon able to speak again, but with difficulty and in a slurred and mumbling manner. The boredom of being confined to his room while forbidden to either read or write reduced him to tears; but Anne was determined that he should have all the peace and quiet the doctor had ordered and she saw to it that there was no breaking of the rules he had set. This time there was no doubt in anyone's mind, least of all the patient's, that it was apoplexy that had struck him. A week later, when at last he was allowed to grasp a pen, he demanded his journal and scrawled details of the ordeal he had been through. 'Whether these precautions have been taken in time I cannot tell,' he concluded. 'I think they have, though severe in themselves, beat the disease. But I am alike prepared,

Seu versare dolos, seu certae occumbere morti.[1]

[1] '[Nerved to either event,] whether to spin his toils, or to fall under death inevitable.' *Aeneid*, Book II, 61.

I only know that to live as I am just now is a gift little worth having. I think I will be in the Secret next week unless I recruit greatly.'

But by the month of May he had so far recovered that he was once more able to dictate to Laidlaw a few more pages of *Count Robert of Paris*. It was a halting and laboured effort. 'The task of pumping my brains becomes inevitably harder when "both chain pumps are choked below,"' he noted despondently. 'My pronunciation is a good deal improved. My time glides away ill employed, but I am afraid of the palsy. I should not like to be pinned to my chair. But I suppose even that kind of life is more endurable than we could suppose. Your wishes are limited to your little circle — yet the idea is terrible to a man who has been active. My own circle in bodily matters is daily narrowing; not so in intellectual matters, but I am perhaps a bad judge. The plough is coming to the end of the furrow, so it is likely I shall not reach the common goal of mortal life by a few years. I am now in my sixtieth year only, and

Three score and ten years do sum up.'

Within a week of writing these words in his journal, at a time when his pride made him delude himself that, although physically he had aged terribly in the previous twelve months, his intellectual ability was unimpaired and that he was still capable of literary composition of a quality that his readers would applaud, he received notification from Ballantyne and Cadell that *Count Robert* was unfit for publication in its present form, and with brutal frankness advising him that if it appeared it might injure his reputation to such an extent that sales of the *Opus Magnum* would undoubtably suffer. For the first time Scott came face to face with the fact that his career as an author was drawing to a close, and that from this time onwards he would have only his past glories to sustain him. 'The blow is a stunning one I suppose, for I scarcely feel it,' he wrote with a heavy heart. 'It is singular, but it comes with as little surprise as if I had a remedy ready. Yet God knows, I am at sea in the dark, and the vessel leaky, I think, into the bargain....I have suffered terribly, that is the truth, rather in body than mind, and I often wish I could lie down and sleep without waking. But I will fight it out if I can. It would argue too great an attachment of consequence to my literary labours to sink under. Did I know how to begin, I would begin this very day, although I knew I should sink in the end. After all, this is but fear and faintness of heart, though of another kind from that which trembleth at a loaded pistol. My bodily strength is terribly gone: perhaps my mental too?'

In the midst of all this anguish of mind, he turned with a fierce purpose once more to his book and dogmatically asserted: 'I am determined to write a political pamphlet *coûte que coûte*;—ay, should it cost me my life.'

16

SCOTT'S POLITICAL SYMPATHIES had long been founded on a now unshakeable belief in the unquestionable merits of a feudalistic society. He firmly believed that there were those who, by reason of wealth or breeding, had been selected by a benevolent Fate as most fit to govern the ignorant masses who formed the immense majority of the British people. Amongst these privileged few he numbered the entire British aristocracy, the squires and lairds and major landowners, and those men of property who could be relied upon to maintain and strengthen the social stockade that protected the upper classes.

He was a firm believer in Falkland's infamous maxim—'When it is not necessary to change, it is necessary not to change.' He therefore bitterly opposed the long-delayed reform of an electoral system that was acknowledged to be rotten to the core, brushing aside all logical and reasoned argument in favour of its alteration. At that time, as Lord Cockburn put it, Scotland was little better than a village in servitude at the gate of a feudal baron, most of the finest elements in public life being totally unrepresented in either local or national government. In 1831, out of a population of 2,365,000 there were only 2,600 voters on the county rolls, and 1,300 town councillors had the job of electing the burgh members. Well over nine-tenths of the adult population were not entitled to vote at all, yet Scott called those who desired to see the introduction of a more just system of representation and a wider franchise 'blackguards and rabble-rousers'. It is little wonder that William Hazlitt, in his *Spirit of the Age*, caricatured him as one who 'stooped to the unworthy arts of adulation and abetted the views of the great with the pettifogging feelings of the meanest dependant on office...who repaid the public liberality by striking a secret and envenomed blow at every one who was not the ready tool of power.'

Scott's Toryism was of the type that the arch-reactionary Lord Eldon was only too ready to applaud, and it is said that he clapped his hands with pleasure at hearing that the Laird of Abbotsford had once raised what he was pleased to call a Buccleuch Legion. This ill-armed rabble of villagers from Darnick, Selkirk, and Melrose was formed with the express purpose of putting down, with the sword if necessary, a rising of half-starved colliers and weavers of the North who had banded together to demand shorter hours and a living wage. His solution for dealing with any attempt by the labouring classes to organize themselves into what later came to be termed trade unions was a simple one—transport the leaders to the penal settlements at Botany Bay, preferably for life.

It is hardly surprising therefore, that despite the precarious state of his health, he insisted in taking part in the political upheaval caused by the proposed Reform Bill. He was determined to travel over to Jedburgh to lend his support to the Tory candidate, and on the 18th May, in spite of the tearful protests of the female members of his family, he set out at seven in the morning, accompanied by Lockhart, meaning to make an impassioned speech to sway the waverers before the election. But as soon as his carriage arrived in Jedburgh it was recognized by the workers crowding the streets as being one that contained an ardent supporter of the anti-Reform candidate. Within minutes a shower of stones crashed against its sides, several of which came through the windows and landed on the seats, fortunately without hurting the inmates. They managed to reach the home of the late Robert Shortreed, whose widow and family gave them shelter and later provided them with breakfast. The election was due to take place that morning in the local court, the hall of which was crowded with a concourse of artisans and working people from Hawick and Jedburgh and other surrounding towns and villages, most of whom were proudly displaying the colourful rosettes of the Reform Movement.

To this hall Scott was now forced to make his slow and painful way, flanked by Lockhart and one of Shortreed's sons, the crowd hissing and jeering him and then taking up the cry of 'Burke Sir Walter! Burke Sir Walter!'[1] as he attempted to push

---

[1] A reference to the notorious criminal, Burke, executed at Edinburgh in 1829 for smothering several unfortunates in a disused cellar after first making them drunk. Their bodies were then sold to surgeons of the city for the purpose of dissection. Burke was assisted in his crimes by William Hare, who later turned King's Evidence.

his way through. On reaching the platform he did his best to speak, despite his continuing impediment, but the catcalls and boos coming from the body of the floor prevented a word he said from being heard. Young Scott of Harden, the Tory candidate, was elected by those present who were entitled to vote by an overwhelming majority, the figures being forty in his favour and nineteen against. No other result was possible with the electoral law being what it was at that time, but even so the news was greeted by the mob with hoots of dismay and cries of vengeance. Lockhart, for one, was seriously perturbed by the threatening appearance of the crowd, and certain of the gentlemen who had served on the side of the Whigs were also fearful for Sir Walter's safety. One of these, a Lieutenant Elliot, who had a villa on the outskirts of the town, persuaded Scott that he ought to seek refuge there, and leaving the hall by the back entrance and using field paths and narrow lanes, they managed to reach it unseen. In the meantime, Sir Walter's coachman, Peter Mathieson, had contrived to drive his master's carriage to the villa by an equally devious route, and Lockhart and his father-in-law thankfully boarded it to make the rest of their way out of the town. But at Jedburgh Bridge, which the mob knew they would be forced to cross, an ambush had been laid. If this had been successful it would probably have resulted in the carriage being overturned with possible serious injury to the occupants. Fortunately for Scott and his companion, Mathieson had enlisted the aid of four muscular Darnick villagers who crowded the rumble seat and menaced the shouting rabble with their cudgels as the coachman laid his whip across the horses' backs and galloped the vehicle through. A final shower of stones and bricks hit the roof and sides of the swaying carriage as it thundered over the bridge, and then they were safely out in the countryside and on their way to Abbotsford.

'I left the burgh in the midst of abuse and the gentle hint of "Burke Sir Walter,"' Scott wrote before retiring to bed. 'Much obliged to the brave lads of Jeddart.' Next day he was off to Selkirk to take part in the election there. This passed off quietly enough, but the countryside was full of rumours of impending trouble and he fulminated in his journal about how the agitators should be dealt with.

During the previous December Cadell had been horrified to learn that Scott intended to write a fiery political pamplet condemning the Reform Bill, and he and Ballantyne posted down to Abbotsford in time to prevent its appearance in the newspapers. The publisher knew the damage it would have done to the author's reputation amongst those of his readers who did not espouse the Tory cause, and Scott was finally persuaded to throw the written sheets on the fire. To soften the blow Cadell gave a nebulous promise that he would consider publishing something of the sort after the election was over, hoping, as in fact happened, that the proposal would eventually be forgotten. James Ballantyne in the meantime had allowed himself to be caught up in the controversy over the reform of the electoral register, and to Scott's horror and disbelief he embraced the Whiggish cause. The first the author knew about Ballantyne's open change of heart was when his copy of the *Edinburgh Weekly Journal* arrived at Abbotsford, and he was so shocked that he immediately summoned the printer to come down from Edinburgh and explain what he meant by such infamous conduct. He had suspected on previous occasions that James might secretly hold opinions of a liberal nature, and once he had threatened to withdraw his support from the paper over some comments Ballantyne had made about the 'Massacre of Peterloo'.

That had happened some twelve years ago, and the friendship that had existed between the two since their school-days in Kelso was patched up again within a week. But the year 1831 was proving a singularly unhappy one for their long-standing relationship. The bickering that had occurred between the printer and Cadell at various times during the previous two years, and in which Scott had been forced to take sides, had rankled with him and made him wish Ballantyne and his printing presses at the bottom of the Firth of Forth. The printer's outright condemnation of *Count Robert of Paris* had wounded him deeply, far more so than any criticism his work had suffered in the past, for he knew he was quite unable to remedy the tale's manifest faults. Another source of irritation was a letter Ballantyne had sent him, doubtless with the best of intentions, advising him to give up drink. 'I suspect it would do both yourself and your printer some good, were both to pin their pledged word to some Abstinence Society,' James had told him in April. What Scott said when he read this piece of unsolicited advice can only be imagined. To Cadell he wrote: 'J.B. wishes to engage himself & I in what he calls a pledge to a temperate Society—that is to proclaim ourselves sots & intemperate fools to the whole world. He be damned – & so much for that.'

So it can be perceived that when Ballantyne entered the lion's den at Abbotsford late in July to explain why his newspaper had decided to support the Whigs over the Reform Bill affair, Scott was in a seething temper and ready to tell the printer exactly what he thought of one who, to use his own words, 'turned his back on his old political friends'. What exactly transpired that summer evening will never be known with accuracy, but early next morning James Ballantyne stalked out of the house without saying goodbye to his host and shook the dust of Abbotsford from his shoes. Thus ended a friendship that had lasted nearly fifty years. The two men never met again, and when the author sent Cadell the first part of the manuscript of *Castle Dangerous*, which, with *Count Robert*, formed the fourth and last series of *Tales of My Landlord*, he expressly ordered that it was not to be discussed with Ballantyne. He told Lockhart that at first he had designed that it should be printed elsewhere than at the Ballantyne Press, but he cooled down sufficiently to permit the printer to tender for the job in the usual way and Cadell later gave him the order to complete.

Ballantyne himself was now a very sick man. The rotund and padded figure of a few years ago, had by this time been replaced by one of almost painful thinness. Those that remembered him in the old days, sitting, at the end of one of his rich and stultifying multi-course dinners, beaming at the assembled company as he called for the dish of broiled bones and steaming bowl of hot rum punch, could now hardly recognize the drawn and anxious little man they saw before them as the genial James Ballantyne they knew so well. The stomach ulcers from which he suffered had not been quelled by the crude and misguided treatments his various doctors had prescribed. The grief and worry occasioned by the loss of his wife, the strains of bringing up a young family and that of running a demanding business, had done nothing to alleviate a condition that was gradually worsening with each passing month. With his brother Sandy editing the *Weekly Journal* and managing the office, and his foreman John Hughes progressing the orders in the printing workshop, he was able to spend many of his worst days in bed. But any recovery he seemed to make was always of short duration and the attacks of intense pain from which he suffered were

257

becoming increasingly frequent. Only complete rest and quiet while adhering strictly to a bland diet would have eventually resulted in any improvement, but for James these conditions were quite impossible to attain. He was the type of person who seemed to take a melancholy pleasure in worrying himself sick even when confronted by a clear horizon, and it now needed only a few days back in the rough and tumble of Edinburgh's commercial arena to put Ballantyne in bed for at least a week. But fortunately John Hughes was an excellent organizer and Sandy saw to it that the books were kept in order, while most of the customers who had deserted them at the time of the financial crisis of 1826 had long since returned to their fold. The quality of the work they turned out was still the best in Scotland and their files contained sheaves of appreciative letters from satisfied clients. Francis Jeffrey, on at last resigning the editorship of the *Edinburgh Review*, gave them a brusque pat on the back before he departed to other fields of glory.

Lanfine.
Thursday 8th August, 1829

Messrs. Ballantyne,
Printers,
Paul's Works,
Edinburgh.

I return the proof which I received this morning—with the further revise—for which, however, I hope the press has not been waiting, as it is of no consequence.

I did not want you to risk a boy on Monday night—but for 2/- you might have got a stout Chairman who would have been thankful for the job. However, there is no harm done—and we must part in peace—my connection with your press (for the moment at least) ends here. The rest of the copy will be sent, and the proofs returned, to Mr. Napier.[1]

You are very good printers—but you are the better for being kept on the alert—and if I have been impatient now and then, it has all been for your own good and did not impart malice. If it has given any pain I ask pardon—and with good wishes for your comfort and prosperity.

I remain,
Your faithful servant,
F. Jeffrey[2]

[1] Macvey Napier, who was editor of the *Edinburgh Review* from 1829–47.
[2] This unpublished letter is in my own collection.

For which testimonial James and Sandy sent him their very grateful thanks.

The younger of the Ballantyne brothers had proved useful to Scott in the past in several ways, not least of which was the providing of musical entertainment at some of the larger dinner parties at Abbotsford. Scott retained unhappy memories of being dragged unwillingly by his wife to concerts in Edinburgh, for he professed to be tone deaf and to have little if any musical appreciation. But he derived real pleasure from hearing Sandy perform traditional Scottish airs on his violin and 'penny whistle', and he made a point of asking him to be present at all important social functions at which he acted as host. The autumn of 1831 witnessed what proved to be the last of these to be held at Abbotsford during his lifetime. All that summer he had been unwell and his doctors were unanimous in advising his family that he ought to spend the coming winter in a more salubrious climate than cold and windy Scotland commonly afforded. Despite the fact that they were well aware in which direction his political sympathies lay, the Whig government of Lord Grey, on being told that the Wizard of the North urgently needed the warmth of the Mediterranean and invigorating salt sea breezes to restore him to some degree of health, magnanimously informed his family that they were prepared to put the frigate *Barham* at his disposal for a winter cruise. In addition, his eldest son would be granted leave of absence from his regiment so as to be able to accompany his father on the trip. This generous offer was too good to be missed and Scott made arrangements for an extended holiday abroad. Guests were invited to a farewell dinner party to be held the evening before his departure for London, and late in September Sandy received an invitation to be present at this special occasion. Amongst others staying at the house were William Wordsworth and his daughter, and the party that assembled at Abbotsford on the 22nd September was a large and distinguished one. Sandy later recalled the event in a letter to his son James. He had been permitted to take along his younger boy John, who was studying to be an artist. 'John and I went to Abbotsford and were most kindly received. We partook of Sir Walter's last dinner, it may be, in that beautiful spot. He left it next morning. John took "The Great Unknown", a picture of a warrior listening to his mistress playing the lute—Sir Walter was extremely pleased with it, as also were Miss Scott and

Lockhart. We caught a dish of trout for dinner. Sir Walter was full of fun and mirth; but his health has received a rude, rude shock! He wrote me a note which says, "I would I could insure our meeting again in life". He harped once or twice on Smollett and Richardson having gone abroad for the recovery of their health and dying there.'[1]

Young John Ballantyne's awestruck reaction to being sandwiched for several hours in the company of the great, can be gauged from a letter he published on the centenary of Scott's birth.

Sir,

At this time, when everyone delights to think of Scott—to think, write and read of Scott—perhaps it might interest some of your readers to have a personal reminiscence of one who dined at Abbotsford the last time the great man ever sat at his table there.

It was on the day before Sir Walter left for the continent, from whence he returned but to die...I was brought up, so to speak, in an atmosphere of Waverley. I have seen my father, night after night, with locked doors, copying the manuscripts of the 'Great Unknown' as if he was engaged on something purely sacred. I have heard him, and everyone bearing the name of Ballantyne who knew Scott, speak of him with not only veneration and respect, but with absolute love. The incident I write, therefore, has always been marked in my memory with a white stone.

The party that assembled around his board that day, September 22nd, 1831, consisted of all the members of his family then in Scotland and several of his intimate friends, including his amanuensis [Laidlaw], Sir Adam Ferguson, Wordsworth, Sir William Allen, my father Alexander Ballantyne, and one or two others whom I did not know, and do not remember, as I was only sixteen years old at the time. Sir Walter sat at the centre of the table, his eldest son, then Major, and Lockhart were seated at the head and foot. I was fortunate enough to be placed facing Scott, and thus had an opportunity of hearing all that he said, and watching every varying expression that lighted up his wonderful countenance. Well do I remember his face, but, alas, at this distant date I remember but as words in a dream the wonderful flow of conversation, the quiet touches of humour in the stories that came so naturally to illustrate any subject on the tapis...All this continued throughout the time of dinner, and afterwards in the library when his 'last' conversations with Wordsworth took place, and, after the party broke up, I

[1] This letter is in my own collection. It was first printed in *Ballantyne the Brave*.

260

remember Sir Adam Ferguson saying to my father that he never heard Sir Walter more brilliant in his palmiest days.

Towards the close of the evening, Sir Walter, with his usual kindness towards youngsters, asked me if I had seen his 'curiosities', and my answering in the negative, he led me into the little room where his treasured relics of antiquity were, and still are, kept; and probably feeling he was parting from them for a long time, he pointed out lovingly, as it were, to my notice, a few of his especial favourites—among them Rob Roy's gun, the thumkins, the Keys of the Heart of Midlothian, etc.,—and then seating himself, he told me various anecdotes and legends called up by the sight of his anti-quarian treasures. Well do I remember his appearance as, seated on a window-seat, his hands crossed on the handle of his stout, in-separable walking-stick, the fading light fell gently on his silvery locks and towering forehead as they were silhuetted against the sombre background of distant trees. At his back the Tweed glit-tered as it passed the abode of him who loved its streams so well.

When the hour came for the departure of the guests who were not staying in the house, Scott accompanied them to the hall, and there, after receiving a kindly pat on the shoulder en pa, standing amongst his old armour and loving friends, I had my last glimpse of Sir Walter Scott.

Yours faithfully,
John Ballantyne.[1]

Next morning Sir Walter and his daughter wished goodbye to the servants and estate workers that had assembled at the gates to see them off, and accompanied by Lockhart, left by carriage for London which they reached by easy stages on the 28th. Scott still insisted on working for an hour or two each day on his notes for the *Magnum* despite the fact that he was under instructions from his medical advisers to rest his brain as much as possible and lay aside all labour of a literary kind. But he was thoroughly frightened when Anne and Lockhart called in three eminent brain specialists to examine him. Dr Robert Ferguson, who had been requested to attend while Sir Walter was in London, advised the family that this should be done, and the author finally submitted to being examined in the middle of October. Lockhart tells how the three doctors with-drew to an ante-room after they had concluded their examination, there to discuss their findings. The door having been left open, Scott moved the wheelchair he now used into a dark corner 'so

---

[1] This letter was printed in *The Standard* newspaper in August, 1871.

that he might see their faces without their being able to read his'. Incipient 'brain disease' had been diagnosed, but the patient was told that he still displayed so much mental vigour that provided he obeyed instructions and kept to a strict diet, at the same time avoiding any undue mental strain and living a life of peace and quiet, then 'the malady might yet be arrested'. His son-in-law informs us that Scott did not attempt to conceal from his doctors 'that he had feared insanity and feared *them*'.

From 25th May to 9th October of that year he made no entries in his journal. When at last he resumed the habit he set down frankly his fears for the future.

> I have been very ill, and if not quite unable to write, I have been unfit to do so. I have wrought, however, at two *Waverley* things, but not well, and what is worse, past mending. A total prostration of bodily strength is my chief complaint. I cannot walk half a mile. There is, besides, some mental confusion, with the extent of which I am not perhaps fully acquainted. I am perhaps setting. I am myself inclined to think so, and, like a day that has been admired as a fine one, the light of it sets down amid mists and storms. I neither regret nor fear the approach of death if it is coming. I would compound for a little pain instead of this heartless muddiness of mind which renders me incapable of anything rational. The expense of my journey will be something considerable, which I can provide against by borrowing £500 from Mr Gibson. To Mr Cadell I owe already, with the cancels on these apoplectic books, about £200, and must run it up to £500 more at least; yet this heavy burthen would be easily borne if I were to be the Walter Scott I once was; but the change is great. This would be nothing, providing that I could count on these two books having a sale equal to their predecessors; but as they do not deserve the same countenance, they will not and cannot have such a share of favour, and I have only to hope that they will not involve the *Waverley*, (which are now selling 30,000 volumes a month) in their displeasure...I have in short no fears on pecuniary matters. The ruin which I fear involves that of my King and country.

He was depressed by the furious political row that was still in progress over the Reform Bill, but the measure finally became law in 1832, amid scenes of wild rejoicing by its supporters. Scott consoled himself with the thought that one day 'education and property will recover an ascendency which they have only lost by faintheartedness.'[1]

[1] *Journal*—14th November, 1831.

He was accompanied by his eldest son and both his daughters when he at last set off for Portsmouth, but although they arrived there on the 23rd October, it was almost a week before the contrary winds died down and they were able to sail. By noon on the 30th the whole party were confined to their bunks by sea-sickness, the ladies being dreadfully ill and Scott scarcely less so. But by the time they had crossed the Bay of Biscay they had all managed to find their sea-legs and the younger members of the party were beginning to enjoy themselves on deck. As they passed Cape St Vincent and Trafalgar, Scott's fierce patriotism was aroused as the captain of the *Barham* regaled him with stories of the sea-battles fought off those rugged peninsulas. The sea air improved his general health and increased his appetite, and his journal was full of the scenes he witnessed in Gibraltar harbour and at the island of Malta where they stayed for three weeks. He felt so refreshed in mind that he became enthusiastic about a proposed new novel, to be called *The Siege of Malta*, and also about a short story *Il Bizarro*, at both of which he worked on and off for the next few months. The manuscripts of these tales have survived, but it is to be hoped that no scholar who examines them will ever be so cruel to their author's memory as to pay for their publication.

They reached Naples in the middle of December and stayed there four months, seeing all the sights in true tourist fashion and being presented at Court to be received by the King. But although Scott's physical health seemed to show an improvement, it had become increasingly obvious to his family that the brain disease from which he suffered was a progressive one and that every passing week found him less able to reason clearly. On 16th January, 1832, he received news of the death of his little grandson, but his ability to appreciate the loss of the child whom he had worshipped in earlier years had become blunted, and he merely noted in his journal: 'Poor Johnny Lockhart! The boy is gone whom we have made so much of. I could not have borne it better than I do now, and might have borne it much worse.'[1] There were times when he believed that all his debts had been paid off and he wrote to Lockhart with light-hearted instructions regarding the purchase of the estate of Faldonside. He had intended to visit Goethe at Weimar on his return journey, but in March word came of the German philosopher's

[1] John Hugh Lockhart died 15th December, 1831.

death. 'He at least died at home,' Scott muttered. Shortly afterwards he started to press his family to allow him to return to Abbotsford. In the middle of April they purchased a light travelling carriage, and into this he was crowded with his daughter Anne, his son Charles (who had come out to replace his brother Walter who had been forced to return to his regiment), and the two servants they had taken with them. In this they made their way to Rome, then through Venice to the Tyrol and so on to the Rhine. Scott made his last entry in his journal on the 16th April, just after they had arrived in Rome, the note ending abruptly in the middle of a sentence. From that point onwards he gradually slipped into a listlessness that the strange sights and sounds outside the carriage windows totally failed to disperse. He was helped into one continental hotel or coaching inn after the other as they progressed northwards, paying little if any attention to what went on around him and continually asking to be reassured that they were in fact on their way back to Scotland and the Abbotsford he was so longing to see.

For Anne and Charles the journey back was a nightmare, a *via dolorosa* that seemed to have no end. To begin with, their father could at least sit in a chair and feed and partly clothe himself, and his valet, Nicholson, was proving invaluable as a male nurse. But on June 9th, when at Nimeguen on the Rhine he suffered his fourth major cerebral haemorrhage which for a time brought him extremely close to death. His valet bled and blistered him and he finally became sufficiently conscious to convey to his son that he wished the journey back home to be resumed at all costs. On the 11th he was carried on a stretcher to the steamboat at Rotterdam, and on the 13th the same method had to be employed at the docks in London to enable him to be taken to a room in the St James's Hotel in Jermyn Street. Most of the three weeks he was there he was in a coma or a stupor of semi-delirium, his family crowding round and messages being received from well-wishers in every part of the kingdom. Newspaper correspondents besieged his doctors as they left after each examination; daily bulletins were printed to give their readers up-to-the-minute news about his condition; and a report soon gained currency that his recent travels abroad had so impoverished him that his state of mind was being made far worse by financial worries. Lockhart shortly afterwards received a private message from a member of the Government to the effect that the Treasury would be only too pleased to advance a sum of money 'to relieve Sir Walter of his pecuniary embarrassments' if the newspaper reports about his difficulties were actually true. The offer was, of course, declined with thanks.

In his lucid moments Scott entreated his family and his doctors to be allowed to return to Abbotsford, all but imploring them to let him die in the home he so dearly loved. There seemed little point in not granting his wish, for all hope of his eventual recovery had long since been abandoned. On 7th July he was carried on board ship, a great crowd lining the pavements outside his hotel, and two days later he was transferred to a carriage at Newhaven to begin his last journey to Tweeddale. He was only semi-conscious for most of the way, but the moment the Eildon Hills came into view from Ladhope he started a restless muttering which turned to a feverish excitement by the time that Abbotsford was reached. A bed had been prepared for him in the dining-room and there his servants and his dogs were waiting to greet him as he was settled by many helping hands under the coverlets. His old secretary, Laidlaw, grasped his hand as Scott managed to whisper to him: 'O man, how often have I thought of you!'

For a short space of time his faculties seemed to return, and on fine days he was pushed in a wheel-chair out on to the terrace overlooking the Tweed, there to sit musing among the rose bushes, swathed in a tartan cloak. 'I have seen much,' he repeated over and over again to those who came and sat with him, 'but nothing like my ain house'. He was content to sit for hours at the library window, while his daughter or Laidlaw read aloud to him from Crabbe or one of the eighteenth century novelists, but it is doubtful if he comprehended what was being said. His condition was now such that he spoke only a single coherent sentence or two during each day, while the irritation his mind was suffering at times made him so violent that his daughters were afraid to approach him. Laidlaw wrote a letter to Skene on the 15th August, in which he gave him news of Scott's distressing condition: 'Your Friend is as helpless and requires to be attended in every respect as an infant of six months old. Of his powerful mind, which as it were shone over the civilized world, there remains only a pale and uncertain glimmering—sometimes, though but rarely, it blazes out for a brief moment, and this makes the melancholy sight more hard to bear. They tell me he is seldom conscious—generally extremely restless and impatient and they tell me irritable—I have rarely seen him show any such symptoms for he always knows me, seems relieved to see me, holds out his hand and grasps mine and looks me in the face and always attempts to speak—often he seems anxious to enquire about or to tell me something, but he rarely makes out a sentence and when he finds he cannot make himself understood he lets his head sink, and he remains silent until I offer to go away when he holds my hand firmly and sometimes entreats me not to go yet.'

Before the end came there was one flash of light, but it flared for only a minute or two before being extinguished for ever. He had been dozing for about half an hour in his wheel-chair, when he suddenly started awake, and shaking the plaids his valet had placed about his shoulders, demanded to be taken to his desk. 'This is a sad idleness,' he told those around him. 'I shall forget what I have been thinking of, if I don't set it down now.' He was wheeled inside the house to his study and the chair placed before his desk where writing paper had been laid in readiness. A pen was inked and placed in his fingers, but the paralysis prevented him from grasping it and it rolled unheeded across the sheet of paper. It was a poignant and deeply embarrassing moment as the old author sank back into his pillows with silent tears coursing down his face. 'Don't let me expose myself,' he said a little later. 'Get me back to bed—that's the only place.'

For the last fortnight of his life he was seldom conscious. Lockhart wickedly concocted a story that his dying father-in-law relapsed into weak-minded piety just before the end. (This about a man who would not have a parson within a mile of his house if he could help it, and despised above all things the death-bed repentance of real or imagined sins uttered as an insurance that the pearly gates would be opened at the appointed hour.) According to Lockhart he was at Scott's bedside (alone, of course) when the great man bade him 'be a good man—be virtuous—be religious—be a good man—nothing else will give you any comfort when you come to lie here.' These statements no doubt brought a warm glow to those readers of his biography who had been caught in the wave of evangelism that swept the country in Victorian days; but to those who knew Scott they rang as false as ever words could be. In the late 1930's a letter was discovered in the National Library of Scotland which seemed to indicate their source. It had been written to Lockhart during the time he was at work on the biography, by a lady relative of Scott. 'When you write anything of the last very melancholy weeks at Abbotsford,' she told him, 'I think it will be most valuable to mention any of the few remarks he uttered when his mind was clear of a religious tendency, such as I heard he said occasionally, Oh be virtuous! It is ones only comfort in a dying state! and anything of that kind, for there *are* wicked people who will take a *pleasure* in saying that he was not a religious man; and *proving the contrary will do much good.*' One other mistake Sir Walter's son-in-law made was to date the utterance of these uncharacteristic words as being on the 17th September, only four days before Scott died. It is known from several sources that the author was deeply unconscious at this time, and his daughter Sophia confirms this when she wrote to a friend five days after his death giving details of what happened during the final weeks of waiting: 'After about forty hours of stupor he breathed his last; for the last fortnight his life was a miracle; every day the doctor took leave saying it was impossible he would outlive the night, and life was only kept in by opiates; his mind never returned for an instant.'

On the 21st September at 1.30 p.m. the Laird of Abbotsford died. His four children were at his bedside and his dogs lay huddled at the foot. When it was noticed that his breathing had ceased his eldest son bent over and kissed his forehead as the weeping servants went from room to room, drawing the heavy curtains and shutting out the light. 'Scott is dead,' wrote Henry Cockburn in his journal. 'He expired yesterday. I had been on a visit to Kirklands...and on coming home today I saw Abbotsford reposing beside its gentle Tweed, and amidst its fading woods, in the calm splendour of a sweet autumnal day. I was not aware till I reached Edinburgh that all that it then contained of him was his memory and his remains. Scotland never owed so much to one man.'

17

SIR WALTER HAD been anything but thrifty during the last few years of his life and his family were dismayed at the load of newly contracted personal debts that had to be cleared up before his estate could be settled. He was buried with befitting pomp beside his wife amid the ruins of ancient Dryburgh Abbey. The line of carriages taking the mourners to the interment stretched for nearly a mile, and at one time an entire black-coated country-side seemed to be walking with bowed heads behind his hearse. The expenses incurred by a funeral of such magnificence were only one of the many bills the new baronet was forced to deal with, for his father's illness and recent journey in quest of health had run up large accounts in several quarters. Including the two shillings allowed as an *ex-gratia* payment by the creditors as being the value of his books and personal possessions, eleven shillings in the pound had been paid towards clearing the debts acknowledged in 1826, but another nine shillings had still to be found even if the interest on the capital sum outstanding was disregarded. During the last years of his life Scott had fallen again into his old habit of drawing bills on his publisher for new editions of his works yet to be printed. His son was well aware of this practice, but his father's mental illness prevented him taking a firm line, and the continuing heavy sales of the *Opus Magnum* was given as an excuse that all in the end would straighten itself out financially. In a letter to Major Walter Scott on the 30th April, 1832, Robert Cadell told him frankly of the bills his father was continually incurring.

> Sir Walter got from his trustees when he left last October   £500
>
> This met his London expenditure, and left a considerable balance over. For this balance he drew from Malta. But on getting to Naples he made so great a howling about money that I paid Coutts & Co   £300

His howling however continued so great that

I sent him further to Naples	£500
Here is in all	£1300

I had scarcely a doubt from the tenor of his letters that this sum must last for many months to come. What was the surprise therefore of Mr Gibson and myself to get advice from Coutts & Co. of two fresh drafts (our advice was only last Friday) one for £500 and the other for £200, making say £2000 in six months! This is Captain Osbaldistone with a vengence—of the £2000 the Trustees will only pay £500 so that here is £1500 from me besides £2000 more your father owes me:

Say his debt to me	£3500
There are many open accounts for which I am constantly dunned they will I am sure come to	£700
There is	£4200

of a new debt running against your father at a speed too which is destruction itself. His whole income just now is about £1200 p.a.; his rate of spending you can form some idea of. He writes me to buy up debts, to buy carriage horses, to buy ponies. *I pay no attention* to these instructions.

Cadell's burning ambition was to secure all the copyrights of the late Author of *Waverley* for himself, and he had already formulated a scheme that he believed would enable him to do this. He knew that if he was once successful in making them the property of Cadell & Company (and half were still owned by the trustees) then he would be able to reap the full benefit of the tremendous profits he believed could be made for many years out of the public's seemingly insatiable desire to own sets of the Collected Works of Sir Walter Scott. He had dreams of producing every sort and size of edition; expensive illustrated editions, cheap editions for the labouring classes, library editions cased in a tough hard-wearing cloth, and large-paper sets bound in sumptuous morocco and fit to grace the walls of a nobleman's stately home.

He managed to frighten the Scott family into believing that the creditors would demand full interest on their father's debts from January 1826 onwards, and succeeded in convincing Walter and Charles that the only way to prevent this happening was for them to offer to pay off the outstanding nine shillings in the pound immediately. This dangling lump sum he thought would so tempt the creditors that they would agree to surrender 'the half copyrights of Scott's Novels, and Romances, Poetical Works, and Miscellaneous Prose Works' and also make over to the family the entailed estate of Abbotsford and other properties still in their hands. This proved to be the case; the creditors agreed to the conditions, and Cadell mysteriously came forward with the sum of £30,000, borrowed, he said, from friends, which, with the £22,000 paid by an insurance company on Scott's death, plus other monies already in the trustees hands, was sufficient to wipe out the debt. Naturally there were strings tied to Cadell's generous offer of help, and in a few months he was the owner of most of the copyrights he so much coveted, the other half being already in his hands. But it was May 1847, before Lockhart was able to write to his friend Croker: 'I have finally settled all Sir Walter's affairs. There remained: debt secured on his lands, £8500; to Cadell £16,000; and sundries £1000. I have taken the £1000 on myself, and Cadell obliterates the £24,500 on condition of getting the whole remaining copyrights of Scott's Works, and also of the Life.'

Lockhart's seven-volume *Memoirs of the Life of Sir Walter Scott, Bart.* referred to in the last paragraph when Cadell managed to scoop the copyright, was issued at intervals of about a month from March 1837, onwards, publication being completed in February 1838. It has been described as standing next to Boswell's *Life of Johnson* in the field of English biography and is undoubtedly a great literary quarry. But modern scholarship has revealed that it is not only speckled with inaccuracies both large and small, but on a number of occasions the author has gone out of his way to slant facts and invent dramatic incidents in order to bolster whatever case he happened then to be making. Lockhart set out with the deliberate intention of blackening the name of the Ballantynes to enable him to whitewash his father-in-law's reputation and explain away his financial ruin by placing the blame firmly on the shoulders of James and John. During their lifetime he had not evinced any particular enmity to either of them, and with James, whom he knew quite well, his relationship appeared to be cordial.

Shortly after Scott's death the printer had become so ill that he was seldom able to leave his sickroom. But hearing that it was proposed that Lockhart should write Scott's biography, he immediately wrote to him offering any assistance he could give.

In particular, he offered to prepare a memorandum of their association as schoolboys in Kelso and in the years that followed; at the same time mentioning that he deeply regretted that political differences had in the end caused Scott and himself to drift apart. Lockhart's reply to his letter was couched in the most friendly terms.

London. Nov. 1, 1832

My Dear Sir,

If any feeling had really existed of the nature of which your letter begins with mentioning, that most touching, most manly letter would have been a thousand times more than enough to do away with it for ever. I can, however, speak for myself, that, though I did observe a certain difference in your relations with your dear friend Sir Walter, I never even for one moment dreamed that anything had occurred to disturb the old, genial feelings which had through your lives been equally marked in both of you as friends.

For two years before his death, Sir Walter Scott was no longer, in all respects, the man of earlier days; and I can perfectly understand, that his political impressions should have been conveyed within that period in a style which would not before have been possible for him. Let us draw a veil over the infirmities of those few sad weary months, and now endeavour to think of him only as he was when you and I so often shared together the delights of his friendship and conversation.

Your Memoranda of him will be expected by me as among the most precious materials for his biography. You knew the man as a boy; and his literary life may be said to have been all in your presence, even from the working of his smallest springs. I earnestly hope your health may soon be entirely re-established; and I am joined in this wish by all the members of my wife's family (they are all at the moment here) as well as in the expression of sincere regret that you should have had the pain of writing such a letter at such a time.

Believe me truly and cordially yours,

J. G. Lockhart[1]

After he had received the extensive notes Ballantyne sent him, the biographer wrote saying that he now felt that he had known Scott 'in the days of Kelso, and the Tavern-club, and the Stage-coach journey. I pray you to continue to draw on your memory for more and more of these invaluable details, ... and may your

[1] Quoted in the *Refutation*, pp. 84–5.

health, and this and a thousand other good works to follow, be strengthened and restored'. Ballantyne was spared the pain of knowing what the writer of this and the previous letter really thought of him, for a few weeks later, on the 16th January, 1833, he died at his home in Hill Street, Edinburgh. A stomach ulcer had perforated a few days before, peritonitus had quickly set in, and there was nothing that his doctors could do but await the inevitable end. His body was laid to rest near that of his brother John, in Canongate Cemetery, and Sandy found himself the sole survivor of the trio of Ballantynes who had each arrived in Edinburgh from their native Kelso bright-eyed with the promise of a prosperous future, only to have their hopes dashed one by one.

James had retrieved his fortunes to an extent that had enabled him to leave his children comfortably off, and the loan Alexander Cowan made to re-establish the firm had long since been repaid. His twenty-year-old son, John Alexander Ballantyne, now managed the business with the help of John Hughes, who was later admitted into partnership. As his nephew grew into manhood, Sandy found himself being gradually eased out of the business, until he finally occupied a position little better than that of a proof-reader. But this was in later years, and it was some time before young John made use of his controlling interest to dispense with the services of his Uncle Sandy. Ballantyne & Company, as the firm was now named (later altered to Ballantyne & Hughes after Sandy's departure), had made an effort to keep up with the times by installing several of the latest steam-presses. For a few years this modern machinery gave them a considerable advantage over their rivals in the trade, for far less labour had to be used and their overhead expenses declined accordingly. There was comparative tranquillity during most of the mid-eighteen-thirties, but later the firm began to suffer increasing pressure from other printing houses, and the price-cutting to which they were forced to resort in order to combat this meant that the salaries drawn by the partners were shaded to a fineness that left little for family luxuries.

In the meantime Robert Cadell had prospered to an extent that must have surprised even himself. He had concentrated almost entirely on re-issuing the works of Sir Walter Scott, dismissing other authors from his stable, both new and old, with a contempt that relegated them to the financial also-rans, at least as far as he, as a publisher, was concerned. His interest in literature was confined to the pounds, shillings, and pence the books he sold brought in, and any firm wishing to be connected with the production of the volumes he commissioned was forced to quote cut-throat prices if they wished their tender to be considered. Ballantyne & Company were pleasurably surprised when he accepted their estimate for the printing of Lockhart's *Life of Scott*; the order was a large one and came at a time when the firm was badly in need of work. It appears today that there might well have been a certain amount of malice aforethought connected with the placing of this order, for neither Lockhart nor Cadell had any love for members of the Ballantyne family, and subsequent events revealed that this was quite possibly a case of wishing to rub salt in the wounds of an old opponent.

The manuscript of volume one was set up in type and passed through the presses at Paul's Works in February 1837: there was nothing in it to give offence to the surviving relatives of either the Ballantyne or Constable families and the book enjoyed an extremely large sale. But when they began to print volume two in April, young John Ballantyne and his uncle were dismayed at what they considered to be Lockhart's lies and calumnies regarding the actions and characters of the late James and John. 'Greatly annoyed with Sir Walter's Life, 2nd Vol.,' Sandy wrote in his diary. 'Don't know what steps to take. A quarrel with Lockhart would go far to ruin our business.' The Ballantynes were in a cleft stick; either they had to go on printing a savage attack on the late members of their family, knowing what was written to be false, or they must ask Cadell to have the last five volumes printed elsewhere. In which case he would more than likely refuse to pay them for work already done, and they would lose one of the best orders their firm had had for many months.

A family conference was called to work out what ought to be done, and it was decided to finish printing the seven volumes without making any comment to either the author or publisher; then, when the order was completed and their account had been settled, to issue a pamphlet denying Lockhart's allegations and giving the public the true facts of the case. They knew that there were plenty of firms in the city only too willing to undertake any printing they might refuse, and, as the work would obviously be published whatever action they took, they came to the conclusion that they must swallow their pride for the sake of keeping their presses busy and their workmen fully employed. There was, however, one voice at the conference raised in furious dissent; that of Hermione, the widow of the late John Ballantyne. She resolutely refused to be muzzled, and a few days later she lumbered into action with a broadside at John Gibson Lockhart that must have caused that gentleman considerable hurt.

To the Editor of the *Kelso Mail*.

Jedburgh. 22nd May, 1837

Sir,

It is with feelings of grief and indignation that I read in your paper extracts from Lockhart's *Life of Sir Walter Scott*, in which the memory of my departed husband (with that of his late accomplished and most worthy brother) has been so cruelly calumniated.

So many false and utterly unfounded assertions I never before saw in print. It is a well-known fact that my husband never was a 'bankrupt' nor in any other than *easy circumstances*; and so far was he from having thrown himself in a 'destitute condition' on the charity of his brother, that it was at the *earnest* solicitation of Mr James Ballantyne that my husband renounced his previous intention of going out to Jamaica, and joined him in Edinburgh, after having faithfully discharged not only his own but his *father's* debts. When Mr Lockhart presumes to assert that, 'as men of affairs they (the Ballantynes) deeply injured Sir Walter Scott,' does he mean to say that they *robbed* him? If so, this (being libellous) calls aloud for an explanation.

That my husband was extravagant, and that his generosity bordered on profusion, I know from bitter experience: nor do I attempt to palliate or deny it. But Mr Lockhart, in the extreme altitude of authorship, has only condescended to make vague or general remarks on the subject of my poor husband's extravagance: he should have told us that, at the christening of his (Lockhart's) eldest child, my husband actually purchased and presented him with Golden Spoons!! So flagrant, so glaring an instance of my husband being occasionally in the habit of throwing away his money, should by no means have been omitted; and this anecdote, being strictly *true*, might have amused Mr Lockhart's readers better than many others which are false and defamatory. In the hideously ugly, hopping, wry-faced, squeaking, croaking, 'scarecrow' portrait, given of my husband, by Mr Lockhart, neither I nor any unprejudiced person can perceive the most remote resemblance. It may be said to be a representation of what my husband was *not* than what he was; and if the other portraits given by this

274

facetious gentleman bear no more likeness to the originals than that of my late husband, they will not be recognizable, unless Mr. Lockhart adopt the plan of a brother artist of yore, who, when he drew the 'king of the beasts' was under the necessity of writing over it— 'This is a lion.'

I am, Sir,
Respectfully your obedient servant,
Hermione Ballantyne[1]

With the appearance of his massive biography came also the birth of the legend that gave such comfort to his countless admirers throughout the world: that the great Sir Walter Scott was ruined not by any extravagant weakness of his own, but by his ill-advised association with tradesmen who dipped their greedy fingers into the treasure chest that his genius had worked so hard to fill. Lockhart's biography enjoyed an immense sale and subsequently went through a large number of new editions, all but drowning the feeble voices of the Ballantynes when they raised them in protest at his allegations. In August 1838, they issued a pamphlet entitled *Misstatements and Calumnies contained in Mr Lockhart's Life of Sir Walter Scott, Bart. respecting the Messrs Ballantyne*, and this sparked off a controversy that the press took up with glee. *The Times* came down heavily on the side of the Ballantynes:

> The main question raised by this pamphlet is, whether Mr Lockhart has taken the true view of the cause of Sir Walter Scott's embarrassments in attributing them wholly to the mismanagement of the Ballantynes, and on this most material point we think the present publication goes far to unsettle Mr Lockhart's conclusion...The accounts now published lead strongly to the inference that Mr Lockhart has misapprehended the nature of the bill transactions to which he ascribes the ruin of the firm of Ballantyne & Co., and that a very large proportion of the money which was obtained by them under the system of mutual accommodation between them and Constable was raised for the personal use of Sir Walter, and applied by him in payment of his extensive and by no means profitable purchases of land.

The Scotsman, the *Spectator*, the *Glasgow Constitutional*, and many other leading papers took a similar view, and for weeks their correspondence columns were filled with letters on the

[1] The letter appeared in the issue for 25th May, 1837. Hermione's second husband, who had earlier fled to the Isle of Man to escape his creditors, had died a few years before. She had again reverted to the name of Ballantyne.

subject, the vast majority of which expressed dismay that men no longer able to defend themselves and tell the other side of the story should have been attacked so viciously by a man with an axe to grind. The clamour reached such proportions that Lockhart was finally stung into making a reply. This took the form of an open letter to Sir Adam Ferguson, under the sarcastic title *The Ballantyne-Humbug Handled*. In it he strove hard to convince his readers that the vast debts of the printing company had been caused solely by James's gross mismanagement and foolhardy extravagance. This brought forth another Ballantyne pamphlet called: *Reply to Mr Lockhart's Pamphlet, entitled 'The Ballantyne-Humbug Handled'*, once more refuting the charges brought against them. The arguments went on for several months until the public grew tired of the whole affair. With the passage of time the defence made by the Ballantynes was forgotten, while Lockhart's *Life of Scott* continued to be printed and retained a wide circulation. The ephemeral, paper-bound pamphlets issued by the Ballantynes quickly disappeared as such things will, and today can be found in only a few of the largest reference libraries; while Lockhart's famous *Life* continues to be prescribed reading for any student of the period.

In later years, Lockhart must have bitterly regretted letting Cadell persuade him to relinquish the copyright of his *Life of Scott*, for it proved to be one of the most profitable works the publisher ever marketed. And the Scott family as a whole soon realized that they had been deprived of the fruits of their illustrious forebear's many years of hard work. They derived no benefit whatsoever from any of the constant reissues of the late Sir Walter's novels, poetical works, and other literary enterprises, most of which reappeared with monotonous regularity during the middle and latter half of the nineteenth century. The new Copyright Act of 1842, on behalf of which Serjeant Talfourd and Thomas Macaulay had argued so eloquently for many years, must have caused Cadell to jump round his counting house with joy, for it played right into his hands. Its terms prevented other publishing houses from issuing any of Scott's works until forty-two years after their first appearance in print. The same rule applied to Lockhart's *Life of Scott*. One could say that the only man who reaped any lasting benefit from the years of labour and mental toil that had done so much to undermine Scott's health, was the tireless and resilient Robert Cadell, a man whose well-timed offers of financial assistance seemed always to contain an angle from which his apparent generosity eventually rebounded to his ultimate benefit. By the time he died on the 20th January, 1849, at Ratho House, Midlothian, at the age of sixty-one, he was the owner of a landed estate of considerable extent and his wealth ran well into six figures. This was not at all discreditable for one who had been declared bankrupt and been forced to go into hiding in 1826. It was Lockhart who described him not only as 'a cool, inflexible specimen of the national character', but also as 'one of the most acute men of business in creation'. He certainly made the most of his chances.

Despite Lockhart's effort to display his subject in the best of all possible lights, the *Life*, when it appeared, contained revelations about Scott's business interests that shocked many of his friends and admirers. Lord Cockburn, a supporter of the Whig cause and as such a political opponent of Scott, was nevertheless a man with the utmost respect for his literary genius. But after reading Lockhart's biography, this otherwise generous-hearted man of letters commented: 'Whether the publication of this portrait will do any good to his memory is a different matter. It has greatly dispelled the fascination connected with his name in the minds of those who only knew him through his work and fame. They thought him purely a literary man. They have now been taught how much he was a tradesman even in the exercise of his genius; and to what extent his taste for those feudal times, which formed the charm of some of his finest works, was united with the practical obeisance of a vassal to his superiors; and how very narrow and shallow were his public views; and how much less he valued fame and literature than those results of them which enabled him to exercise an intellectual and splendid hospitality.'[1]

Scott's frenetic urge to prove to the world at large that he was not only entitled to the place his genius had carved for him in high society, but that he was capable of sustaining in feudalistic splendour the establishment that, in his eyes, set the seal on his success, was his fatal weakness, the blind spot that made him unperceptive of the obvious dangers that loomed larger with each passing year. In an age of Gothic revival he left his competitors in the same field far behind, matching Horace Walpole's earlier

[1] *Journal: Being a Continuation of the Memorials, 1831–54*, Henry Cockburn, 2 vols. Edinburgh, 1874.

gimcrack effort at Strawberry Hill, with its pseudo-medieval plasterwork, by the solidarity of the turreted granite and carved oaken beams at Abbotsford. Unfortunately for Scott and the others concerned with him, the folly he reared to perpetuate his name turned out to be a Delilah whose demands were unceasing and he was seduced by an image of grandeur into increasing excesses to satisfy its claims. Early in his career he had salved his conscience by the arrant assumption that his pre-eminence in the world of letters entitled him to adopt an attitude of amoral indifference to the soundness or otherwise of the commercial concerns of which he was the secret owner. He roused himself to prop them by loans raised from friends only when his business interests seemed in imminent danger of collapsing: on all other occasions he viewed them merely as milch-cows, means of gratifying his insatiable thirst for funds. To suggest it was his love of secrecy for its own sake that made him shelter behind the Ballantynes is nonsense: in this, as in many other affairs, he revealed himself to be a snob, fearful of the social odium that the knowledge of his involvement would have brought from the very friends whose generosity saved him from certain disaster on more than one occasion.

Throughout his life his nostalgic longing for the feudalistic chivalries of an age that was past, coloured his thinking to a degree that led him to resist social change in any form. He condemned out of hand, with arguments as passionate as they were irrational, any attempt to alter what he considered to be the natural order of society, while defending with equal vigour the way of life handed down by generations long since dead. It is hardly surprising, therefore, that in politics he was tenacious in clinging to a philosophy that sought to perpetuate a system which gave the reins of power to a privileged elite, a narrow circle of aristocracy that Scott was determined should not be enlarged. His belief that Parliament's function was to represent property, not the people, led him, as a sick man, to brave the brickbats of a mob eager for his blood; while his obsession to turn his home into a seat of baronial magnificence equates exactly with the political thinking of a man who respected wealth only when it was displayed in the form of landed estates.

His financial success, which at times must have dazzled even his own extravagant dreams, could never quite keep pace with the rate at which he squandered the money his writing brought him. He was never able to ground his fortune on foundations that could withstand the buffetings of commercial speculation or the vast inroads his greed for land made on the immense sums he received for his books. He was haunted by a sense of insecurity and by the fear that one day his popularity would wane and the reading public turn to a new and more fashionable literary idol. And there can be no question that he was commercially astute enough to realize that by making over the estate to his eldest son, he was putting Abbotsford and its domains beyond the reach of his creditors if things should really go wrong. Yet even in this desire, the longing to found a dynasty securely based on the Border empire he had created, his hopes were due to be disappointed, although he was in his grave before the events that thwarted them occurred. All his children died at comparatively early ages. His eldest son Walter, who succeeded him in the baronetcy, died on the 8th February, 1847, less than fifteen years after his father. Charles died at Teheran in 1841, while an attaché to the British Embassy. Of his two daughters, Anne died soon after her father, in June, 1833; Sophia Lockhart was laid to rest in May, 1837, while the first volumes of her husband's biography were still issuing from the Ballantyne Press. With Walter's death the baronetcy became extinct, but happily for his father's memory, the home he created on the banks of the Tweed remains in the hands of surviving members of the Scott family to this day.

Thomas Macaulay's comment on the man whom countless thousands of readers had come to love was a particularly bitter one, even making allowances for the famed acidity of a wit renowned for its cutting edge. 'I have not, from the little I know of him, formed so high an opinion of his character as most people seem to entertain,' he wrote to Macvey Napier in declining an offer to review the *Life* for the *Edinburgh Review*. 'He seems to me to have been most carefully, and successfully, on his guard against the sins which most easily beset literary men. On that side he multiplied his precautions, and set double watch. Hardly any writer of note has been so free from the petty jealousies and morbid irritabilities of our caste. But I do not think that he kept himself equally pure from faults of a very different kind, from the faults of a man of the world. In politics, a bitter and unscrupulous partisan; profuse and ostentatious in expense; agitated with the hopes and fears of a gambler; perpetually sacrificing the perfection of his composition, and the durability of his fame, to his eagerness for money; writing with the slovenly haste of Dryden, in order to satisfy wants that were not, like those of Dryden, caused by circumstances beyond his control, but which were produced by his extravagant waste and rapacious speculation; this is the way that he appears to me. I am sorry for it, for I sincerely admire the greater part of his works; but I cannot think he was a very high minded man.'

The final comment on a character that left an indelible mark on the literature of his time and on the age in which he lived can perhaps be left to Henry Cockburn. He was privileged to count Scott as a personal friend; had shaken his hand when fortune smiled and when adversity, on a scale that would have broken many a lesser man, had revealed to the world that their idol was beset by faults and weaknesses common to us all. 'How much, how very much, there was to admire and love in such a man!' he wrote in remembering the passing of the Wizard of the North. 'What extraordinary combination of genius with industry; of the poetical powers without any of the defects of the poetical temperament. If the acquisition of money entered too much into his literary thoughts, who ever made so liberal a use of it, or one that so much extended the renown of his country?...How noble the spirit with which he bore up against the wreck of his fortune! How honourable the feeling of justice, and the ambition of ultimate independence, with which he struggled for his creditors!...I still hear his voice and see his form. I see him in court, and on the street, in company and by the Tweed. The plain dress, the guttural burred voice, the lame walk, the thoughtful heavy face with its mantling smile, the honest hearty manner, the joyous laugh, the sing-song-feeling recitation, the graphic story—they are all before me a hundred times a day.'

Bibliography

Memoirs of the Life of Sir Walter Scott, Bart. by J. G. Lockhart; seven volumes, 1837–8.

Recollections of Sir Walter Scott by R. P. Gillies, 1837.

Refutation of the Misstatements and Calumnies contained in Mr Lockhart's Life of Sir Walter Scott, Bart., respecting the Messrs Ballantyne by the Trustees and son of the late Mr James Ballantyne, London and Edinburgh, 1838 (fourth edition 1839).

The Ballantyne-Humbug Handled, in a letter to Sir Adam Fergusson. (by J. G. Lockhart) 1839.

Reply to Mr Lockhart's Pamphlet, entitled, 'The Ballantyne-Humbug Handled' by the Trustees and son of the late Mr James Ballantyne, 1839.

Memorials of His Time by Henry Cockburn, 1856.

The History of the Ballantyne Press and its connection with Sir Walter Scott, Bart., Edinburgh, 1871.

Archibald Constable and his Literary Correspondents by Thomas Constable; three volumes, 1873.

The Life and Letters of John Gibson Lockhart by Andrew Lang; two volumes, 1897.

The Ballantyne Press and Its Founders. Edinburgh, 1909.

The Private Letter-Books of Sir Walter Scott edited by Wilfred Partington, 1930.

The Letters of Sir Walter Scott edited by H. J. C. Grierson; twelve volumes, 1932–37.

Sir Walter Scott, Bart. by Sir Herbert Grierson, 1938. This work was issued as being 'supplementary to, and corrective of, Lockhart's biography'.

The Journal of Sir Walter Scott. The text revised from a photostat in the National Library of Scotland. With a foreword by W. M. Parker, and a preface by J. G. Tait. First published in three volumes, 1939, 1941, 1946; in one volume, 1950.

Index

Abbotsford, 11, 12, 19, 55, 56, 65, 67, 70, 72, 74, 79, 81, 82, 83, 95–100, 107, 109, 110, 115, 121, 129, 134, 135, 138, 139, 140, 149, 151, 152, 162, 167, 171, 175, 176, 178, 179, 181, 185, 187, 188, 191, 198, 199–203, 207–211, 214, 215, 220, 225, 226, 227, 232, 234, 239, 242, 246, 249, 250, 255–257, 259, 260, 264, 265, 267, 270, 278, 279
Abbot, The, 136
Abercorn, Lady, 22
Abercromby, Dr, 225
Abud & Company, 213
Adelphi Theatre, London, 220
Ainslie, Mr, 114, 119
Allen, Sir William, 260
Alvanley, Lady, 56
An Apology for Tales of Terror, 22
Angelica's Ladies Library, 20
Anne of Geierstein, 236, 237, 238
Ann Street, Edinburgh, 219
Anti-Jacobin Review, 42
Antiquary, The, 98, 101, 109
Applegarth & Company, 204
Ashiestiel, Scotland, 25, 41, 46, 54, 56, 57

Baillie, Joanna, 51, 185
Ballantyne & Hughes (printers), 272
Ballantyne, Agnes, 20
BALLANTYNE, Alexander ('Sandy')
  Boyhood in Kelso, 20
  Kelso Mail, 24, 37, 43, 148, 162, 163, 218
  Transcriber of Scott's MSS, 82, 83, 101
  Loans to his brother and Scott, 91, 92, 100, 220, 221, 226
  Financial difficulties, 219
  Last meeting with Scott, 259, 260
  Other references, 44, 150, 156, 171, 199, 207, 235, 257, 272, 273

Ballantyne, Hermione (John's wife), 32–34, 43, 50, 144, 152, 155–157, 274, 275
Ballantyne-Humbug Handled, The, 276
BALLANTYNE, James (printer)
  Life in Kelso, 20, 21
  Kelso Mail, 21–24
  Early days in Edinburgh, 25–29
  Publishing ventures, 43–46, 61, 62, 64, 71
  Marriage, 99–101
  Last partnership with Scott, 160–166, 167, 232
  Critic and proof-reader, 164, 165, 224, 237, 243, 244, 247, 251
  Troubles with Cadell, 229, 237–243
  Quarrel with Scott, 236, 256, 257
  Illness and death, 257, 258, 270–272
  Other references, 33–37, 51, 54, 59, 66, 68, 75–78, 81–83, 89–98, 102–106, 109, 112–115, 118, 134, 137, 142–148, 150, 152, 154, 156, 158, 163, 176, 178, 179, 181, 182, 186, 196–208, 216, 218, 219, 225, 226, 230, 234, 235, 244, 259, 270, 273–276
Ballantyne, James (son of Alexander), 259
Ballantyne, James, & Company (printers), 29, 30, 49, 65, 76, 91, 99, 100, 140, 161, 165, 166, 167, 172, 173, 196, 200, 202, 206, 209, 230, 238, 272–275
Ballantyne, Jean, 20, 33
Ballantyne, John (father of James), 20, 32, 33
BALLANTYNE, John (publisher)
  Early life in Kelso, 20, 32, 33
  Marriage, 32
  Life in Edinburgh, 34, 37, 50, 51
  Publishing career, 43, 44, 48, 49, 59, 91

Ballantyne, John (publisher) — *cont.*
  Auctioneering, 88, 89, 103, 114, 145
  Illness, 141, 143, 144, 146, 152
  Death, 153
  Other references, 52, 54, 55, 61, 63,
    64, 66–72, 76–78, 83, 86, 87, 92–
    94, 97, 98, 101, 103, 106–109,
    112–115, 118–120, 133, 135–137,
    140, 142, 143, 147–156, 160, 270,
    274, 275
Ballantyne, John (son of Alexander),
  259, 260
Ballantyne, John Alexander (son of
  James), 272, 273
Ballantyne, John, & Company (pub-
  lishers), 43, 50, 51, 60–66, 75, 78,
  85–88, 91, 142
Ballantyne Press, 23, 25, 31, 46, 61,
  65, 76, 77, 90, 99, 113, 162, 172,
  173, 178, 179, 205, 206, 218, 234,
  238, 239, 242, 257, 279
Ballantyne, Randall (wife of Alexan-
  der), 100, 163, 220
Ballantyne, Robert Michael, 163
Ballantyne, 'Sandy' — see Ballantyne,
  Alexander
Ballantyne's Novelists Library, 146–
  148, 152
Ballantyne the Brave, 219, 260
Bank of England, 189, 190
Bank of Scotland, 203, 104, 212, 222
Barber, Stephen, 134
Barham frigate, 259, 263
Beaumont and Fletcher, Works of, 52,
  64
Bell, William, 229
Belmont Place, Kelso, 100, 162
Belsches, Williamina, 22
Bentley's Standard Novel Series, 183
Betrothed, The, 176
Biographia Literaria, 128
Black Dwarf, The, 104, 109
Blackwood, William, & Company,
  103–107, 115, 116, 124–126, 224
Blackwood's Magazine, 121, 124–128,
  187, 242
Blore, Mr, 158
Blücher, General, 96
Border Press, 23
Boroughmuir Head, Scotland, 147,
  150
Bridal of Triermain, 57, 58
Bride of Lammermoor, 133
British Linen Bank, 20, 204

Broadmeadows estate, Scotland, 27
Brooks & Company, 190
Brougham, Henry, 38
Brown, Mrs, 226
Bruce, Miss, 44
Bruce, Robert, 95
Buccleuch, Dukes of, 17, 19, 24, 37,
  54, 58, 68, 72, 73, 75, 77, 98, 115,
  132, 137, 138, 245
Buccleuch Legion, 254
Byron, Lord, 79–82, 86, 96, 194

Cadell and Davies (booksellers), 23,
  29, 78
Cadell, Mrs R., 202
CADELL, Robert (publisher)
  Partnership with Constable, 62, 117,
    118, 145, 175
  Financial difficulties, 85, 86, 93,
    122, 174, 190–196, 198, 204
  Bankruptcy, 210–212, 229
  Financial recovery, 217, 218, 221–
    225, 230–234, 272, 273
  Quarrel with Ballantyne, 327–244
  Loans to Scott, 268, 269
  Other references, 66, 67, 97, 106,
    115, 119, 120, 136, 156, 158, 200,
    201, 251, 255–257, 262, 270, 276,
    277
Cadell, Robert, & Company, 230, 243,
  269
Caledonian Mercury, 216
Callot, Jacques, 56
Cameron, Mr, 146
Campbell, clan, 19
Campbell, Thomas, 29, 30, 109, 110
Canning, George, 36, 42, 224
Canongate, Edinburgh, 25, 87, 153,
  168, 219, 222, 272
Carlyle, Thomas, 126
Carlton House, London, 95
Carpenter, Charles, 137
Carpenter, Charlotte Margaret — see
  Scott, Lady
Carpenter, Mrs Charles, 139
Carstairs & Company, 190, 191
Castle Dangerous, 247
Castle Street, No. 39, Edinburgh, 22,
  38, 49, 83, 94, 107, 109, 129, 130,
  131, 135, 167, 170, 179, 194, 198,
  200, 201, 205–208, 211–214, 220
Cathcart, Robert, 117
Cauldershields Loch, 65
Chaldee Manuscript, 125, 126

284

Chalk Farm, London, 129
Charles I, 57
Chase, The, 22
Cheape, Mr, 191
Childe Harold's Pilgrimage, 79, 80
Child, William, 219
Christie, Mr, 128, 129
Chronicles of the Canongate, 230, 232, 234, 244
Clarkson, Dr James, 250
Clarty Hole, 55, 176
Cleghorn, William, 124
Clephane, Miss, 175
Clifford, Arthur, 31
Cobbett, William, 42
Cockburn, Henry (Lord Cockburn), 86, 116, 207, 253, 267, 277, 280
'Cockney School of Literature', 126
Coleridge, John Taylor, 188
Coleridge, Samuel Taylor, 79, 128, 205, 244
College Wynd, Edinburgh, 18
CONSTABLE, Archibald
  Bookseller's apprentice, 15, 16
  Edinburgh Review, 16, 17, 18, 38–40
  Friction with Scott, 41–43, 49
  Help with Scott's publishing concern, 62–65, 67, 71, 75, 86, 87
  Waverley, 83, 85
  Financial difficulties, 102, 122, 140, 172, 173–175, 189–198
  Partnership with Cadell, 117–119
  Constable's Miscellany, 181–185, 187, 190, 193, 216, 217
  Illness, 189, 201
  Bankruptcy, 204–211
  Death, 217
  Other references, 25, 29, 31, 37, 66, 68, 69, 72, 93, 95, 97, 98, 106, 107, 115, 116, 120, 121, 124, 145, 158, 164–166, 176, 177, 185, 187, 200, 202, 203, 212, 218, 229, 232, 234, 238, 243, 273, 275
Constable, Archibald, & Company, 39, 68, 85, 87, 93, 102, 116, 135, 140, 148, 173, 179, 192, 196, 198, 200, 202, 204, 205, 209, 210, 218, 222, 229, 234
Constable, Archibald, and his Literary Correspondents, 93
Constable, David, 216
Constable, George, 48, 265
Constable, Thomas, 217

Constable's Miscellany, 181–185, 187, 190, 193, 216
Coral Island, 163
Count Robert of Paris, 247, 249, 251, 256
Court of Session, Edinburgh, 28, 32, 34, 35, 53, 71, 85, 109, 134, 136, 186, 204, 222, 223, 225, 226, 233, 246
Coutts, Mrs — see Duchess of St Albans
Coutts & Company, 268, 269
Cowan, Alexander, 215, 218, 235, 272
Cowan, David, 219
Cowan, Duncan, 156
Cowgate, Edinburgh, 18
Crabbe, George, 48, 265
Cranstouns, family of, 17
Cranstoun, George, 88
Croker, John Wilson, 73, 224, 239, 270
Cruikshank, George, 247
Cummins, Maria S., 184

Dalgleish, Mr, 227, 248
Dalkeith, Lord, 43
Dance of Death, 96
Darnick, Scotland, 79, 135, 158
Dick, Dr, 143, 144
Disraeli, Benjamin, 187
Dixon & Company, 190, 191, 195
Douglas, Dr, 55
Douglas, David, 194
Downshire, Lord, 22
Dramatic Characters by Mrs Siddons, 90
Drapier's Letters, 224
Drumlanrig Castle, 68, 70, 72
Dryburgh Abbey, 111, 268
Dryden, John, Works of, 30, 31, 280
Dudley, Earl of, 213
Duke, William, 155
Dundas, Robert, 53, 55, 225

Edgeworth, Maria, 60, 169, 170, 171' 181, 185, 189
Edgeworth, Harriet, 170
Edgeworth, Sophy, 170
Edinburgh Annual Register, 51, 53, 62– 66, 96, 106, 109, 130, 181
Edinburgh Evening Courant, 90
Edinburgh High School, 19, 58
Edinburgh Monthly Magazine — see *Blackwood's Magazine*

Edinburgh Review, 16–18, 38, 39, 41, 42, 52, 57, 79, 93, 116, 124, 125, 187, 258, 279
Edinburgh University, 20, 21
Edinburgh Weekly Journal, 113, 141, 162, 163, 166, 199, 218, 219, 224, 235, 256, 257
Eldon, Lord, 253
Elliot, Lieutenant, 255
Ellis, George, 30, 41, 42
Encylopaedia Britannica, 83, 93, 117, 181
Endymion, 127
English Bards and Scotch Reviewers, 79
Erskine, Charles, 77
Erskine, William, 29, 62, 82, 88
Essays on Ballad Poetry, 246
Evans, Edmund, 184

Fair Maid of Perth, 232, 244
Faldonside estate, Scotland, 139, 239, 263
Ferguson, Sir Adam, 112, 169, 171, 177, 178, 227, 260, 261, 276
Ferguson, Dr Robert, 261
Ferguson, The Misses, 202, 227
Fielding, Henry, 148
Field of Waterloo, The, 96, 97, 164
Firth of Forth, 18, 34, 50, 142, 168, 256
Flodden Field, 37, 80
Floors Castle, Roxburghshire, 149
Forbes, Sir William, 68, 91, 204, 213, 214
Foreign Quarterly Review, 217
Fortunes of Nigel, 82, 153, 158, 159, 165
Foulis Close, Edinburgh, 25
Fox, Charles James, 36
Frere, Hookham, 42
Friars, near Kelso, 144

Gala river, 54, 55, 111
Galashiels, Scotland, 55, 111, 179
Gale & Company, 204
George IV—see also Prince Regent, 95, 112, 135, 167, 168, 169, 227
George Square, Edinburgh, 18, 27
Gibson, John, 193, 207, 208, 212, 213, 218, 220, 223, 231, 234, 262, 269
Gifford, William, 42, 52, 104, 105, 187
Gifford, Lord, 186
Gillies, R. P., 108, 217
Glasgow Constitutional, 275

Glen, James, 167
Gleig, G. R., 19
Glover, John, 156
Glover, Mrs John—see Ballantyne, Hermione
Glyn & Company, 195
Goethe, Johann Wolfgang von, 263
Gordon, George Huntly, 233
Grant, Anne Randall, 37
Green, Mr, 190
Greta-Bridge, Yorkshire, 58
Grierson, Sir H. J. C., 167
Grieve, Mr, 66, 67
Griggs, E. L., 205
Guy Mannering, 94, 95, 102

Halidon Hill, 175
Hall, Capt. Basil, 183
Hall's Voyages, 183, 217
Hanover Street, Edinburgh, 51, 63, 71, 86, 88, 101, 104, 107, 120, 144
'Harmony Hall', Edinburgh, 34, 50, 142–145, 156
Harold the Dauntless, 109
Hartsonge, Matthew, 77
Hazlitt, William, 126, 252
Heart of Midlothian, 120, 121
Heber, Richard, 42
Hedderwick, James, 233
Heriot Row, Edinburgh, 218
Hill, Peter, 15
History of Scotland, 231
History of the Culdees, 52
Hoare, Mr, 75
Hogarth, Christina, 99, 100, 236
Hogarth, George, 99, 113, 155, 162, 176, 179, 201, 207
Hogarth, Robert, 99, 100
Hogg, James, 23, 124, 125
Holland, Lord, 106
Holyrood House, Edinburgh, 25, 168, 222
Home, George, 28, 54
Hours of Idleness, 79
Hughes, John, 166, 257, 258, 272
Hunt, Leigh, 126, 127
Hunter, Alexander, 39, 49, 62, 85, 117
Huntly Burn, 179
Hurst, Robinson & Company, 122, 158, 189, 190, 192, 195–198, 200, 208, 210, 222
Hurst, Thomas, 204

'Il Bizarro', 263

Iona, Scotland, 51
Irving, Washington, 109, 110, 112
Ivanhoe, 133, 135, 159, 164, 227

Jamieson, Dr John, 53
Jedburgh, Scotland, 254, 255
Jeffrey, Sir Francis, 16, 38, 41, 42, 52, 57, 58, 79, 88, 258
Jobson, Miss Jane, 177, 178, 179, 180, 184, 185
Jobson, Mrs, 178, 179
Jokeby, 60

Kaeside Estate, Scotland, 79, 202
Keats, John, 127, 128, 188
Kean, Edmund, 90
Keepsake, The, 244
Kelso, Roxburghshire, 12, 20, 22, 23, 32–34, 37, 82, 90, 92, 144, 146–152, 156, 162, 163, 236, 238, 256, 271, 272
Kelso Grammar School, 20
Kelso Mail, 21, 22, 24, 37, 148, 162, 163, 218, 274
Kemble, John, 90, 143
Kenilworth, 136
Kirklands, Scotland, 148–150, 152, 155, 156, 267

Lady of the Lake, 46–48, 54, 58–61, 66, 78, 85, 112, 156
Laidlaw, William, 23, 133, 199, 247, 248, 260, 265
Laird's Jock, The, 244
Lamplighter, The, 184
Lardner's Cyclopaedia, 231
Lasswade, Scotland, 22, 25
Lay of the Last Minstrel, The, 17, 25, 28, 78, 79
Legend of Montrose, The, 133
Leigh & Sotheby, 89
Letters Left at the Pastry Cook's, 184
Letters of Malachi Malagrowther, 224
Letters on Demonology, 231, 247
Lewis, M. G. ('Monk'), 23
Leyden, John, 23
Life of John Bunyan, 246
Life of Lord Herbert of Cherbury, 31
Life of Napoleon Bonaparte, 184–186, 203, 208, 213, 224, 227, 230, 231, 234
Listener, The, 212
Liston, John, 90
Loch Katrine, 47

Lochore Estate, Fifeshire, 177, 180
LOCKHART, John Gibson
    Textual alteration of Scott's letters, 105, 106
    First meeting with Scott, 123
    Blackwood's Magazine, 125–127
    Quarrel with John Scott, 128, 129
    Marriage, 130
    Dislike of John Ballantyne, 142, 143
    Description of John Ballantyne's last days, 152, 153, 155
    Meeting with Maria Edgeworth, 171
    Visit to Ireland, 184, 185
    Quarterly Review, 187, 188, 194, 197, 246
    Reform Bill agitation, 254, 255
    Scott's death, 266, 267
    Life of Scott, 270, 271
    Attack on the Ballantynes, 273–276
    Other references, 11, 23, 27, 28, 31, 50, 52, 61, 83, 84, 100, 120, 131, 136, 147, 149, 160, 164, 168, 176, 181, 182, 186, 191–193, 204, 206, 210, 244, 245, 257, 260, 261, 263, 264, 277
Lockhart, John Hugh, 177, 231, 263
Lockhart, Violet, 245
London Magazine, 128
Longman, Hurst, Rees, and Orme, 25, 49, 66, 78, 86, 87, 95, 107, 118, 122, 135, 137, 223, 227, 230
Lord of the Isles, 51, 81, 94, 95, 170
Luttrell, Henry, 244

Macaulay, Thomas, 276, 279
Mackenzie, Henry, 88
McDougal clan, 19
Maggs Bros. Ltd., 134
Marmion, 37, 38, 57, 79, 80
Mathews, Charles, 143
Mathieson, Peter, 255
Mayhew, Horace, 184
Meadowbank, Lord, 249
Melrose Abbey, 56, 110
Melville, Lord. 24, 35, 36, 53, 130, 224
Memoirs of Capt. George Carleton, 31
Memoirs of Robert Carey, 31
Memoirs of the Life of Sir Walter Scott, Bart., 12, 28, 31, 105, 106, 142, 164, 270, 276, 277, 279
Memorials of His Time, 88, 207
Miller, William, 30, 49, 80
Milne, Nicol, 139, 239

Minstrelsy of the Scottish Border, 23, 25

Misstatements and Calumnies...respecting the Messrs Ballantyne, 275

Monastery, The, 136

'Mons Meg', 169

Montrose, Marquis of, 57, 142

Moore, Thomas, 60, 186, 244

Morrison, John, 141

Morritt, John, 58, 75, 76, 77, 89, 108, 227

Moss, John, 79, 202

Mull, Scotland, 51

Murray clan, 19

Murray, John, 31, 41, 80, 81, 95, 103, 106, 115, 116, 187, 188, 223, 247

Murray's Family Library, 246

My Aunt Margaret's Mirror, 244

Napier, Macvey, 258, 279

Naples, Italy, 263

National Library of Scotland, 209, 218, 266

Naughton, Sir R., 31

Nelson, Mr, 238

Newark Abbey, Scotland, 27

Nicolson, John, 248, 264

North Castle Street, Edinburgh — see Castle Street

North St David Street, 226

Old Greyfriars Church, 122

Old Mortality, 104, 109

Original Memoirs Written during the Great Civil War, 31

Osborne's Hotel, London, 203

Opus Magnum, 230, 234, 238, 239, 241, 251, 261, 268

Parker, Hermione — see Ballantyne, Hermione

Park Place, Edinburgh, 216

Partington, William, 242

Patmore, Mr, 129

Patronage, 170

Paul's Letters to his Kinsfolk, 95, 97, 109, 181

Paul's Works, Edinburgh, 25, 31, 34, 102, 158, 163, 165, 166, 196, 199, 201, 238, 239, 258, 273

Percy, Thomas, 23

'Peterloo Massacre', 256

Peveril of the Peak, 169, 172

Pirate, The, 148, 158

Polton, Lasswade, Scotland, 191, 192, 195, 216

Pontefract Castle, 122

Popular Tales, 64

Porteous, Captain, 121

Portobello, Scotland, 37, 217

Prince Regent (see also George IV), 71, 72, 74, 80, 132

Pringle, Alexander, 95

Pringle, Thomas, 124

Purdie, Tom, 199

Pye, Henry, 71, 72

Quarterly Review, 42, 52, 104, 181, 187, 188, 194, 197, 246

Queenhoo Hall, 31

Quentin Durward, 172, 174, 175

Raeburn, Henry, 169

Ramsay, George, & Company, 166

Ramsay's Bank, 204

Ratho House, Midlothian, 277

Ravensworth, Lord, 186

Redgauntlet, 176, 185

Reform Bill, 254, 256, 257, 262

Regent Moray's House, Edinburgh, 219

Reliques of Ancient English Poetry, 23

Reply to Mr Lockhart's Pamphlet, 46, 171, 276

Representative, The, 187, 188

Reynolds, Frederick Mansel, 244

Richardson, John, 169, 186

Richardson, Samuel. 260

Roberton, Hermione, 144, 155

Roberton, William, 144

Robinson, J. O., 189, 190, 193, 195, 201, 203, 204

Rob Roy, 107, 109, 114–116

Roby, John, 60

Rogers, Samuel, 42

Rokeby, 55, 57–63, 66, 68, 76–78, 81, 86

Rosebank Cottage, Kelso, 24

Roxburghe, Duke of, 149

Royal George yacht, 168

Russell, Colonel, 202

Russia, Czar of, 96

Rutherford clan, 19

St Albans, Duchess of, 186

St James's Hotel, London, 264

St John Street, Edinburgh, 34, 90, 91, 100, 103, 146, 152, 218, 236

St Ronan's Well, 176
Sale Room, The, 141
Scots Magazine and Edinburgh Literary Miscellany, 94
Scotsman, The, 275
Scott, Anne (mother of Sir W.S.), 18, 19
Scott, Anne (daughter of Sir W.S.), 110, 112, 171, 179, 181, 184, 206, 225, 226, 227, 245, 249, 250, 259, 261–264, 279
Scott, Anne (niece of Sir W.S.), 225, 226
Scott, Charles (son of Sir W.S.), 110, 206, 264, 269, 279
Scott of Harden, 255
Scott, Janet, 20
Scott, John, of Gala, 95
Scott, John, of London, 128
Scott, Major John, 46, 55, 107
Scott, Lady (wife of Sir W.S.), 22, 38, 57, 74, 95, 96, 132, 137, 170, 179, 181, 200, 206, 219, 225, 226, 230
Scott, Robert, 24
Scott, Sophia, 48, 112, 130, 177, 188, 263, 267, 279
Scott, Thomas, 27, 53, 80, 88
Scott, Walter (father of Sir W.S.), 18, 19, 24
Scott, Walter (son of Sir W.S.), 21, 48, 110, 138, 177, 180, 184, 185, 221, 239, 260, 263, 264, 268, 266, 279
SCOTT, Sir Walter
  Boyhood and student life, 18, 19, 21
  Marriage, 22
  Commercial speculation, 25–27, 29, 30, 43–46, 60–64, 68–71, 90–93, 99–101, 160–162, 166, 167
  Court of Session work, 28, 34, 35, 53, 54, 134, 186, 226, 233, 246
  Political affairs, 35, 36, 41, 43, 253–256
  Marmion, 37, 38
  Quarrel with Hunter and Constable, 39, 40, 49, 117
  Quarterly Review, 41, 42
  Lady of the Lake, 47, 48
  Book publishing schemes, 51–53
  Abbotsford purchase, 55, 56, 57, 65
  Rokeby, 57–59, 60
  Land and building purchases, 65–67, 79, 98, 99, 135, 158, 167, 175

Laureateship, 71, 72, 74
Financial difficulties, 72–77, 86, 87, 93, 97, 102–104, 115, 139, 140, 172–185, 192–212, 268–270
Byron and Scott, 79–81, 96
Waverley, 82–85, 118, 170, 235
Paris visit, 95, 96
Illnesses, 107–109, 114, 115, 119, 133, 144, 244, 245, 249–251, 260–262, 264–266
First meeting with Lockhart, 123, 129, 130
Baronetcy, 132, 135
Royal visit to Scotland, 167–169
Ireland visit, 181, 184, 185
'Last cast for freedom', 212–215
Quarrel with James Ballantyne, 256, 257
Italian visit, 263, 264
Death, 267
Other references, 11, 12, 17, 23, 24, 30–32, 50, 51, 72–75, 89, 94, 101, 105–107, 111, 112, 118–121, 129, 131, 136–139, 142, 145–147, 150–159, 163–165, 170–172, 176–183, 186–191, 217, 219–248, 252–254, 259, 271–280
Scremerston, Berwickshire, 99
Seccombe, Thomas, 121
Seward, Anna, 51
Seven Gables Cottage, Kelso, 163
Shelley, Percy Bysshe, 244
Shepherd, Lord, 186
Shortreed, Robert, 186, 254
Siddons, Sarah, 90
Siege of Malta, 263
Skene, James, 202, 206, 211, 247, 249, 265
Skene, William, 249
Slingsby, Sir Henry, 31
Smith, John, 134, 158
Smith, 'Sandy', 190
Smith, Sydney, 16, 38
Smollett, Tobias, 148, 260
Somerville, Lord, 54
Southey, Robert, 42, 73, 74, 79, 80, 126, 188, 244, 246
Specimens of the British Poets, 30
Spectator, The, 275
Spirit of the Age, 253
Standard, The, 261
State Papers of Sir Ralph Sadler, 31
Steevens, George, 72
Stewart, Dugald, 117

Stewart, Douglas, 98
Story of Rimini, 126, 127
Strutt, Joseph, 31
Stuart, Lady Louisa, 97
Swanston, John, 248
Swift, Jonathan, Works of, 39, 66, 78, 85, 86, 93, 176, 224
Swinton clan, 19

Tales of a Grandfather, 177, 231, 232, 237, 246
Tales of My Landlord, 103, 105–107, 115, 119, 120, 122, 133, 257
Tales of Terror, 22
Tales of the Crusaders, 176, 177, 181
Tales of the East, 64
Tales of Wonder, 23
Tait, J. G., 194
Tait's Magazine, 141
Talfourd, Serjeant, 276
Talisman, The, 176, 177
Tennyson, Alfred, 129
Terry, Daniel, 57, 67, 90, 135, 220, 221, 238
Times, The, 275
Tixal Poetry, 52
Toftfield estate, Scotland, 112
Tofts, 'Sandy', 102
Tory Party, 123–126, 168, 253–256
Traill, Mr, 128, 129
Trinity Grove, Edinburgh, 34

Tweed, River, 12, 20, 54–56, 65, 111, 149, 163, 205, 209, 261, 265, 267, 279
Two-penny Post-Bag, 60

Usher, Laird of Totfield, 112

Vision of Don Roderick, 53, 64, 86, 96

Walker Street, Edinburgh, 232
Walton Hall, Kelso, 147, 150, 156, 162, 163
Waverley, 32, 67, 82–84, 86, 87, 94, 95, 101, 117, 118, 133, 164, 165, 170, 235, 241, 260, 262
Weber, Henry William, 52, 64, 238
Wellington, Duke of, 41, 96
Whig Party, 16, 18, 19, 35, 36, 41, 123, 125, 255, 257, 259, 277
Whittaker, George Byrom, 194
Whittaker, Treacher & Company, 183
William and Helen, 22
Wilson, John, 123, 125, 128, 171
Woodstock, 186, 197, 203, 208, 213, 223, 224, 227, 231, 234
Wordsworth, William, 79, 126, 244, 259, 260
Wright, William, 191, 192

Yates, Frederick, 220
Young, Dr, 245
Young, Miss, 245